Copyright © 2023 by Darryle Purcell

All rights reserved.

No part of this publication may be reproduced, distributed, or transmitted in any form or by any means, including photocopying, recording, or other electronic or mechanical methods, without the prior written permission of the publisher, except as permitted by U.S. copyright law and in brief quotations embodied in critical reviews and certain other non-commercial uses.

For permission requests, contact: OffBeat Publishing at OffBeatReads@pm.me; "Purcell Permissions" in subject.

All names, characters, and incidents portrayed in this production are fictitious or used in a fictitious way. All stories and commentaries, and all names, characters, and incidents, are included and intended for entertainment purposes only.

ISBN (PAPERBACK): 978-1-950464-50-0

ISBN (EBOOK): 978-1-950464-51-7

HELL
TO
HUMOR

Contents

Preface	1
1. Animals and Attitudes	7
2. Issues and Actions	49
3. Romantic Expertise	85
4. War and Remembrance	105
5. Frightening Conspiracies	139
6. An Arizonan's View of Modern Science	150
7. The Culture War	159
8. The Home Front	203
9. Random Thoughts	231
10. B-Western Therapy	261

Preface

ARIZONA IS A SPECIAL place. Individuals from all over the United States, Mexico and Canada come here to work, play and live in this land of diverse culture and climate.

One has to look closely to find a commonality among this mass immigration of unique personalities. The same qualities that brought the original settlers to America, first to the east coast, then westward across the country, brought our growing population to Arizona. That would be the quest for freedom from thought control, which has been known throughout the late 20th and early 21st centuries as political correctness.

A growing cabal of Communists, Socialists, alleged Progressives and other autocrats have demanded their rights to berate us all, at the same time punishing, banning and silencing those of us who disagree with their dictates. These battles rage across the country on campuses, in legislatures, "homeless" camps, beer distribution facilities and newsrooms and on the streets of big cities. In many states, the left-wing activists have declared victory. But, some states have held fast to citizens' U.S. Constitutional rights to free speech. The Great Southwest stands out as a beacon of freedom.

One of the deciding factors that brought me to Arizona was the receptiveness of residents to discuss popular and unpopular subjects, something that, at the time of my immigration, was beginning to vanish in my prior home of southern California. That was in 1993. Today, that state has clamped down hard on any voices to the right of official "beloved leader" Gavin Newsom.

Having been a conservative, newspaper editorial cartoonist in the Golden State, I had always enjoyed open political discourse, including the many letters, both pro and con, that I received at my office every day. In the 1980s and early '90s, the Internet, e-mail and Twitter didn't exist. People had to sit down at their desks or kitchen tables and write letters. And I appreciated the correspondence no matter how the writers felt about my editorial stance. Expressing a political position had yet to become offensive. Most people didn't demand that opposing views be silenced — not back then.

But, by the early 1990s, many southern California daily newspapers had been purchased by large national and multi-national publishing corporations. With that came an amalgamation of accepted editorial viewpoints that wouldn't outrage special-interest activists. In other words, newspaper publishers were replacing local editorial writers and cartoonists with syndicated columnists and artists whose work had little effect on local issues and advertisers. That kind of pandering was the beginning of a trend that has, at this point in time, led to my reference to my former home state as the People's Republic of California.

Today, like California, many other states tout their acceptance of diversity — as long as one agrees completely with their version of that philosophy. And state officials, Hollywood activists and a variety of movers and shakers often silence individuals who may have other points of view. One only needs to remember that in the late 1940s and early 1950s, Sen. Joseph McCarthy was the leader of political correctness. The song and the singers may have changed, but the pressure for all of us to carry the same tune is still there. Just ask anyone who has been shunned by today's cartel of social media platforms.

Now don't get me wrong. There was, and still is, just as much political and social silliness going on in Arizona, which you will notice in the following pages, as any other state. The difference is, in Arizona we are still free to be critical of the social order without having to suffer a whole bunch of retaliation, yet. Yes, some city, county and state officials threaten reprisals, but those actions are seldom carried out as there are still a couple of news publications that are not in the pockets of elected officials, activists or back-room political bosses.

I, like older folks throughout history, often say that life was simpler when I was younger. And, as you will see when you've read a few of my commentaries from prior years, I would often get my (choose a body part) in the ringer now and then over issues that hardly seem important today. Some readers in those days didn't think life was so simple, only that I was simple minded. Nobody's perfect.

Oh, I can remember, back in 1983, a newsroom getting rather hissy with me over a cartoon that depicted Sally Ride bursting into the Space Shuttle cockpit and demanding to know "Who left the seat up?" And the same attitude was thrust at me in 1993 when I illustrated a frontline infantryman in a combat situation foxhole. His eyes were wide with surprise as a clean-cut soldier reached over to light his cigarette and said, "So. You come here often?" Clinton had just announce his "Don't ask, don't tell" policy. But those were newsrooms, traditionally full of left-leaning, non-veteran reporters. Most readers responded well to those cartoons.

After moving to Arizona, most of my columns were a bit like those cartoons – tongue in cheek silliness about the current culture. Of course, questioning mad cow disease and Teddy Kennedy's sobriety were certainly not as serious or earth shaking for the late 20th Century readers as current issues are to today's population, such as rejecting a low-calorie beer because the company chose a rather-silly young man in a dress to be a social-media spokes-being.

I believe that current in-your-face form of product branding is a bit, shall I say, un-enlightened to us traditional, beer-drinking dinosaurs (men who don't wear dresses). Product spokesmen should never be embarrassing to a company's long-time customers. Thinking back, I can remember when I considered the Hamm's Beer bear as a member of the family. That bear was a morally acceptable mouthpiece for his "refreshing" hops brew, unlike those multi-colored, toilet-paper bears we see today who like to shake their rear ends at the camera while touting Charmin.

We were very accepting a while back when Mickey Spillane and Billy Martin used to argue about the benefits of Miller Lite. And the thought of tossing back a couple of brews with the old Yankee's manager and the hard-boiled mystery writer was something we all (dinosaurs) would have enjoyed. But, not many of us would get a kick out of sipping tranny-cans with Dylan Mulvaney these days. In fact, if that happened, I'd wonder if I had already had a few too many beers and had accidentally entered the wrong establishment.

But, getting back to my original premise, Arizona is truly a diverse state in that there are many philosophies professed and many discussions and arguments held both in the legislative world and the world of private citizens and business. And since so many of our residents have come from areas where they had experienced pressure from the alleged "majority," or from those in social power, they are thankful for their Arizona rights to be themselves. Of course, ex-Californians like me would probably not be welcomed back to our former state.

Hell to Humor is a look back at some local and national issues during a time of change in America, although I have to say, today is also a time of change. Most of the following essays appeared in a small daily newspaper along the Colorado River in Arizona where I served as managing editor from 1993 until 2005. A few of them were published in some Arizona weeklies in more recent years and dealt with topics not necessarily widely criticized by the mainstream (usual suspects) media. And although not all of them involve politics, most of them probably would not appear in today's newspapers from other (more PC) states. And as far as Left-Coast techies are concerned, Twitter hearts would probably go all-aflutter as they co-conspire with Google and Facebook to turn banning into an art form. The columns are quite facetious — "smart ass" – according to at least one of my former publishers. They are my opinions, at the time of publication, and not those of anyone else including (especially) the management of those publications.

Although readers probably will not recognize most of the local Arizona characters in these opinion articles, they will likely be familiar with public officials and activists in their own communities who might just fit the bill. Of course, many of the national politicos and entertainers mentioned are still either famous, or infamous, today.

Most of the following columns include the date of publication. Some, by today's standards, seem naive while others come off as angry or caustic. All are views over the last few decades through a time-specific window of a rural Arizona newspaper editor, smartass cartoonist, neo-pulp writer and grumpy old man. And, this particular grumpy old fart will most definitely add a few contemporary issues concerning those columns as they relate to today's politically correct insanity.

I am thankful to the people of Arizona for the prevalent acceptance of individualism during the past and right up to this afternoon. I am truly thankful for the American Constitutional freedoms, highly honored in this southwestern state, that give us all the right to be wrong.

Publisher's Note:

When known, the editorials which follow include the original date of publication after the title.

Current day comments by the author follow each article in quotes.

1. Animals and Attitudes

ALTHOUGH I LIVED QUITE some time in the big city, I also grew up on a ranch in northern California and now live in rural Arizona. Animals have played a big part in my life. I've always enjoyed pets, farm animals and wild critters, and delighted in their unique personalities, even the ones that Chuck Jones and Tex Avery masterfully animated for our enjoyment. So, obviously, I found animals to be especially useful in communicating a variety of points of view.

California birdbrains take a dive

July 15, 2004

Ever since Charles Darwin communicated the Law of Natural Selection, there have been those who have attempted to repeal it.

During the last 20 years we have heard a lot about spotted owls, desert tortoises, razorback chubs and a variety of snail-darting minnows, gnat-catching mud suckers and cross-dressing root rats. I'd swear that some "rare" species are being created just so a group of otherwise out-of-work bureaucrats will have something to protect.

Darwin's theory is that some species are better adapted to survive than others. For instance, a desert tortoise won't do too well in the Antarctic region, and penguins are quite scarce in Arizona. They are both well designed to survive in their respective neighborhoods.

Humans have an advantage on other species in that most of us possess the intelligence to come in out of the rain, put on a jacket in cold weather and grab a chilled brewsky when it's hot. This places us at the top of the evolutionary scale — even with "Lite" beer.

But the attempt to keep some species with us may just be a lost cause.

The *Mohave Valley Daily News* printed an Associated Press story out of Phoenix Sunday headlined "Endangered pelicans mistaking Arizona asphalt for lakes."

According to the article, some endangered brown pelicans have come to Arizona looking for fish (first sign that these creatures may be too stupid to survive) and are mistaking mirages, created over hot asphalt, as lakes. This can cause an incredible road-rash problem for the big-beaked Bozos.

California environmentalists should be alarmed, since the birds are native to the People's Republic of Santa Monica and other Left-coast hubs of enlightenment. Those folks can't afford to allow a single endangered species to leave as government restrictions and taxpayer-funded programs depend on keeping the creatures local.

Perhaps they should print flyers warning the birds against the Republican state of Arizona and its desert asphalt traps. Of course it would be hard to distribute the flyers to the birds because that would be littering. It would also be quite expensive since, in California, government flyers have to be printed in several languages.

Another possibility would be to build pelican helmets with tinted goggles so the birds wouldn't be bothered by the mirages, and, if they were, the helmets would protect them from birdbrain damage. This program could create a lot of government jobs in the Golden State — pelican helmet manufacturers and distributors — and may just be a major part of John Kerry's job growth plan.

And then maybe Darwin had it right and it should be up to Mother Nature as to the survivability of some creatures. Pacific Coast brown pelicans that fly into the desert looking for fish and kamikaze dive into highways and parking lots are not necessarily a benefit to the rest of us. They could be looked at as dinner from heaven for Arizona transients hanging around parking lots. But for the rest of us, those creatures are showing signs of terminal stupidity and don't deserve protection.

And in the same category, there are Hollywood "entertainers" who demand we put our tails between our legs and surrender in the Mideast. They consider Americans to be the barbarians and offer only love and acceptance to the terrorists.

The brown pelicans are smarter than that.

Okay. I may have understated the fact when I said much of my work was "facetious." And there are plenty of folks in Arizona as well who found my columns "in poor taste," "over the line," and "beyond mainstream" to the point that I should have been "muzzled." Their opinions were also published in "letters to the editor" as part of the newspaper's acceptance of diversity, at that time.

Tombstone gives scoop on new 'Old West'

Sept. 22, 1995

The *Mohave Valley Daily News* printed an Associated Press story Thursday about the Tombstone (Arizona) City Council's vote to force horses that travel on city streets to wear diapers. The council calls them "dung bags." They claim the animal wraps may not do anything for the "Old West" image of the area, but they will help keep the streets clean.

The story went on to say, "Horse owners who fail to equip their animals with dung bags will have to pay a misdemeanor fine ranging from $25 to $300 and face a possible jail term of up to 30 days."

The City of Tombstone should be proud of the progressive thinking of its elected leaders. I am sure western towns would have done the same thing over one hundred years ago if they had thought of it. Perhaps it just took until now for politicians to acquire enough expertise in horse manure.

Whatever the reason, the new policy can become an entrepreneurial boom. Designer horse diapers could be produced for the discriminating cowboy. Think of it: horse diapers with pictures of Phoenix Suns players, city council members, first ladies or rock stars on them; cartoon characters for children's ponies; special designs by Calvin and Ann Klein (which could come with an accessory package including a lace sneeze guard and a happy-trails headband); Marlboro brands for the macho cowboy; and the ever-popular Elizabeth Taylor Black Biscuit design.

Construction companies could jump on the horse wagon by building street corner changing stalls. Mr. Ed, of course, could make a comeback to rival June Allyson as the spokescreature for "Deep Ends" horse diapers. On the other hand, horses that assist Sheriff Joe's chain gangs would have to be issued pink diapers to avoid contraband selling of same.

Retailers would experience an increase in the sales of industrial-sized baby wipes and powder containers.

If the policy had been established in the Old West, the area would have become civilized sooner. Lives might have been saved. Just think. Wild Bill Hickok could have thrown down his poker hand of aces and eights and quietly excused himself to go change his horse. Instead his horse relieved itself in the street and Wild Bill was shot.

Such a waste.

Seriously, this is the kind of thing that makes one appreciate our own (Bullhead City) council. I realize some of them have felt many of my earlier columns were filled with the source of the above topic. And we all have made judgments in the past about some of the Bullhead City issues and actions. But historic Tombstone, Ariz., wins my vote to receive the golden shovel award for silliest political action.

Randolph Scott must be spinning in his grave.

Arizona has its share of animal activists. And I support the rights of all property owners to follow their dreams even if they value pit bulls over people. But many of those folks didn't find humor in some of my opinion-page blather. In the days when most people still wrote letters, as opposed to today's email and online "social media" comments, I would receive about five angry letters for every four that were complimentary.

As we used to state, "at least they are reading the paper."

Ferret aficionados put the bite on prairie dogs

June 21, 2001

They say it's a dog-eat-dog world out there.... that is unless you're a prairie dog. Then, according to an Associated Press story that appeared in Sunday's *Daily News*, it's a ferret-eat-dog world.

The story reports that Kaiser Permanente attempted to "relocate" 500 prairie dogs that just happened to live where the company is building an assisted-living facility in Colorado. Kaiser spokesman Steve Krizman is quoted as saying, "There is no one taking prairie dogs right now." Therefore, the company is shipping the prairie dogs to an Arizona black-footed ferret breeding program to become ferret chow.

The last paragraph of the story reads, "Prairie dogs are typically quarantined for a period to make sure they aren't carrying disease. They are usually killed before being given to the ferrets."

Now, I'm not your typical animal-rights kind of guy. Oh, I like dogs, except for those mincing little yappers with Richard Simmons haircuts. But I also like hamburgers and a snake can really tick me off by just looking at me.

However, in this case, I feel a bit sorry for the prairie dogs.

I'm sure Kaiser will build a very nice assisted-living facility. And, obviously the 500 prairie dogs should be moved. Otherwise they might mess up the miniature golf course with extra holes, trip a few walker-assisted residents, or foul the hot tubs. But do they really need someone to take them? Did Kaiser look in the classified section for "prairie dogs wanted," or "room to rent, prairie dogs preferred," only to find "There is no one taking prairie dogs right now"?

Does Kaiser have an employee who solves problems such as what to do with extra critters?

I can picture the board meeting where Third Vice President of Rodent Remedies Michelle Marmot pipes up, "Let's sell the little beasts for food. We can tell everyone we are relocating them, herd them onto miniature cattle cars and deliver them to our ferret camps in the Arizona desert. We'll medically check them out for a couple of weeks to make sure they are disease-free, then we just make sure most of them are dead before we feed them to the ferrets. We'll call it Code Name: Soylent Brown."

Now, I know there are some local politicos who might think I would tend to favor weasel-like creatures. But they also know I am against any form of affirmative action. Programs that discriminate for any reason are wrong. Therefore, what makes ferrets, black footed or not, more important than prairie dogs? Prairie dogs have a society. They live together in communities while the infamous untrustworthy ferrets are loners that raid those rodent civilizations, dragging helpless dog-children off in the night to devour them.

If they had been born animals, Franklin Roosevelt, Jonas Salk, Henry Kissinger and Whoopi Goldberg could have been prairie dogs. On the other hand, Bela Lugosi, Ho Chi Minh, Dr. Mengele and James Carville could have been ferrets. Which creatures would you rather deal with?

I would think there is a lot of uninhabited desert land out there, miles from everything, where a community of displaced prairie dogs could move in without even being noticed.

As for the ferret-breeding program, Arizona Game and Fish could come up with a less-insidious dining plan. Perhaps desert tortoise on a half shell or spotted owl under glass could be served. And there is always an abundance of the little yapping lap dogs with Richard Simmons haircuts running around.

Had I written the prairie dog column today, I probably would have moved Whoopie Goldberg over into the ferret category along with Michael Moore, Ho Chi Minh, Dr. Mengele and Hanoi Jane. Does anyone even remember James Carville?

New Arizona resident has plans to help state Fish and Game Department manage wildlife

June 29, 2001

I recently wrote about a ferret-feeding program that I considered questionable. Now, according to the Associated Press, a Marana, Ariz., resident is proposing an even more questionable wildlife-feeding program.

The AP story reports that Wallace Burford's cat, Jake, was killed by a coyote near his home. Burford, who had moved to Arizona only two weeks earlier, is angry and blames the state Game and Fish Department for his loss.

He paid $328.21 to have Jake cremated and he wants the offending department to reimburse him.

"They (Fish and Game) are responsible for all the wild game," Burford said.

The AP story reports that Burford wants the department to "post signs warning people about roaming wildlife, feed the animals so they're not hungry enough to seek out pets, or reimburse people whose pets are killed."

Since people who have smoked tobacco for many years can legally blame the tobacco companies for health problems, and get away with it, why can't someone who's not "worldly" enough to know that desert coyotes consider cats succulent morsels blame a government agency for his problem? After all, the Arizona Game and Fish Department is designated to *manage* wildlife.

Perhaps the agency should consider tagging all animals with warning signs. "Warning! This coyote may be hazardous to your cat's health," signs could be branded horizontally on the sides of the wild canines. Of course government diversity law would demand one side would have to be in English and the other side in Siamese. I'm not sure the signs will save all cats, especially if they are Persian or dyslexic.

I still haven't figured out how to post the warning signs on snakes.

Burford, AP reports, has a new indoor cat. I wonder if he has been warned that it may be hazardous to his tropical fish collection. Perhaps it needs a sign.

Burford's idea of a feeding program for wild animals could also save a lot of pets and bring a lot of government jobs to Arizona. I wonder how many state animal feeders it would take to keep the wildlife full and away from our frightened kitties.

For instance, how many times per day will the animals have to be fed? Can we get all the animals to agree on a specific dinnertime as a cost-cutting measure? Perhaps night-feeders, like owls, could pick up their government handouts around dusk to avoid an overtime situation.

And what could we feed them? Could we take ground meat and pat it into the shape of kittens to feed to coyotes, bobcats, snakes, hawks and other feline aficionados? And where will we get the meat? The only place I can think of that would have that many expendable carcasses to turn into coyote food would be animal shelters. Unfortunately, due to some pet owners not spaying or neutering their animals, the shelters have to "euthanize" a lot of cats. Of course, a little common sense would eliminate this as a source of coyote munchies.

And we all know the ferrets will be a problem. They are hard to organize. I'm not even sure they will meet and confer.

The AP story reports that Burford believes all residents whose pets become victims of wild animals could be reimbursed. He believes the dollars could come out of funds from hunting and fishing licenses.

Seriously, I don't believe there is enough money in that state department's budget to fund Mr. Burford's proposals. And, I'm sure the Game and Fish Department has much higher priority programs that make much more sense than Burford's — such as the construction of restrooms for the bears.

I can't be completely sure, but I've heard that President Joe Biden may have considered a Mr. Burford for the position of director of the (ATF) Bureau of Alcohol, Tobacco, Firearms and Explosives before he settled on appointing Steven Dettelbach. It may have been another Burford; I don't know. Apparently Dettelbach exhibited his unequalled expertise, or lack thereof, to the world while being questioned by Congress.

Editor takes a stand on cockroach survival

June 23, 2000

People for the Ethical Treatment of Animals (PETA) is a large organization well known for its advocacy for animal rights. We've all either seen, heard about or read about their work against the use of animals in circus acts. These are people who really love animals.

Most of us are animal lovers in our own way. I like dogs and cats…. and I really love a good steak. The only hunting I ever did was in Vietnam — and it was a mutual situation — so I can understand those who want to protect Bambi and Dumbo from what they perceive to be uncaring acts by man.

But a letter I recently received from the PETA people really bugs me. They are no longer just complaining about sadistic circus clowns poking slapsticks into elephants and cosmetic scientists forcing bunnies to wear experimental tacky lipstick and eye shadow. They have launched an assault to protect the persecuted cockroach!

In the letter dated June 9, PETA staff writer Paula Moore states, "Instead of reaching for the Raid, why not show a little kindness to a cockroach?"

She goes on to explain that cockroaches "are really quite fascinating once you get to know them." She states that cockroaches "smell with their mouths and with the long antennae" and describes their cute little versions of eyes and ears.

"They also feel pain," she claims.

Well, maybe Bill Clinton would, but when it comes to cockroaches, I just don't feel their pain. Call me just plain mean, but I really don't care whether these disgusting creatures smell with their mouths or any other filthy chunks of their slimy bodies. And I don't want to "get to know them."

I can picture animal-nut actress Kim Basinger cuddling up to a sad-eyed crippled-up cockroach on a PETA public-service television commercial to explain the horrors that particular bug had to endure at the hands of some uncaring "speciesist." Perhaps Sally Struthers could also launch a "feed the cockroaches" program for PETA. (She should be very careful where she steps while filming.)

Will their next press release advocate a meals-on-wheels program for sewer rats? Will they sue Marine sergeants for calling recruits "maggots" on behalf of the Maggot Anti-Defamation League? How many Hollywood stars will wear Save The Roach ribbons at the next Academy Awards celebration?

Although many of us have considered the PETA people to be extremists, I think we all gave them credit for standing up on their hind legs for their beliefs. But their stand on cockroach preservation has dramatically increased the number of nuts that their image has over the average fruitcake.

In regards to the aforementioned Marine sergeants, I guess I was bit prophetic back in 2000. Today, sergeants not only can't call recruits "maggots" anymore, they aren't allowed to use detrimental expletives of any kind, whether they rhyme with maggots or not. In fact, recruits today have to make sure to keep straight faces when being "kindly" yelled at by sergeants who might just be men who think they are women.
The recruits are obliged to join in the pretense.

PETA believes silence is golden for retrievers and others
Sept. 20, 2017

We all have special interests that we support at one level or another. One of mine is free speech, so it boils my turnips when one side of an issue demands silence from anyone who disagrees. Of course I have said telephone solicitors that cold-call in the evening, or any other time, with requests to speak to the "woman of the house," or offer resort rewards or seek ridiculous polling information should not only be silenced, they should face the death penalty. But I guess the Supreme Court probably disagrees, and they certainly have that right.

Other folks are embroiled in efforts to protect the 2nd Amendment and ensure legal hunting is not restricted. While there are also people who give their time and energies fighting for the rights of dogs and cats not to be abused. I support a lot of goals that people have, as they are usually launched with the best of intentions.

But some activists are evil, such as Antifa, Nazis, Communists, homeowners' association leaders who measure lawn lengths, and those really nasty folks who want to tax cigar companies out of the country while making it illegal for businesses that hire employees to discriminate against potheads. I think that about covers it.

However, there is one group of caring people who aren't evil, yet they often go over the line. On the surface, PETA (People for the Ethical Treatment of Animals) seems like it is on the right course in defending the "rights" of other species. And I certainly support any efforts to protect Fido and Fluffy from abuse.

But now and then, they go too far – such as wearing pig suits to protest hot dog and hamburger restaurants. They look ridiculous in the suits and that discredits any good the organization does. It's as if I were to wear a pig suit with bunny ears in protest at the next Gloria Steinem appearance. That woman could swear about chauvinists all she wants, pigs or otherwise, while I would be the one with the funny captions pasted all over Facebook.

No, don't get me wrong. I love animals, especially chicken and steak. (*I believe I've been a bit too forthcoming in these columns about being a meat eater.*) And I believe there is a happy medium in the issue of animal welfare, especially since many of those animals also eat meat. I'm sure a few of the vegan PETA people look quite delicious to some of their meat-starved pet hawks, snakes, owls and, probably, some cockapoos. Perhaps the PETA R&D Department could develop a kind of bread that would be a decent alternative to carnivores' prey. If so, sadly they won't be able to name it after their organization, because someone else has already come up with Pita Bread.

I remember several years back when, as the editor of a newspaper, I received a PETA press release on saving innocent cockroaches. The PETA PIO wrote that cockroaches "are really quite fascinating once you get to know them." She stated that cockroaches "smell with their mouths and with the long antennae" and described their cute little versions of "eyes and ears." Sorry, but the concept of having any kind of compassion for allegedly cute cockroaches actually makes pig suits look debonair.

But finally, I've found a PETA issue I might support and, of all things, they are seeking silence. Last week the organization put out a release concerning their efforts to silence New Year's Eve in Seattle. The PETA president wrote a letter asking for a silent New Year's high-tech fireworks show "to offer a stress-free celebration for noise-sensitive animals, children, veterans and the elderly." Apparently, the group's efforts have been successful in Costa Mesa, and I would think that PC California city's explosive entertainment probably comes with subtitles – which now makes me wonder if they also have to put up a large screen to project a woman in a black sweater with moving hands that continue to sign "Boom" in American Sign Language (ASL).

As a Vietnam vet, I've never been a big fan of surprise booms, bangs and popping sounds. Many years ago, I was on my first day of a week of RR in Japan. It was raining. I went to a place that specialized in renting nice suits to guys who just came out of the jungle, so we could at least start out looking spiffy. I left the building in a blue pinstripe suit and walked across a rainy street. Some youths, who probably pulled the same stunt every time it rained, threw firecrackers behind me. I dived into the gutter only to see the laughing #@^&%*#s running off. Then I went back inside, dried off and rented another suit.

That's a long time ago, but even today there's that shudder that hits when I hear a surprise backfire or firecracker. So fireworks shows are never part of my New Year's Eve plans. And, let's face it; no official fireworks show is as colorful, exciting and adrenaline-laced as a napalm strike.

So I believe I have finally found an issue where both the PETA people and I can agree, silent fireworks. I'm probably alone, again, in my thinking, but it's nice to realize that extreme advocates can find some common ground. And I also think anyone who beats a puppy or kitty should be staked out in a Bullhead City yard for the majority of July.

Bullhead City summer heat gets up into the 120s in June, July and August. So, since many current liberal attorney generals and district attorneys claim to be looking for alternatives to incarceration for thieves, armed robbers, rapists and basic low-life scum-suckers, I recommend chaining the assholes up on a Bullhead City parking lot for just about any summer they choose.
I wrote this previous article for a weekly in 2017. It basically shows that maybe my maturity level peaked many years ago.

Pet psychics may have uses

Feb. 14, 1997

I just finished reading an interesting Associated Press feature out of the Peoples' Republic of Berkeley, California. The story is about pet psychics.

One woman claims to be able to talk to animals through her telepathic powers. She solves animal problems either on the phone, or for a few extra bucks, through house calls.

"While I'm on the phone with the person, I form a picture of the animal in my mind," the psychic claims. "Then I begin communicating with the animal by exchanging sounds, feelings and pictures."

The story describes one visit the psychic made to settle the squabbles of a dog, a cat and a rabbit that live together. She closed her eyes and, while holding each animal tightly, spoke for them. The channel discussion apparently solved their furry little problems.

Another pet psychic from Kansas pines for the acceptance of California. "In California people don't laugh at you when you tell them you're an animal psychic."

Well, I can't speak for a whole state, but I am from California. And I laugh at a whole lot of things going on in that land of fruits and nuts.

Anyone crazy enough to hold a cat up to a phone so some Ace Ventura wannabe can "read its mind" and solve its psychosis is either a candidate for the West Hollywood City Council or the Shady Rest Funny Farm.

In case you haven't figured it out, I'm not really a New-Wave kind of guy. I believe that if there were real psychics they would be doing productive things like averting disasters and making killings at the track, not guessing at how long John John Kennedy's marriage will last, predicting what Michael Jackson will impregnate next and holding psychiatric sessions with Bunny Foo Foo.

Even our own newspaper astrologer Jeane Dixon is questionable. For one thing, she died last month. We have her predictions through March, which we are running in the *Daily News*. But how good can they be? If she had really been a psychic, wouldn't she have put a note in her column last month saying, "Please forward all my mail to my syndicate editor after Tuesday as I will no long be alive"?

If so-called pet psychics were really able to communicate with animals, wouldn't they be conversing on a more basic level than solving disagreements between dogs, cats and rabbits? After all, most pets' needs are really basic: food, shelter, a place to relieve themselves, a pat on the head once in a while, a few disgusting things they do for their own pleasure and a little social intermingling with their own species. I have a feeling that any self-respecting cat wouldn't discuss his/her private life with some nosy California fruitcake anyway. And while we're at it, I believe it's illegal in several states to allow a dog, a cat and a rabbit to live together.

Of course the story does come out of Berkeley, the only town in California that makes Santa Monica seem like right-wing militia country.

But perhaps I'm wrong. (I'd like to say I'm the first to admit when I'm wrong, but there are usually quite a few other folks who beat me to the punch.) Maybe these pet psychics aren't nuts or larcenous fakes. Perhaps they really have a God-given ability to "walk and talk and squawk with the animals." If that is so, they could be put to better use than playing Frasier Crane to neurotic collies. They could be used to direct Benji movies; several could periodically swim along the California coast and persuade sharks to leave the surfers alone; some could legally assist military K9 dogs in species harassment litigation; perhaps some could help foul-mouthed parrots clean up their language; and one Republican pet psychic could help Whitewater investigator Kenneth Starr interrogate Socks.

Protesting has changed immensely in the last few decades. Complaining about PETA putting people in pig suits to protest Weinermobiles seems very naïve by today's standards, although putting ANTIFA thugs in pig suits would definitely be an improvement.

Make sausage, not war

Aug. 14, 1997

One would think the fine art of protesting is in monumental decline.

The angry crowds that used to fill the streets to hear Hanoi Jane denounce American imperialism are now sweating to the oldies with her workout tapes. The outraged college students who staged campus sit-ins to protest ROTC programs, conservative newspaper opinions, Ronald Reagan or the lack of black- Hispanic- women- and gay-studies classes presently sip the right kind of wine as they watch HBO Barbra Streisand specials in their time-share vacation condos.

Times they are a-changin'. And protesters have become a thing of the past ... until just recently.

It seems American whining has increased, again, to the level reminiscent of the 1960s.

It began with a religious group announcing a boycott of Disney. On the surface, that action could be equated with Bill Clinton being shocked by the *Sports Illustrated Swimsuit Edition*. But, as Southern Baptists pointed out, Disney isn't just Pooh-bears and friendly dwarfs anymore. The corporation is now involved in a lot of entertainment offerings, some of which contain sex and violence and not-so-G-rated humor.

The Disney-produced "Ellen" TV sitcom, which features a comic lesbian portraying a comic lesbian, sent the Baptists into their protest. One would think that if they were shocked by the content of the program they could simply watch a different show with more social acceptance, like "Men Behaving Badly."

Now that the economy seems to be improving and unemployment is at a low level, some unions have begun flexing their collective muscles. The Teamsters' strike against United Parcel Service looks like it may take a while. Unfortunately, the strike may result in giving UPS the same status as Railroad Express.

But the big Kahoona of protesters for the '90s is People For the Ethical Treatment of Animals (PETA). These animal rightists are known for their Missing-In-Action style raids on laboratories where they rescue mistreated rats and such.

PETA is presently deployed in an anti-Weinermobile operation. Everywhere the Oscar Meyer Weinermobile shows up, PETA people also show up dressed as pigs with meat protest signs. They attempt to hog the spotlight to preach their tasteless baloney against the eating of meat.

Once again, it would seem that free people have a choice not only in what they want to read and view on TV and at the theater, but in whether they eat meat and/or vegetables. And maniacal vegetarians certainly have the American right to carry signs demanding everyone else stop eating meat. But PETA people in pig suits are hard to take seriously. (I would hope they don't wear their costumes when they protest in the town near where "Deliverance" was filmed.)

I've always wondered what PETA people feed their pets. Do they give their dogs a daily diet of PETA bread? Can a cat live on grits? Do they avoid vitamins derived from shark livers? Would one squeeze melon balls into the shape of a rat to feed to a pet boa constrictor?

Now that I think about it, today's protesters haven't quite reached the level of the whiners of the 1960s. The hippie costumes were rather silly looking, but they outclass pig suits.

Anyway, this is America. And people have a right to protest things they don't like as long as they don't resort to violence. And thank God, even Hanoi Jane still has the right to send her oldies-work-out tapes through UPS and eat a hot dog while watching "Ellen."

> *Snap forward to the early to mid 2020s. Disney has gone beyond "Ellen," to a point that I wonder if Scrooge McDuck will soon be attacked for systemic white-duck species-ism while having to share his wealth with the Biden-pardoned, Marxist Beagle Boys and the parrot from the Three Caballeros will have to cross-dress while the rooster will advocate for Beak Lives Matter. That company is in transition in more ways than one.*
>
> *Protests are now even more violent than the screaming, whining anti-war nuts of the 1960s. Back then, they blocked roads, started fights, burned banks and made fools of themselves all to support Communist North Vietnam's invasion of the South Vietnam democracy. Today's big city protesters look more like the PETA whiners of the 1990s in their pink hair and freak costumes, all the while blocking highways, burning neighborhoods, flash-mob looting stores, attacking non-protesters and screaming that people who don't believe as they do must be silenced.*
>
> *I miss the pig suits.*

Politics play part in pups' park proposal

January 17, 2002

Recently the Bullhead City Rotary Park finished building a skate park for local youth. And from what I have seen, it has been a success for those young folks on small wheels.

But, one of the realities of doing good things for people is, as soon as an organization does something like this, there are other folks who become upset because it wasn't done for them. Bicyclists, who had been using the skate park improperly and had been blamed for some damage to it, complained that no one had built a park for them.

The city has, however, been working with a group of caring folks who are attempting to build a BMX park for bicyclists. When this project is finished, it will help another group of local youths enjoy their free time in Bullhead City.

It will not, however, assist any Pogo Stick aficionados, Hula Hoop hipsters, Yo-yo flippers or spiritual snake dancers. The city leaders should apologize in advance for their slight to these folks.

But our city is moving forward in its attempt to take a bite out of our lack of recreational facilities. The City Parks and Recreation Commission has discussed the development of a dog park. And, oddly enough, the proposal does have a lot of community support.

One dog park supporter proposes the park should be three acres where dogs could run off the leash. She would like to see the area fenced to separate big dogs and little dogs.

I'm not sure we should get involved in any separate-but-equal park areas, canine or not, at this time. Signs that read "no coyotes allowed," "small dogs only" or "you must be this tall to urinate on this tree" could eventually lead to future discrimination lawsuits. However, allowing the petite and plus-sized canines to frolic together could be almost as dangerous as allowing camouflage-fatigue-wearing owners of hunting dogs to mingle with lap dog owners. Those lap dog owners can be pretty mean.

Now, I'm not necessarily against the building of a park for dogs. But I do think the proposal should be thought out thoroughly. For instance: Who's going to design the seats on the swings? And how high should the doors be on the restrooms?

In a *Daily News* story Wednesday, the city parks and rec director pointed out that the Lake Havasu City dog park had a problem with snowbirds taking the doggie bags to use in their RVs. Those must be really large doggie bags.

I would suggest that retired police dogs should probably be hired to handle the security. There's more than just doggie bag theft to worry about. After all, a cat may disguise itself to look like one of those disgusting little yapping dogs that look like walking dryer lint just to enter the park.

Which brings us to another point: To avoid complainers at City Council meetings, should we also develop a cat park, weasel park, ferret park, chicken park or even a nice boa constrictor park (which shouldn't be placed too close to the small dog area)?

Whatever our city leaders decide on this issue is fine with me. We are, after all, in a recreation area and all parks assist in drawing tourists. Perhaps our city could even make a few bucks by selling visiting dog owners special scoops decorated with the printed message, "Bullhead City is piles of fun."

It was a kinder, gentler era when I could question what kind of dogs would be allowed to use the dog park restroom. Today, somebody's gonna be offended if one animal breed is restricted from the puppy potty. And what terrible misfortune could happen to the city puppy park posse member who dares to reject the cat that looks like the dryer lint yapper? After all, that cat may really identify as a terrier.

PETA claims are an udder story

April 27, 2003

A few years ago we were all worried about Mad Cow Disease and whether our bovine brothers and sisters would all have to be restrained at a funny farm. Well, time has passed and Mad Cows have been placed on the back burner. We are now faced, according to the People for the Ethical Treatment of Animals (PETA), with the problem of falsely labeled "Happy Cows." (Wouldn't it be interesting if some of the Happy Cows were also Mad Cows? Would that make them manic-depressive cows?)

Apparently, the San Francisco-based California Milk Advisory Board launched a "Happy Cows" advertising campaign, which ticked off the PETA folk. One of the board's television commercials shows cows frolicking in a beautiful pasture with the slogan, "Great cheese comes from happy cows. Happy cows come from California."

PETA sued the board demanding an end to the campaign because, according to PETA's wisdom, the cows are really miserable.

Now, I grew up on a farm, and I have seen a lot of cows, and bulls, engaged in a lot of bovine activities. And, truthfully, I have never seen a cow smile (although I have seen a horsefly). Cows have perfect poker faces — it's impossible, for me, to tell what they are thinking. Perhaps PETA has the assistance of Shirley MacLaine in communicating with the cloven-hoofed complainers, but I wouldn't think grumpy cow channeling would be admissible in court.... no matter what they would have to beef about.

To me, the burden of proof should be on PETA. And let's face it, from what I've heard is growing in many parts of California, especially near Frisco, those cows may not only be happy, they may be Robert Downey, Jr., ecstatic.

According to an Associated Press report, the California court (for once) made a decent decision to throw out the case. But, typical of California, they didn't base it on the stupidity of PETA's allegations. The court ruled that a government agency (California Milk Advisory Board) is exempt from false advertising laws that would apply to private individuals.

So basically, a La La Land government agency could have claimed the milk comes from zootsuit wearing, prurient tap-dancing weasels with skin problems and not have been responsible for honesty. On the other hand, that private canned cream company that claims its cows are contented could be the next target of a PETA lawsuit.

PETA's actions, as well as most California court rulings, are, once again, enough to drive a happy cow mad.

> *Okay! I did find PETA to be an easy target back in the old days.*

The following cartoon and column continues the protest theme, while updating it to some of the more recent craziness. It appeared in a weekly publication during a time while I wrote a series of columns dealing with old-movie westerns.

Free Speech is a right

April 2017

Writing about white-hatted cowboy good guys is out of the question this week. Today's topic is on the other side of the spectrum – contemporary villains. These are people who know nothing about the values of the Code of the West. They don't respect anyone else's rights to live and speak freely. And they have channeled their lack of values into a destructive, Machiavellian hatred. Obviously, I'm referring to the current crop of violent, anti-free-speech protesters.

The people who scream the loudest while destroying property just to make sure other opinions aren't voiced do not deserve our attention. They deserve the attention of law enforcement. Break the law; go to jail.

You know the protest gatherings I'm referring to. On the other hand, there are many valuable rallies and parades in this country that profess a point of view. And, in Arizona, most of them are peaceful and end up being a lot of fun. I wouldn't be surprised to see a Pit-Bull-Pride Parade on Bullhead City's Miracle Mile this year as a replacement for the River Regatta. But I digress.

This country has bent over backward to accommodate political expression of all kinds. Americans have the right to say some very wacky things, as long as they do so peacefully. Since the 1960s, protesters have taken to the streets to rally for every issue from anti-war to anti-death penalty, anti-vaccination, anti-meat, anti-guns and anti-restroom "discrimination." And no one steps in the way to stop these naysayers while the law is being followed. Peaceful protest is our First Amendment right; violence is not.

Today, whenever protesters seem to be being ignored, they tend to get out of hand. And just like our parents used to say in the 1950s and '60s when a bunch of us kids would get carried away with our toy swords and BB-guns, "It's all fun and games until someone loses an eye." Many current protests seem to be premeditated crimes of violence and should be dealt with as such.

I've noticed issues are now less important to protesters than personalities. For instance, in California (the land of openness, diversity and acceptance), professional agitators always gather to disrupt any speaker to the right of Ho Chi Minh or Jerry Brown. Civilized discourse has become a thing of the past for the Golden State. Of course that state looks upon current federal immigration laws a lot like southern states once viewed the

Emancipation Proclamation. (Just thinking about that brought an odd image of Nancy Pelosi in a Confederate general's uniform to mind.)

Anyway, lots of things have been said in this paper and others about the behavior of today's protesters. I believe lawbreakers need to be dealt with by the law. But I also think that many liberals who share the anti-Trump, anti-wall, anti-Republican values of the protesters also do not believe that violence is the answer. And those folks should unite with the rest of us and denounce the violence. Then, maybe, we could get back to civil discourse.

And I, for one, would look forward to a peaceful Bullhead City Pit-Bull-Pride Parade, as long as there is no discrimination against Jack Russell terriers, Weimaraners, Shih Tzus, miniature Pinschers or Pekingese pups. I'm sure we could all get along. But cats can be prohibited.

Just in case there is a Feline Anti-Defamation League, I really don't hate cats. Most of them are really wonderful pets.
Then again, there are Persians. I believe they're on the no-fly list.

Nutty idea becomes a swinging success

July 11, 2001

In 1997 I wrote a column about a new product on the market. A Kansas City candy maker had come up with the idea of testicular implants to ease the suffering of male pets going through "post-neutering trauma." He called them Neuticles.

Now, four years later, with a slightly flaccid economy, the Neuticles market is still quite potent. An Associated Press story in Friday's *Mohave Valley Daily News*, "'Neuticles boost dogs' self-image," updates us on the masculine canine falsies.

Dr. Thomas Allen, veterinarian, pointed out how the product helps dogs' "self-image" and went on to say it also makes the owners feel better about sterilization. "It's a pretty common thing for a family to be in a squabble when the wife wants to do it and the husband is against it. This could be a compromise," he said.

I don't want to doubt the good doctor's philosophy, but, if I thought my wife's idea of a compromise was the implantation of artificial nuts anywhere, I'd be somewhere in the Sierra Nevada Mountains by now. It's not a good precedent to set in one's relationship.

The story went on to describe the "standard model" implants as being made of polypropylene. But for a few more bucks one can purchase the Cadillac of artificial dog testicles, which are made of silicone. The AP story says the silicone Neuticles have a "more natural feel." Now how did the reporter find that out? I know that some AP reporters will go to all ends to get a story, but this one worries me.

One pet owner quoted in the story remarks about her English bulldog who had recently had the procedure, "He's got the cutest rear end I've ever seen." Where do they get these people?

Neuticles are offered in sizes ranging from Chihuahua to Great Dane and are more popular, according to the 1997 information, with shorthaired dogs where they can be noticed (by people like the above mentioned pet owner, I assume). Cat Neuticles are also available. (Why? How could you tell? And who's gonna check?)

This is the kind of procedure that one would believe only Hollywood dog stars like Benji or My Dog Skip would go through. But, apparently, many preppie suburban canines are profiling the product as well. And, obviously, there must be quite a market for this product throughout modern America or it would not have survived the last four years.

Perhaps Mohave County *(Arizona)* Economic Development Authority (MCEDA) could get back into the County Supervisors' good graces by getting a Neuticles plant built along the I-40 industrial corridor. It wouldn't take as much electricity as a steel mill. It certainly wouldn't use as much water as a power plant, and, unlike Griffith Energy, if it sells its entire product out of area, no one will be shortchanged.

With the right marketing and economic development assistance, other competing product manufacturers could be lured to the I-40 industrial corridor. MCEDA could exonerate its image and get the last laugh on its detractors by making Mohave County the artificial dog testicle capital of the world.

But perhaps I'm being too optimistic. It's quite possible that, over time, recipients of silicone Neuticles could develop certain medical problems like warm noses and misshapen doohickeys. If that begins to happen, hordes of lawyers will join in class-action suits to take a bite out of the industry, and our county could be subject to some liability in the case.

Maybe we should be a little more conservative and keep an eye out for other more positive and profitable clean industries such as manufacturers of desert tortoise Speedos or birth control devices for rabbits.

Okay. So some of my old columns weren't exactly Drew Pearson, Jack Anderson or Thomas Sowell-worthy. But even by today's standards, artificial dog nuts is a much less cringey topic than some of the things big city school boards are approving for elementary school curriculums.

Now for some hard news...

Texas scientists cough up cloned hairball named 'Cc'
February 22, 2002

The scientific community has once again amazed the rest of us with a startling announcement: They have cloned a cat.

I only have one question regarding the situation: Why?

The kitty, named "Cc" which probably stands for "cloned cat," is the product of experiments at Texas A&M University. Apparently the researchers had 187 failures before their final success in producing Cc, the feline of the future. One would think that if those Texas scientists really wanted a kitten that much they would have just put a male and a female cat in the same vicinity. Their success ratio would have been better.

But, then again, this makes one wonder if we are going through a period of not having enough cats. Are those four-legged, furniture-clawing, sand-pooping, aloof felines on the endangered animals list? I don't believe local community animal shelters would say we are having a cat shortage.

Besides the cat, researchers have now been able to clone sheep, goats, cattle and mice.

Although I believe the natural reproduction process to be far superior to sci-fi cloning theories, I can understand why some would experiment with cloning sheep, goats and cattle. People eat these creatures and perhaps, someday, it will be necessary to use high-tech means to feed the growing population.

But mice are another thing. Do we really need cloned mice? Maybe that is why the brain trust cloned the cat — to catch their cloned mice.

Japanese scientists have reported recently that most of the mice they have cloned have died young of liver and lung problems. Perhaps cloned lab-mice have a predisposition for use of alcohol and tobacco.

According to another recent news story, the city of Scottsdale, Ariz., would not welcome any cloned mice at this time. Apparently, the area residents are under siege from an infestation of roof rats. These rodents allegedly live, party and reproduce in trees and roofs. The problem is so bad that local officials have requested federal funds and services to help exterminate the fuzzy rodent trespassers.

Perhaps Cc could lead a small army of cloned super-soldier cats in an assault on the Scottsdale vermin. The Texas A&M scientists could dress the future felines in Santa suits so they could sneak up on the roof rats before terminating them.

But I may be stretching my imagination a bit as I think the use of cloned super soldiers in Santa suits has been in at least three of Arnold Schwarzenegger's recent films. It would probably be wiser to see what traditional exterminators could do about the situation before we send in the clones.

Anyway, I can understand why scientists may want to experiment with cloning endangered species. But the idea of cloning cats and mice makes about as much sense to me as attempts to clone cockroaches and mosquitoes.

Cloning has been a frightening topic for quite some time, although scientists are still dabbling in a variety of strange genetic experiments. I guess our fears might have been a bit over-stated twenty years ago. But today, the fact that Artificial Intelligence (AI) might eventually begin cloning experiments without human oversight is a tad worrisome. It's sort of like having Frankenstein's monster creating its own monsters.

Some of the following columns may cause readers to think I am not very conservative and am picking on Republicans a little too much. The fact is, most, if not all, elected officials in Mohave County are Republicans. In recent elections (2020 and 2022), 75 percent of Mohave County voters chose Republican candidates over those from that other party. So suck it up, buttercup.

News scoops pigeon poop problem
Aug. 14, 1998

The *Mohave Valley Daily News* has covered some interesting topics in the last couple of weeks including killer bees, poopy pigeons and snotty Republicans.

Supervisors have decided that pigeons with loose bowels have become a deadly menace for Mohave County. They contend that these winged pariahs have not only reached critical mass population-wise, but are now hell-bent on a rampage of destruction through aerial poopy bombardment of civilian and government rooftops. And, unlike killer bees, they cannot be scooped up in a vacuum cleaner.

Therefore, county residents have been saddled with the draconian rule now commonly known as "feed a pigeon, go to jail."

Already, I understand, there has been a backlash to this law, which has created a whole new category of criminal. It may only be a rumor, but an unnamed informant has told me that a new category of criminal gang has been created in reaction to the ruling. The gang, known as the Pigeon Putsch, is made up of elderly ladies, many who fought in the underground during the big war, who hang around parks and street corners flaunting their distaste for the law. They can be recognized by their black leather jackets with pictures of a Walter Lanz' cartoon character, Homer Pigeon, painted on the backs. They carry large bags of contraband popcorn that they criminally disperse to the feathered manure spreaders. It's said they are armed with bird-head topped canes. (One has a bird-head topped walker.)

Certainly there must be some more-reasonable reaction available to our county leaders in dealing with our feathered friends' potty problems. Possibly, the county could allow the feeding of pigeons as long as the popcorn is laced with Kaopectate. This would allow the birds to pucker up and clean up their act, and, as a possible side benefit, improve their image among other birds. (This may help the above-mentioned Republicans as well.)

Another possible cure for the problem would be to tie a hungry coyote on the top of every roof in the county. It has been found that rubber snakes and owls do not scare pigeons. They make nests on the snakes and I can't tell you (in a family newspaper) what they do with the owls. But hungry coyotes are another matter. I guarantee that no pigeon would roost on a roof protected by a hungry coyote. Of course there probably would be a slight problem of what to do with the piles of coyote poop that would end up on the roofs.

Then, of course, the county could follow the example of Bullhead City's pet ordinance, and make it a law that all pigeons should be licensed. People would have to license the pigeons they wanted to keep and all unlicensed pigeons would be taken to the fowl pound to wait for adoption.

If this last example is successful, it may also work on killer bees and snotty Republicans.

Truth be told, Mohave County is, and has been for a long time, a very conservative area. And anyone who wants to be elected here probably should register Republican. That said, there are quite a few Republican social groups in the area and not all of them get along together. One might say that in Mohave County we have a three-party system. And all of those parties are Republican.

Fad of the past could be a holiday blessing
Nov. 7, 1997

Fads are fleeting, and it seems the once trendy Vietnamese potbellied pigs have gone the way of the pet rock and Nehru jacket.

A few years ago, these immigrant porkers were touted as more intelligent and cleaner than dogs, and destined to remain small, cute house pets. According to a Scripps Howard news story, house-pig buyers were told the little beasts wouldn't grow to be over 50 pounds. After a couple of years, those people, some of whom paid more than $1,500 per pig, are waking up to 250-pound wallowers in their homes.

And, according to Patty Williams, bureau manager of the local animal shelter, people are losing their once welcome house pets at an alarming rate. Last week the shelter picked up five conveniently lost potbellied pigs.

Only 60 percent of animal shelters will even take in the pigs, according to the Scripps Howard story. The shelters are designed for dogs and cats, not livestock. What's a humane society to do?

Well, folks, the holidays are coming. And the Salvation Army and community service clubs will be doing their best to feed the homeless and less fortunate during those special days.

It seems to me that a lot of poor folks would be pleased to have "the other white meat" for Thanksgiving and Christmas. I'll just bet the shelter would be happy to donate these creatures, which have overgrown their welcome, to any service club willing to "prepare" them for holiday services.

Think how happy this will make our hungry transients this holiday season, as well as how thankful it will make many turkeys.

> *Concern for feeding transients was no big deal back in the 1990s. But today, it's a major problem in big cities like Frisco, L.A., Portland and Seattle. Especially since the number of "homeless" residents in those cities have begun to rival the official populations. I don't think there are enough pet pigs left in those areas to serve a decent brunch to the drug-addled squatters who currently use city sidewalks as both beds and toilets.*
>
> *But the aforementioned "poopy pigeons" could be of use.*
>
> *After all, the only difference between a "flying rat" pigeon and a squab dinner is a little preparation.*

How should community react to biting fish tale?

Sept. 15, 1999

A front-page story in Sunday's *Mohave Valley Daily News* tells us that "piranha-like fish" have been caught in the Colorado River. To me, this is a bit like "nuclear-like missiles sighted."

The recent catch was by Everett Martin in the Devil's Elbow area of the river. The Brazilian fish, apparently unhappy about being caught, took a bite out of Martin's fellow fisherman, Carl Hill, who "bled like heck for a while." A third fisherman, Mike Exted, described the fish as having "a mouth full of teeth similar to a human's, but sharper."

Havasu Wildlife Manager Greg Wolf identifies the fish as a relative of the Red Piranha, of which there have been other sightings and/or catchings and he believes the breed is reproducing in the river. Wolf, however, says not to worry, as this relative, the paku, is only a "nut eater." Now if I was Carl Hill, I'd probably be a little insulted.

This reasoning is somewhat like "The fisherman was wounded by a John Gotti family member. John Gotti would be dangerous, but these family members have a history of only shooting rats."

Say it to yourself. "Piranha family!" Does that give you a nice warm-fuzzy feeling along the line of the Osmond and King Family Christmas shows? Or does it tend to lean toward Manson family?

Wolf's contention that this fish is a nut eater is a bit unnerving. For the present, I, for one, don't plan on wading into the water beyond my knees. And I think most of our elected officials should completely avoid going into the river.

Perhaps Carl Hill had been snacking on Planters' Peanuts while fishing and his victim finger may have had a salty barbecue flavor about it, thus leading the illegal immigrant fish, already in shock from being caught in its new North American homeland, to snap, literally.

But even with that scenario, I still question Wolf's contention that this fish is relatively harmless. After all, the Colorado River area is not known as the almond capital of the country. Where are the rest of these breeding Brazilians getting their nuts?

Exted looked up both red piranha and paku on the Internet and claims the fish Martin caught looks just like the red piranha, not the paku. Is this beginning to sound like a screenplay for Jaws 5 with Wolf playing the part of the resort town mayor?

I believe, no matter whether this is a nut or meat eater, the Tri-state area has to go all out to rid the Colorado River of this Brazilian menace — and I think I know how we can do it. First we must lure the devils into one area by chumming the river with an offer it can't refuse. We then tow the bait through a gate into a special netted area of the river and cut the bait loose in the trap, at the same time closing the gate. We then lift the huge net out of the river and have a gigantic community fish fry — perhaps during this year's Hardyville Days.

The hard part will be choosing bait that would be applicable to the feeding habits of either type of piranha. Now, lacking an outlet for specialized Purina Piranha Chow, I suggest we tie one of our local politicians (candidates requested) to a long drag rope and troll the Devil's Elbow area of the river. Perhaps he (or she) could wear a Mr. Peanut outfit as an added attraction. I'm sure one of our dedicated Republican leaders would jump at the chance to clear the Colorado of this red menace. Besides, the next regular election is less than a year away — not to mention possible recall elections.

Of Course, I may just be overemphasizing the problem. Perhaps Wolf is correct that this fish is really harmless. In that case, everything I said is probably an exaggeration and there really is no danger — except the part about the coming elections.

I think back and wonder about why I made a joke concerning worry over coming elections. That was in 1999, prior to hanging chads, computer-ballot-counting machines with minds of their own and vote counting that gets halted due to an alleged water leak only to continue after the appearance of a massive amount of mail-in ballots that can't be validated. Even Alfred E. Neuman has a reason to worry about today's elections.

Dog days of summer arrive

Aug. 27, 1999

Readers of the *Mohave Valley Daily News* realize by now that we have entered the dog days of summer.

Monday's front-page story about poor Geronimo the lap dog being carried off by a marauding hawk kicked off the week's canine capers. Luckily, Geronimo's story had a happy ending, as according to the dog's owner, the hawk "must have dropped him at the school..."

Geronimo's picture accompanies the story and, from his expression, one would believe his airborne experience was traumatic — that is unless he always looks like that. In that case, perhaps the hawk was justified in thinking he was some kind of mutant bunny.

Wednesday's front page presented Mayor Diane Vick with her new, cute, little spotted Dalmatian puppy that she adopted from the City's animal shelter. This is what we call a "feel-good" story filled with kindness and sacrifice.

On the other hand, it's rumored that some of the mayor's political critics are spreading the story that she plans to adopt 100 more just like this one and then use them to market a line of spotted fur coats. Although I know some local Republicans plan to put on the dog for the upcoming GOP picnic, and that there will be some pretty Mickey Mouse political speeches made, I can't believe there is any truth to that Disneyesque rumor.

And finally Thursday's front page led with the story of Councilwoman D'Arcy Downs-Vollbracht's questions concerning Robbie the overheated police dog. Apparently there is some question about how this northern European dog "over-exerted itself..." causing it "... distress from the heat." My question is how often does it reach 120+ degrees in northern Europe? I would believe that any dog that grew up around yodeling, alp-climbing beer guzzlers would also yelp "Ach der leiber!" and fall flat on its Germanic muzzle the minute it hit the summer Bullhead City pavement.

What this city needs to do is to recruit specialized police dogs that are bred for the Tri-state area's climate, specific terrain and criminal element. Possibly Australian Outback dingoes could do the job.

Another animal that is proving to be heat resistant and, although they would be a little too hard to train for police work, could really take a bite out of crime is an alligator like the one that remains at large in Lake Mead. Thursday's paper contained a continuation of our own version of the recent movie "Lake Placid." The movie was about a couple of large crocodiles living in a lake in the northeastern United States. Our version started with the capture of a two-foot-long 'gator in Lake Mead along with a tale of the one that got away. Rangers are still looking for the second 'gator.

If the creature is able to survive the winters and grows to a healthy size, he or she could become quite a tourist attraction. Californians could bring their cameras to record "Meady" sightings, or possibly view rangers trolling the lake with a live burro on the line.

However, the little 'gator probably won't survive the winter. It could also get bashed by a Sea Doo or choke on a carp bone. Then again, a marauding hawk may have already carried it off.

The 'gator was never seen again. And with Lake Mead water levels on a downward trend, we may yet find the bones of the poor creature, much like some of the ones recently found inside a rusty 50-gallon drum.
On a brighter note, I don't believe the mob had anything to do with Meady's disappearance.

Bullhead City canine capers continue

Sept. 5, 1999

Robbie the dog's celebrity status is heating up again.

The Arizona Department of Public Safety (DPS) has been brought into Bullhead City's political kennel to investigate the police department regarding actions concerning the recently medically retired rookie police dog and a councilwoman.

Bullhead City residents have gotten used to the Council taking on a periodic circus atmosphere, but we have never been able to capitalize on it ... until now.

Thanks to the all-consuming need for local controversy, Robbie has become one hot dog — and he is in need of a new career. I believe, with the right management, Robbie could parlay his local popularity into a movie of the week and possibly a spokes-animal contract with Alpo or Dandy Doggie Bits. And the City would be wise to appoint him as mascot or, at least, grand marshal of the next rodeo, to ensure national coverage even if it's only a short feature next to Bat Boy in the *Weekly World News*. Perhaps he could ride in the rodeo parade in a vintage Belgian automobile driven by Councilwoman D'Arcy Downs-Vollbracht, in disguise, and followed closely by a Model T loaded down with men in Keystone Kops costumes.

Robbie possesses star-quality looks that will play well in a movie of the week. A good makeup man will have very little problem getting rid of the Nixon-like five-o'clock shadow that was noticeable in the photo that appeared on the front page of the *Mohave Valley Daily News* Wednesday.

I can picture Robbie playing himself in the docudrama titled "Dog of Bullhead," "Teaching Ms. Vollbracht," "Robbie Brown Eyes," "Heat Factor" or possibly just "Paws." The cameraman trucks in for a close-up as a misty-eyed tongue-dragging Robbie, gasping for air in a kennel shaped like a frying pan, chokes Brando-style, "I kooda beena contenda. Ya shooda took care of me."

Notice he isn't speaking German this time. I received a note from Republican P.R. guy Tom Criser telling me the correct expletive "Ach du Lieber" should have been used the last time I put words in Robbie's mouth. (I incorrectly quoted the beast as saying "Ach der Leiber.") In my defense, the dog is actually Belgian and, for all we know, could have a lisp. Besides, I worry more about right-wing Republicans who speak German just a little *too* well.

Anyway, this may be Bullhead City's best chance to be noticed by the rest of the country. Perhaps we could put a sign at the end of the Bullhead Parkway that could say something like "Now entering Bullhead City: The home of Robbie the Wonder Dog" or "This way to Bullhead City: The Land of the Perennial Investigation."

Bullhead City, Arizona, was incorporated in 1984 and, during the nineties was simply going through a troubled adolescence. The issues and actions of that time were as serious to the mayor and city council as they were humorous to the rest of us. Over the years, I've found that life is like that. Sometimes the situations one finds most vexing are also the ones that, in later years, one laughs the hardest about.

Remember how some folks reacted to Dan Quayle?

Those same people currently might attempt to understand a Kamala Harris speech and, looking back, consider V.P. Quayle to be brilliant.

They shoot horses, don't they? Not with vaccines

August 1, 2004

A recent Associated Press news story pointed out a political issue so far avoided by this year's crop of candidates.

The story concerns the plight of the West's wild horses in that they face West Nile virus unvaccinated.

The AP reporter stated horse owners are able to vaccinate their equine friends to help protect them from the latest publicized virus.

So, why the long face?

According to the article, wild horses do not have access to vaccinations.

Some would think that maybe it was a slow news day at the Associated Press. But I see the reporter's reason for pointing out this tragic issue, and perhaps political conspiracy, regarding the lack of health care for our majestic wild mustangs.

I would have thought someone at the Democratic Party convention would have made an issue of the Bush Administration's failure to protect wild horses from this dreaded disease. After all, just because they are wild does not mean they shouldn't be given everything Smarty Jones has.

Certainly the Kerry campaign could show a little compassion for those needy animals who have less, through no fault of their own, than your average cowboy-Republican-owned, pampered, domestic horses. I feel their pain.

By using a little horse sense, Kerry/Edwards could devise a job program that would put wild people (transients) to work vaccinating wild horses (as many of them do have experience handling needles) against West Nile virus, thus bringing the unemployment level to zero.

With a little government training, the newly employed could also give the wild horses needed basic dental exams, hair and nail rejuvenation, therapeutic massages and colonoscopies.

I would think the Demo-contenders could propose a tack-tax that would pay for the equine assistance. Your average horse owner or dominatrix probably won't complain about ponying up a little extra to pay for riding crops, bridles and saddles if it is to be used for a good cause.

Kerry could expand the program over time, with the assistance of Ted Kennedy and Ron Reagan, to vaccinate bats against rabies, rats and Michael Moore against plague and to send mad cows to anger management classes.

Obviously the Associated Press did us all a favor by pointing out an as-yet unsolved problem. Maybe the liberal media conspiracy serves a purpose after all.

> *Oddly enough, there were no calls to vaccinate wild horses against the recent Red China-released bat disease. In fact, I don't recall seeing any horses, wild or not, wearing paper masks or staying home from equine schools. Where have all the caring Associated Press reporters who championed the mustangs in earlier years gone? Anyway, so much for silly fuzzy, furry and feathered issues.*
>
> *The following columns deal with mostly serious topics that impact all of us on a more local level.*

2. Issues and Actions

Is it time to save the children, again?
May 7, 1998

As a child I was told drinking coffee would stunt my growth and/or turn my fingernails black. This kind of java-jive was served up in the 1950s without explanation to any preteen kid who asked for a cup of coffee.

Well, it must have been a slow news day in Phoenix last week when the *Arizona Republic* printed an exposé on kids who drink coffee. The focus of the story is that the Starbucks coffee houses have become for late '90s kids what the malt shop was to the '50 and early '60 kids.... and that for some reason we should be worried about this trend.

It quotes one high school girl as saying, "I'm totally addicted to coffee."

Now obviously, most common-sense parents won't serve their preteen children coffee because of the amount of caffeine it contains. But those same parents will make sure their kids don't over indulge in soda and chocolate either, both substances rich in caffeine.

But teenagers of all generations have to have a place to socialize. Hanging out at a coffee house with friends certainly beats hanging out on the street corner, in front of a liquor store or paraphernalia shop or any one of a dozen other places where they could get in trouble.

In fact, I believe the trend of teens hanging out at coffee houses is a step back to a more innocent era. Today's coffee houses are clean, well-lit establishments where high school and college students go to meet their friends, work on homework and discuss dating, philosophy, parents and politics ... and have a cup of coffee or cappuccino.

The *Republic* story, however, contained a hard edge of fear. It mentioned many problems associated with over-use of caffeine. I'm sure upon reading the article, some legislators, already high on their successes in the war on tobacco companies, have begun to salivate over the possibilities of creating another evil empire out of coffee companies and the monetary rewards government agencies could derive from punitive taxes.

Perhaps John McCain, Grant Woods and President Hillary are even now planning their propaganda campaign to stir up a prohibitionist-fervor against Juan Valdez in order to once again "save the children." If they are thinking of embarking on such a campaign, old Juan should begin to worry about loosing his ass; the brothers should think about heading for the Hills; and Maxwell could very well lose his House. Nothing seems to stand in the way when a politician smells money.

I can picture the anti-coffee commercial showing the Tasters' Choice couple being arrested for domestic violence after getting too buzzed from an afternoon coffee break. A variety of cartoon characters will suffer the fate of old Joe Camel as Folgers and Yuban executives testify before Congress that they "really weren't advertising to hook kids" on java. And insurance companies will force businesses to ban coffee drinking inside buildings.

And, of course, taxes would be raised about a dollar a cup to stem the use of coffee and "save the children."

Then again, maybe I'm just a little paranoid about the misuse of government power. Perhaps I'm just a little over sensitive, possibly from the large mug of Yuban I have been sipping while writing this column.

And I think my fingernails are getting a little dark.

All right. I said "mostly serious topics," didn't I? They are coming. Trust me. Perhaps the importance of this next issue regarding the state Legislature will be appreciated.

Arizona politicians debate prehistoric representation

Jan. 22, 1998

Sometimes, state legislators take a long time to deal with issues: deciding on an official state dinosaur for instance.

There is a little Jurassic flap going on at the state capitol between the pro meat-eating-dinosaur people vs. the pro vegetable-eating-dinosaur people. The fierce meat-eater dinosaur species, dilophosaurus, roamed northern Arizona a couple of hundred million years ago, while the more liberal vegetarian Sonorasaurus came along in a more enlightened age, only 100 million years ago, in southern Arizona.

Once again, the age-old battle of rural Arizona vs. the Pima-Maricopa power base raises its ugly, and in this case reptilian, head. Sonorasaurus fossil remains are housed at the Arizona-Sonora Desert Museum in Tucson. State-found remains of its northern meat-eating rival are kept in, of all places, Berkeley, California.

While legislators and special interests battle over which dinosaur will receive the honor of representing the great state of Arizona, one senator has suggested letting school children vote on the issue. That's a great idea. Kids will get a good lesson in democracy, and perhaps our legislators will be freed up to deal with a real issue or two.

Kids are fascinated with dinosaurs and, usually, bored to death with politics. Letting children decide which extinct beast will be crowned with the state title will teach the students about expressing their desires at the voting booth. They will also learn that, whether they win or lose, they will see a lot of political hoopla while nothing much will be accomplished. What better lesson can they learn about the election process?

Some may find it a little sad that the winning dinosaur will be honored posthumously. Perhaps a descendant of the beast, such as a sewer alligator or a horny toad, could be on hand to represent his/her/its ancestor as one of our political leaders announces the triumphant creature. And if the meat eater wins this scaly pageant, maybe our elected representatives will find a way to rescue its remains from Berkeley before they rename it Hippiesaurus.

I find it interesting that our hard-working legislators can spend the time to debate such topical issues as naming a state dinosaur. Perhaps soon they will engage in more of this activity, such as naming a state cowboy, posthumously of course. They could choose both a real cowboy from the 19th century and a reel cowboy from the 20th century film world.

I know we have a state flower, but do we have a state weed? How about a state pest, such as from the vermin, insect, environmentalist or slimy water-creature groups?

And, of course, we voters are seeking other near-extinct creatures in Arizona — politicians who take their jobs seriously and spend time representing voters on *important* issues.

> *I admit that I didn't take a lot of what our state Legislature and local government officials were doing too seriously.*
> *But I did find them entertaining. At least they couldn't declare war.*

Cowboys, Indians Duke it out over freeway name

June 11, 1997

John Wayne has been dead for almost 20 years and he's still having Indian troubles.

Pinal County supervisors recently renamed the refurbished Arizona Highway 347 as "John Wayne Parkway." The highway, soon to reopen as a four-lane freeway, runs by where the Duke once owned a ranch. Unfortunately, it also runs through the Gila River Indian Community.

In another instance of life imitating art, many tribal officials were angered that movie cowboy Wayne would be honored in their backyard. After all, Wayne offed a lot of movie Indians in his John Ford classic western films. He also killed a lot of movie Japanese soldiers, black-hatted bad cowboys and a variety of no-goodnik celluloid characters.

But that's show biz. And so is naming a freeway. Street, highway and freeway names are supposed to be publicly accepted as a positive for communities. Indians have a right to dislike Wayne because he played a cowboy just as much as they might like Tony Curtis, Jeff Chandler or Boris Karloff because they played movie Indians. Well, maybe that's not a good example. But communities have a right to support, or not, any image they want.

The supervisors are now planning on voting June 18 on a proposal to name the freeway "American Indian Veterans Memorial Parkway" on the Gila River reservation and "John Wayne Parkway" everywhere else. This may sound a little gutless on the supervisors, part, but, even though it's impossible, why not try to please everyone?

John Wayne is dead. I'm sure he wouldn't care if his named freeway was cut off at the pass with equal billing for the Indians. In fact, I think freeway names are about as un-John Wayne as an airport would be. If anything is named after the Duke, it should be a battleship, a riding club, an Irish pub, a shooting range or a college conservative think tank.

But using celebrity names for public roads, parks and airports is about as American as Dolly Madison cupcakes. And we Tri-state folks could spruce up our area's image by rounding up a few western celeb monikers.

For instance, when Highway 95 is finished being widened, (God knows when that will be) segments could be renamed for a variety of celebrities. Our area may not be large enough for a John Wayne stretch of road, but we could name a portion of the highway after, say, Hoot Gibson or Lash LaRue. That part of the highway that crosses reservation property could be named after Jay Silverheels (Tonto) or Little Beaver from the Red Ryder series.

Ronald Reagan Way would also be a nice western image for our area. Of course we would have to appease liberals with a Larry Parks Way, or a Lyndon Johnson Lane. The airport might adopt a more Old West image by renaming itself Crash Corrigan Airport while Telephone Cove could become Buster Crabbe Cove.

Even our Bullhead City Council chambers could be renamed after an appropriately successful B-western star such as Gabby Hayes or Al "Fuzzy" St. John.

These names could do for Bullhead City what Andy Devine has done for Kingman.

And then again, I could be wrong. Perhaps Pinal County supervisors should stick with Route 347, and we should keep Highway 95. After all, it would sound slightly silly to complain about construction delays on Lash LaRue and Little Beaver Boulevard.

That was 1997. Unfortunately, today cowboy stars would be the last folks to be honored by the naming of a road, airport or structure. For instance, there is still a big effort to remove John Wayne's name from the airport in Orange County, Calif. The Duke, who lived in Newport Beach until his death in 1979, was guilty of being a conservative Republican from the 1930s through the 1970s. How could he? The man was so non-woke that he supported US soldiers during the Vietnam War. He actually owned guns, publically supported Barry Goldwater for President, and he was never seen wearing a dress in public. There are those who want to ban his name from the airport because of his retroactive crimes against the current crop of cross-dressing Progressive, Socialist, Communist Democrats. Soon we'll probably see an ABC, CBS, NBC, CNN (etc.) celebration broadcast of the airport renaming to honor either Hanoi Jane Fonda or Admiral FUBAR (Rachel Levine).

What kind of weasel?

April 22, 2001

Councilman Dale Collins blasted the *Daily News* editorial staff recently for publishing a follow-up article regarding Bullhead City legal expenses. Collins called the staff "chickens**t weasels."

One might think that being called that would stick in my craw, but, on first hearing the tape of Collins' interview, I laughed so hard I stepped on my own tail. Collins, on the other hand, stepped on another appendage with his remarks concerning city staff.

I have to give Collins credit for originality. Usually politicians who dislike a story will use cliché names on their media targets. I've been called a fascist, communist, Nazi, redneck, member of the "liberal media conspiracy" and a variety of areas of the human anatomy. "Chickens**t weasel" is a new one.

I kind of like the weasel part. With today's acceptance of animal-rights activists' philosophy, this rather adaptable creature is not as negative an image as it used to be. In fact, since the media gets blamed for just about everything it reports, Collins would have been better served by blasting us as "journalists," probably the second least respected occupational category today — the least respected, for honesty anyway, is the lowly "politician."

Having been a cartoonist, I like to visualize characterizations. And I've had a hard time trying to depict what a chickens**t weasel would look like. I can see a dirty, rotten weasel or a sneaky weasel, but one made of, or covered with, fowl excrement? That's just hard to picture. I guess this particular weasel would have to be a little slow, perhaps chicken-pen challenged, to have that particular personal-hygiene problem.

Collins blasts again with "You're going to hell, you're looking like the *Bullhead City Bee*..." Should the *Daily News* be insulted by that remark? Should the *Bee*? I don't know what *Bee* Publisher Thom McGraham's opinion is on the matter, but I like to think both local newspapers are doing the best we can to present the news.... and scoop each other whenever possible.

Collins says he lets us know when we do a good job, which can be interpreted to say when he agrees with the essence of a story. If he doesn't like a particular story, he, and others, demand the newspaper "get the article straight."

I believe a local newspaper's job is to report what officials, such as council members, say and do. For those who say we print "lies" and a large amount of "negative news," I say of course we do: We quote politicians and cover Bullhead City politics.

Collins complains that the city finance department is not doing its job. He says he has told his concerns to the department and City Manager Dan Dible, who he says is like "talking to a bump on a log." Perhaps, once again, Collins is just upset that the answers he gets from city personnel are not what he wants to hear. Perhaps he finds opposing opinions on issues a little hard to swallow, a situation a bit like what an egg-sucking snake would encounter in an ostrich nest. (Once one starts animal references, it's hard to stop.)

Anyway, I'm a bit put out by the fact that I am only labeled "Weasel #2." Publisher Chuck Rathbun has the honor of the title "Weasel #1." And, like a true publisher, he has found a way to save money with this situation. We have been looking at plans to expand the *Daily News* newsroom. But now, Weasel Uno has scrapped the blueprints for new walls and offices and just wants to put in a little larger area surrounded by chicken wire. Thanks a lot, Collins.

Of course, after Collins' remarks about city personnel, he might think about putting a little chicken wire around his Council office, along with a few trip flares and anti-personnel mines.

All of my columns appeared on the one page in the newspaper that had the word "OPINION" plastered across the top. It was the only page where editorials, political cartoons and letters to the editor appeared. And although some politicos got their panties in a knot over the paper's coverage and my columns and cartoons, I never got truly upset by their hissy fits. I found that a little bit of humor could communicate a point of view to the readers as well as the officials better than an expletive-riddled attack. True masters of that form of column writing were Mike Royko, Lewis Grizzard and Erma Bombeck. I miss their work.

Restaurant chain fires first shot in war for 'a man's right to choose'
Nov. 19, 1995

There has been a lot written and spoken about freedom of choice in the last few years. Questions and opinions abound on how far we should allow our government into our wallets, bedrooms and onto our backs.

The majority in Congress has produced a budget that will trim some of our wasteful government spending, thus partially removing their hands from our pockets. When President Clinton was served the budget package, he called it a turkey and sent it back to the kitchen. Obviously he ordered pork.

Clinton, no stranger to bedrooms, believes government, as a whole, should not invade America's bedrooms. Of course he probably doesn't think this should apply to a variety of campaign aides. It's said this policy came to him one night after receiving Flowers.

The federal leviathan is continuing to litigate and legislate our national persona into a gaggle of divergent viewpoints, alternative lifestyles, none of which may say anything negative about the other. In other words, allowing freedom to be different as long as everyone pledges acceptance of each other.

The Knights of the Irish Snake Hunters may have their Diamondback Parade in Fruit Loop, Calif., as long as they allow the Loyal Order of Lithuanian Sheep Fetishists, Rwandan Rotifer Worshippers and the Brotherhood of Ricky Lake Look-Alike Transvestites to join their march. It seems the more diversity the government approves, the less individuality we have.

Our present administration has embraced the right to diverse lifestyle choices to such an extreme that they seem to be drawing the line at cannibalism. And for God's sake, and I may be breaking a federal law by bringing God into this, don't let the feds catch you teaching your children that "traditional values" are "normal."

This week we find freedom of choicers, those who believe in the rights of the individual over the power of the thought police, have a new, unlikely, champion. The Hooters restaurant chain has fired the first shot in the battle for "a man's right to choose."

The Equal Employment Opportunity Commission has recommended the restaurant chain, which is known for its well-endowed waitresses, hire men waiters as well. Hooters says, "No way."

"Hooters is fighting back," Mike McNeil, a vice president of Hooters, said in an Associated Press story Wednesday. "...A lot of places serve good burgers. The Hooters Girls, with their charm and All-American sex appeal, are what our customers come for."

Basically, if a company specializes in selling all beef hamburgers, and is well patronized and profitable, does the government have the right to demand the company also sell soy-burgers and kosher hot dogs? In the Hooters case, does the government have the right to force the business to hire men where none are wanted? And what kind of men would want to wear the Hooters Girls' costumes? Where does the right of the individual to patronize the business of his/her choice end and the government's power to dictate personal choice begin?

Certainly there are those people who think Hooters is a tacky, sexist establishment, just as others find it a delightful restaurant atmosphere. They both have the right to choose what establishments they desire to patronize.

And the federal government needs to spend more time finding ways to get off our backs and out of our wallets and less time keeping abreast of Hooters.

> *Some of the same battles we are having today were foreshadowed in the 1990s. Certainly people have the right to spend their hard-earned money where they want. The government should not be telling citizens where they will be allowed to go out to eat, what kind of music they want to listen to or what silly hats they can wear to a polka, hip-hop or Lady Googoo concert.*
>
> *But the government should also not be telling bakeries that offer traditional wedding cakes that they have to offer alternative designs for men marrying men, women marrying women or any mixture of unique peoples, animals or mythical creatures, some of which live in Frisco. If I were a traditional baker and the feds forced me to also offer "alternative" designs, I would have a set of traditional cakes with figure toppings that would give the clients a dozen or so all-American options. As for the "alternative" "others," I'd have another set of designs from which to choose, all of which would depict somewhat disgusting (perhaps accurate) behavior toppings that no one in his, her, its right mind (giving them the benefit of the doubt) would consider.*
>
> *And while I'm on that subject, why does the President demand businesses kowtow to leftist restrictions at the same time he's claiming it's no one else's business to know what various Biden family members, including grandchildren, did to deserve the millions of dollars they've been paid by Red China, Ukraine and other foreign powers?*

The Aging Art of Outrage
May 2017

Apparently, geezer-rocker Madonna Ciccone would like to "blow up the White House." And, it seems that a large number of today's Hollywood celebrities are onboard with the former superstar's desire. My question is, when did members of the entertainment industry turn from patriotic Americans of a variety of political viewpoints into a gaggle of far-left whiners?

As a lifelong fan of western movies, I've always enjoyed sitting in a darkened theater (and sometimes a darkened living room) while experiencing wonderful adventures with the likes of Clark Gable, Jimmy Stewart, Wayne Morris, William Holden, Audie Murphy, Hoot Gibson, Randolph Scott, Ken Maynard, Gene Autry, Tim McCoy, etc. These wonderful action stars, like so many of their peers, were all veterans of either The Great War or World War II. Some, like McCoy, served during both wars. Western star Buck Jones served two terms in the military and was wounded in combat during the Moro Rebellion in the Philippines.

Their wartime experiences brought credence to their performances as rugged individualists who lived by the Code of the West: Straight shooters always win; good will triumph over evil; have respect for the law; be kind to horses and courteous to women and children; fight to win but be a good loser.

During the same years, starlets like Mary Pickford (WWI), Bette Davis, Rita Hayworth, Marlene Dietrich, Betty Grable and Carole Lombard (WWII) entertained the troops and worked to promote the sale of war bonds. Martha Raye entertained our military during World War II, the Korean War and Vietnam. Ann-Margret, Raquel Welch, Connie Stevens and Phyllis Diller kept soldiers, sailors and Marines entertained in South Vietnam.

I could go on for quite a few inches of copy listing off Hollywood's patriots of the bygone era. Some were Republicans. Some were Democrats. All put America first.

Flash forward to 2017. Today's entertainment industry lacks military veterans. Many current "stars" haven't shared the experiences of working Americans. They have set themselves apart and above the rest of us.

World War II and Korean War veterans are vanishing. And there aren't that many of us who served in Vietnam still working in any capacity, especially government and entertainment. Yet there are some of those burnout 1960s protesters hobbling around who had supported the North Vietnam Communists who invaded our democratic ally, South Vietnam. And, from seeing news videos of angry protesters breaking windows and blocking uniformed military members from entering a gate to view the recent presidential inauguration, I'd say today's whiners are made of the same traitorous slime as those who spewed hatred toward Vietnam-era soldiers and veterans close to 50 years ago.

And the leaders of the current election deniers are old enough to have learned better. Madonna, for instance, has been around a very long time. I'm not saying she is really old, but I've heard she started out as a warm-up act for Sophie Tucker. Time has taken its toll on her career. It's been reported that Don McLean has rejected her bid to join him during his current concert schedule. Her long-time stage routines of crotch-grabbing and crusty sexuality have gotten to the point where, if he were still alive, Michael Jackson would have taken his 10-year-old date and walked out of her concert in disgust.

But, like her odd performance behavior, Madonna's explosive threat did get her noticed and she is once again a topic of *People*, *Entertainment Weekly* and *National Hog Farmer* magazines. Of course, had she been active in the 1940s, her "blow up the White House" threat would have caused Democrat President Franklin Roosevelt to open up a special wing of Manzanar just for her.

And on that same note, another long-in-the-tooth former rebel, Gloria Steinem, used the same protest to denounce the recently elected administration. She stated, "If you force Muslims to register, we will all register as Muslims." I wonder how many of the women in her audience thought to themselves, "Speak for yourself, Gloria."

One, conservative supporters have said many times that America is not at war with Muslims. We are at war with Radical Islam – or basically, nutcase-terrorist Muslims.

Two, President Trump is not President Franklin Roosevelt, so putting American citizens of any race or religion into concentration camps is not the answer. Eliminating terrorist organizations is the answer. Three, if Steinem wants to align herself with nutcase-terrorist Muslims, it would be interesting to see if she could be deported. I don't think she would be welcome in Iran or Syria today. If it were back in the 1970s, they might have accepted her – if she brought along her old bunny costume.

Another old-timer who seems to be channeling his gangster-film characters is Robert De Niro. Having spent more than 40 years trying to equal his Godfather Part II performance, this actor is now better known as a political activist who said he would like to "punch" President Donald Trump. That's certainly tough talk, very much like the lines that screenwriters put in his mouth for many years.

De Niro's recent film performances are, like John Barrymore's later film and radio character parts – bad imitations of his public image. In the late 30s and early 40s, prior to his death, the great stage and screen star Barrymore sleepwalked through many scenes as a washed-up, over-the-top ham actor. De Niro seems to be doing the same thing as he mumbles his Casino-like lines during leftwing political events.

I could continue, but why? Old Hollywood worked hard to bring class entertainment to the rest of us. But, the great cowboy stars, western films and the Code of the West are all dead. And class is the last thing Hollywood is offering.

And, as for Madonna's bombastic announcement, I suggest she practice by blowing something up slightly smaller than the White House. Michael Moore comes to mind.

> In the last half-dozen years, most of these same activist/celebrities have periodically continued their well-worn songs and dances critical of those of us who are to the right of Alyssa Migraino. And just like the rest of us they have that right, thanks to the U.S. Constitution. But what happened to Gloria Steinem and her National Organization for Women feminists? Gloria and the gals fought throughout the last half of the 20th Century for equal rights. And, up until just recently, I would have to credit them with a win. Women are in all of the branches of our military, in corporate CEO chairs and boardrooms and making their presence known throughout local, state and federal governmental agencies.
>
> Now, I'm not saying I fully embraced every action they made since the late 1960s, but I can remember being a tad supportive of them when many stepped forward to burn their bras. Anyway, NOW battled the political correctness of their time to bring equality to women when it came to jobs, paychecks, property ownership, political opportunity and support for their own sports competitions.
>
> Flash forward to 2023. Where are all the feminists now that men can simply put on a skirt and demand everyone address them as real women? Why has NOW allowed "guys" to compete in women's sports? A few literally nutty male athletes, who had competed poorly against other men, have simply put on globs of sloppily brushed eye shadow, smeared their mouths with outdated 1950's lipstick and squeezed into ill-fitting women's swimsuits to break the gals' aquatic speed records. Those dudettes, as well as a bunch of other drag-clowns, are figuratively claiming that men can be better women than women.
>
> NOW seems embarrassingly quiet. It would seem to me that any real woman would be as outraged by the assault on their legitimate sports endeavors and the torturous drag performances inflicted on children in schools, public libraries and, now, on military bases, as members of the NAACP rightfully would be if they witnessed a 21st Century blackface minstrel show. We're talkin' about the ultimate in cultural appropriation. Lia Thomas, Sam Brinton and Admiral Levine are flat-out, in-your-face insults to real American women and their hard-fought victories in their quest for equality. Wake up, Gloria Steinem!

The following cartoon and column shows just how much things can change in just a couple of years. The 2017 "gateway bill" was sold on the fact that it wouldn't lead to recreational use of pot. Oh, well. Time marches on and it's now legal to get high on marijuana in Arizona. At least the acceptance of drug usage is not as totally nutso here as, say, Oregon.

Senators high on industrial hemp bill
May 2017

As we all grew up in this great nation, we stood tall and sang about "amber waves of grain, for purple mountain majesties above the fruited plain." But if one state Senator gets his way, Arizonans will be rockin' out to "olive-drab waves of hemp, for rainbow mountain highs thanks to Senators Moe, Curly and Shemp."

The Arizona State Senate has passed Senate Bill 1337, which would legalize the cultivation, distribution and sale of industrial hemp. The Bill, described as a tool of economic development, is currently in the hands of the State Legislature. Mohave County Republican Sen. Sonny Borrelli is hoping the House members will not Bogart that Bill.

According to a Cronkite News release, "Borrelli praised the benefits of hemp production as an economic driver," stating "It's good policy. It's economic development, and it's good for the agriculture community."

Proponents claim the concentration of tetrahydrocannabinol (THC) in industrial hemp is quite low. Which, they say, would make the plant about as popular with local potheads as watery lite beer is to an Australian crocodile hunter.

And the plant has many uses. The most well known is rope. At least, with fields of pot plants growing all along the river, smoking rope will not be an issue. Hemp is used in the manufacturing of insulation, plastic and paper. In fact, it is used in cigarette papers. What are the odds? The seeds can be used in birdseed, which, if you think about it, is probably a humane way to mellow out any birds that get lost during the summer and accidently migrate into our delightful Arizona Desert.

Wikipedia lists a whole variety of uses for hemp in the production of food. That online information source notably left off brownies. That's fake news for you.

Kidding aside, I see SB 1337 as a gateway bill. So what if the fields of marijuana farmers will be growing are low on THC? Once Arizonans get used to seeing olive-drab waves of hemp, we probably won't even bother to think that some folks might actually plant an acre or two of the more potent variety. Of course the state could hire inspectors to make sure the plants are all benign. I'm sure I would trust the state inspectors just as much as I trust those federal inspectors who have ensured us that Iran's nuclear facilities are not part of the construction of an atomic arsenal.

Some folks believe marijuana is harmless. If they ever get their way, the state might as well start growing a benign version of industrial opium poppies. I'm sure there's money, and tax dollars, to be made in that, as well. Then law enforcement could concentrate on proponents of medical methamphetamine. But then I'm probably just biased and my argument is more blowing smoke.

Medical marijuana is now a reality in Arizona. But, currently, recreational use of the weed can lead to a stretch in the joint. Many of us see marijuana as a gateway drug that leads to the use of some very dangerous hard drugs. And SB 1337 is a gateway bill to the eventual legalization of recreational use of that gateway drug.

> *I really don't want anyone to think that all of my predictions are this accurate. Then again, even Nostradamus had to start somewhere.*

Whether to suffer the slangs and arrows of outrageous English
Dec. 30, 1996

Many black Americans are rightfully angry at the Oakland, Calif., school board.

The (Oakland Unified School District) board recently voted to recognize "Ebonics" as a legitimate language on the same level as Spanish or German. "Ebonics" is their term for street slang such as "She be late fo work." The board contends the "language" is part of being an African-American and to consider it street slang or "jive" is racist. They say it is legitimate Black English.

However, a large number of black leaders across the country realize black kids need to learn regular English if they want to compete in the American economy. There are only so many job opportunities as rap singers. The rest of us have to communicate on a different level.

Not many corporations are ready to hire Ebonic-speakers. For instance, how many people would feel comfortable having a house designed by "Homey's Homes; We be architects"?

However, if the idea does catch on we will have to legitimize other languages. Jeff Foxworthy will lose his whole act if the country's teachers have to accept Honkyese. I can visualize third graders having to watch Gomer Pyle reruns to learn the proper inflection to pronounce "Y'all."

Some immigrants would study old Charlie Chan movies to improve grades in their Pidgin English class. Can you see network anchor Connie Chung having to be politically correct during an interview with Charley Sheen by saying, "You no likee, Chollie?" I don't think so.

Can you picture any American government agency trying to do business in our country if slangs become official languages?

"I'm sorry, sir," the Department of Employment receptionist said. "You are a Brooklynite and the person you need to talk to is a Chicanista from the Nicaraguan neighborhood of Los Angeles. Unfortunately our Brooklynese-Chicanista interpreter is on family leave. Do you happen to speak Nebraskan? If so, I can interpret Nebraskan to Rio Grandese and Maria can then pass on the information in Chicanista to the proper official."

Thank God the Beatnik culture of the 1950s didn't get government approval as an official form of English. The slang of the late '60s hippies wouldn't seem very groovy today either. In twenty years the "we be" slang will be in the same scrap barrel as "hubba, hubba," "far out!" "reet pleats," "bee's knees," "sho nuff?" "hodads and grimmies," and "hepcats," for sure. Can you dig it?

Certainly the English language does evolve with the times. And slangs will always exist. It does not, however, make sense to divide the country any more than it already is by adopting various street slangs by race and calling them official languages.

Lucky for us, Ebonics had its 15 minutes of fame before vanishing into history like the funny hats from a variety of generations. Now, if we can only live through this era of weird folks demanding we use "they" and "them" as pronouns for individuals who consider themselves more than singular.

Celebrity threats are not civilized

September 2017

President Trump is truly a topical leader who either garners exuberant support or extreme criticism.

We've seen this situation before, but not to the same level. For instance, Pres. George W. Bush had very high approval ratings at the time that Saddam Hussein was captured and when the first Iraqi elections were held in 2005. But, after the downturn in the economy in 2007, his ratings dropped. At that time, his political enemies began calling him "stupid," mostly because of his non-professorial Texas accent. But life continued under his watch without violent threats and actions.

His successor, Barack Obama, campaigned on Hope and Change. And he certainly delivered on the Change part. He also was on the receiving end of a lot of allegations of wrongdoing, but was never called stupid, as he spoke very much like a liberal university professor. Most of the harsher complaints about his actions were easily pushed aside by his supporters as being "racist," because the man is half African American. Oddly enough, when Ben Carson and other blacks complained about him, he didn't call them "racist" because his half-white part was offended.

But the current President gets a plethora of extremely hateful remarks out of his liberal critics, many in the entertainment field. One over-the-hill actor said he would like to punch the President in the face. Others have gone much further with their allegations and threats. A z-list, bottle-redheaded comedienne posed with a fake bloody Trump head and a geezer rocker said she would like to blow up the White House. A couple of other "celebrities" have actually said they would support a coup or assassination. Just like when the police looked the other way during the recent violent actions of Antifa revolutionary thugs in Berkeley, celebrity threats against a sitting President have also crossed the line beyond what is acceptable in our alleged civilized democracy.

Let's look back in time and picture what earlier Presidents might have done in the face of such behavior.

If Ricardo Cortez (Jacob Krantz) had publicly made the same death wish against FDR that Charlie Sheen made against Trump, I believe Roosevelt would have found a nice place in the desert south of Manzanar in which to re-educate the actor. And if little Shirley Temple had proposed a "Push FDR off a cliff" game like Rosie O'Donnell did with Trump, she probably would have come up for parole sometime during the Ford Administration.

Let's consider what might have happened if Leo Gorcey had said the same thing as current B-movie mug Robert De Niro did about Trump. If the late Bowery Boy had been quoted in 1950s newspapers as saying he'd "like to punch" Pres. Dwight Eisenhower "in the face," old Leo might have looked out onto his front porch the next morning to a scene not unlike Normandy Beach on June 6, 1944.

Johnny Depp's allusive threat concerning Trump ("When was the last time an actor assassinated a President?") would not have played well either if, say, Sonny Tufts had asked that during the Truman Administration. I'm not saying Sonny might have been at the center of a mushroom cloud, but, if Truman's reaction to criticism of his daughter's piano playing is an example, there would have been repercussions.

There have been quite a few years of unanimous condemnation against U.S. Sen. Joe McCarthy's and the House Un-American Activities Committee's attempts to purge alleged Communists from government and Hollywood in the late 1940s and early '50s. What's not discussed is those efforts obviously failed in that, today, anyone who *doesn't* spout Marxist clichés while threatening conservatives has been thoroughly purged from Hollywood, universities and many federal agencies.

What I'm saying is that, times have certainly changed and self-proclaimed compassionate liberals have crossed many lines in the sands of civilization. And, perhaps, our federal administration should quit accepting public threats as a way of life and start handing out a few Truman-like repercussions to those who advocate violence, murder and revolution as their political norm.

Advocating violence is not going to end. Today the Left complains when conservative politicos suggest voters "fight for" an issue. Then the Left describes a burning neighborhood as a "summer of love." Potato tomato. Semantic issues. I think Americans would learn not to be too judgmental of each other if they just saw both sides ridiculed on late-night talk shows, network sitcoms or even "Saturday Night Live." For instance, Alec Baldwin did an amazing job of ridiculing President Trump on that program. Unfortunately, the producers kept all of the featured comedians firing in one direction. I'd probably begin watching that show again if Darrell Hammond used his impressionist skills to portray Alec Baldwin as a movie cowboy who solves his problems by shooting women performers in each skit. (Oh, God! Will that statement be interpreted as advocating violence? Probably. But I would like to see Hammond show how Baldwin can fire his pistol without pulling the trigger.)

Stupid actions cause carnage; if we can't stop it, let's cash in on it
July 8, 1998

Local entrepreneurs are missing out on a super moneymaker.

We've all seen the advertisements for the "World's Wildest Police Chases" video, as well as "Greatest Motorcycle Race Accidents," "When Monster Trucks Explode," "Europe's Outstanding Soccer Riots," "Fishing's Funniest Casting Accidents" and "Candid Shark and Train Fatalities." They all seem to come as three-video sets for only $19.95.

After the recent Fourth of July weekend, I have come to the conclusion that these Colorado River communities are sitting on a gold mine. Our local investors could reap a fortune by packaging video volumes of "Personal Watercraft's Bloodiest Smashups:" a compilation of the most exciting fatal and near-fatal accidents ever sold on tape.

Personally, I've never understood why people will come here from Southern California on crowded holiday weekends to do things on the Colorado River between Nevada and Arizona that James Bond's stuntmen wouldn't attempt. The actions of some of these people tell me they must have acquired brain damage from prior accidents. Possibly some of them have head wounds from Southern California freeway road-rage shootings. (Having just returned from the Los Angeles area, I now believe road rage has been given a bad name. Many Southern California drivers otta be shot.)

Perhaps we could get Bob Sagat to do humorous voice overs for the tapes. For instance, our cameraman could catch Joe Middleclass slugging down a beer and leaving the can with several others on the beach as he boards his (brand deleted) water rocket sled to go out and show the kiddies a few tricks. Sagat could then do his W.C. Fields voice, "Watch this my little (hic) sand fleas." After Joe falls off a few of times, swallows a couple of quarts of river water and sand, he opens the throttle full tilt, launching himself directly in front of a Burbank Soap Opera producer's ostentatious speed boat. The water rocket is pulverized much the same as Joe. The producer drops his bottle and kills the engine as his two well-endowed starlets-to-be vomit off the side of the boat with Sagat adding appropriate sound effects.

Cross-dissolve to next sequence: Mike Macho, his wife, Beatrice, and their three-year-old son, Derwood, launch their family-size personal watercraft. Beatrice starts to put a flotation vest on Derwood and Mike puffs up with an indignant look. Sagat uses the Fields voice (I think he only has two) again. "Take that sissy thing off our little man. He's three now and that's too old for such childish falderall. When I was three I didn't wear life jackets." Beatrice gets in Mike's face and Sagat now uses his squeaky voice, "When you were three they hadn't invented them yet! And if they had they probably didn't have any big enough to cover your beer belly!"

Mike eventually wins out and I'm sure you can guess the result.

Anyway, if cameramen were hired to tape from both sides of the river over each of our three-day holiday weekends, we could end up with enough outrageous accidents and stupid actions to fill several $19.95 video packages for early-morning cable advertising. The activities could be separated into individual categories such as drunks who try to swim the river, stupid teens who jump off cliffs and metal pipes that stick up out of the water, methamphetamine freaks who try to walk across the river and the ever-popular idiots on water rocket skis.

Obviously, common sense and the fact that stupid, dangerous activities on the Colorado River are illegal have been about as successful in stopping the carnage as the U.S. Border Patrol has been in stopping illegal immigration. The nut cases come here thinking they can get away with anything. Then they either kill themselves or other people.

Since we can't seem to stop it, let's make a buck off it. And Bob Sagat could use the work.

Even though law enforcement offers warnings to visitors, Colorado River carnage continues to happen. And, sadly, there are still folks who deserve posthumous Darwin awards for stupid behavior. Not much has changed during the last quarter of a century. But I do miss Bob Sagat.

I stand by the following column.

Real men don't need a parade
June 23, 1996

According to an Associated Press story, a group of American men have created an organization called the Order of Manly Men. Last weekend they gathered in the town of Roslyn, Wash., for their annual Manly Men Parade and Spam Festival. The festivities include the parade, open to both sexes; a tool belt competition; and a Spam cook-off.

The organization's president, R.M. Crane, a Tacoma florist, said, "Our wives razzed us about being manly men and we said, 'Sure we're manly men and we're going to do manly things in the woods.'"

That's about the meat of the story.

I can't help but think if these guys are our front line in the battle of the sexes, we've lost. Not just lost in the sense that "Oops. We should have gone on into Baghdad." Or even "Holy cow! Didn't we sign peace accords with North Vietnam?" More like Hiroshima-devastation lost.

Women's organizations like the take-no-prisoners National Organization of Women (NOW) have captured a lot of ground for their side. Some deserved, some not. While women's groups have grown and all-women colleges have survived, men's clubs and colleges have been opened to both sexes. Women are now swabbing the decks of Navy ships, peeling Army potatoes and complaining about someone leaving the toilet seat up on a space shuttle.

Most of us guys just consider this life in the '90s. Times have changed, maybe a little faster than some of us guys would like, but most of us adapt well. We now have big screen TVs for baseball, football and Arnold Schwarzenegger movies. We still shoot pool, argue politics and drink beer, even if it is Lite.

Then we hear of this "manly" organization. This is the type of group NOW would never protest: a group of guys who, with their wives' blessings, call themselves "manly men," parade around eating Spam and talking in phony deep voices. I wouldn't be surprised if they had a "wabbit-hunting" competition.

We all know that folks aren't always what they call themselves. President Clinton could call himself a war hero if he wanted. Janet Reno could call herself Miss America as well. It doesn't make it so.

Real men don't wear T-shirts advertising how manly they are. They don't demand Irish Spring soap to wash the Spam grease off their hands. And they don't need a parade to feel "manly."

The "manly men" is a caricature depicting the last American cultural element political correctness allows to be ridiculed, males, as a bunch of Bozos. And although some of us are Bozos all of the time, and all of us are Bozos some of the time, we aren't all Bozos all of the time. (Not the best of political slogans.)

Many real men have what NOW would call archaic political beliefs and public images. That doesn't really matter. What really matters is that real men are good fathers, sons and husbands.

Real men take responsibility for their actions, and their children. Oh, yes. They also oppose the American League's designated hitter rule.

> *Some local issues had little to do with the rest of the country.*
> *But what one interest group could attempt to do to a rural Arizona community might be a wakeup call for other areas to be on the alert.*

Mohave Valley is getting dumped on — literally

May 23, 2003

Residents of Mohave Valley are rightfully using their freedom of speech to weigh in on the spreading of biosolids (human feces) on local farmland.

Over the last nine years Mohave County has been quite strict in the placement of septic tanks on lots and multi-acre properties in the valley. This has slowed the development and increase in property values in the area.

The government alleges, even though many valley properties are large and separated by quite a distance, the nitrates from septic tanks filled with human feces can impact the quality of groundwater. Some valley residents even had to put in alternative waste systems to meet county specifications.

Accepting the government premise as fact, one would think the covering of complete sections of land with the same stuff, human feces, would not be an issue at this time.

Apparently the low-grade California poopy presently being dumped in the valley is limited in that it cannot be used as fertilizer on crops for human consumption but can be used for alfalfa, hay and other animal feed crops. This is an admission there are some health problems possible from its use. But if it can cause problems with human food, why can't it cause problems with animal food? After all, Mad Cow disease, presently having a revival in Canada, has been blamed on tainted animal food.

That may not be something we have to worry about in our valley, but then we could be a launching place for Mad Sheep disease, or even household pet problems. We don't want to wait until we see our ferrets stumbling around our living rooms or our dogs and cats drooling while watching daytime television.

Perhaps the stuff really is safe, but the concept still stinks. Having grown up on a farm, I have shoveled a lot of cattle and horse manure. (And in my present occupation, I have been accused of continuing that practice.) But cattle and horse manure fertilizer has a much cleaner image than human waste. Obviously, cows and horses eat grass; humans eat everything — garbage in, garbage out.

One reason I might be a tad biased against human fertilizer is that years ago in Vietnam I had to fill my canteens quite often from ponds and streams that may have been tainted by water from rice paddies. Enough said about that.

Another reason is that I escaped the People's Republic of California over 10 years ago and I resent that haven of condo-dwelling tree huggers using Arizona as their sewer dump. First that state wanted to close their dumps and use trains to haul their trash to Arizona landfills (the waste-by-rail proposal of the late 1980s and early 1990s) and now they want to flush all their poopy into our state. The land of pot-smoking fruits and nuts who fly into a rage if a good Dominican cigar is lit up or someone is caught carrying Oreos should find something better to do with their waste.

Hopefully our county, state and federal officials will represent us on this issue.

As for me, I feel a lot cleaner and safer spreading horse manure in my garden than being anywhere near an agricultural area that is using the sewage sludge of even one San Francisco or West Hollywood residential household.

> *Life's number one rule is that shit happens.*
> *But I'm pleased to say that southern California's crap is no longer being sent to western Arizona.*
> *I have no idea what the Golden State is currently doing with its sewage,*
> *but I did notice the last time I visited that many of the local surfers were looking a little flushed.*

One Western Arizona rural city dabbled in leftist Cancel Culture behavior more than 20 years ago. At least I was able to make fun of the situation. Then again, I don't have that job anymore.

Should Bullhead City blacklist the founder of Hardyville?
October 31, 2001

A news article appeared on page one of the *Daily News* that "Honeymooners" character Ralph Kramden might have had a good "Hardy, Har Har" over.

Bullhead City Parks and Recreation Commission is apparently unhappy with the name "Hardyville Hall." Commissioner Olivia Moya Krok allegedly made a remark that (area founder) Mr. William Harrison Hardy was prejudiced against Indians.

What marvelous timing our city officials have in their very important quest for the historical purification of our area. We have just finished the community-involved Hardyville Days Celebration where civic and fraternal organizations joined with other community groups to have fun and raise money for various charities. Now we find out that the founder of "Western" civilization in our area is considered by some to be the Simon Legree of the Colorado River area.

One would have thought that anyone as smart as we tend to think Mr. Hardy was when he founded Hardyville in 1864 would have been enlightened enough to have embraced diversity with the gusto of Barbra Streisand. In fact, perhaps he was just that. History has such a miserable record of portraying early American entrepreneurs as hard-driving, uncaring cusses. Historians probably just want us all to think that pioneers had to be tough to survive in the 19th Century. Poppycock!

I can picture William Harrison Hardy as he leads a diverse group of politically correct prospectors, pioneers and buffalo skinners in a Zen Buddhist chant one Saturday afternoon in 1864 at the Hardyville Saloon and Yoga Parlor.

"If a tree falls in the forest," he mentors, "and there is no one to hear it, does it really bug the squirrels?"

His message of acceptance and equality was a little rough edged, but, then again, it was 1864.

If we all think very hard we can visualize Hardy in 1866, dressed in rattlesnake-skin Speedos and an owl-feathered Fedora, as he leads the first annual Hardyville Gay and

Lesbian Pride Parade from Dirty Sally's Vegetarian Fern Bar Restaurant to Wild Bill's Hair, Nails and Open-air Tanning Salon. A couple of years later, the same group, under Hardy's leadership, protested the so-called Indian Wars with a wicked hunger strike. The town was packed with "Shucks no, we won't go!" signs in both glass windows.

Okay, maybe it didn't really happen that way. And just maybe old Hardy didn't like Indians at that time. I'm sure the feeling was mutual. But just because 19th Century folks had a different view of each other than today's kinder, gentler enlightened officials, should we really start purging their names from our world? Should the successes of those who came earlier be ignored because the individuals didn't have 2001 sensibilities?

Perhaps members of the 101st Airborne Division should stop yelling "Geronimo" as they leap into the sky from perfectly good flying airplanes. That particular Indian leader was not known to be fond of white illegal immigrants.

Maybe the famous Crazy Horse Saloon should have a more politically correct name as well. Perhaps it should be renamed the Martin Sheen Saloon. And for the same reasons, John Wayne Airport may have to be renamed after Tipper Gore.

When one thinks of blacklisting historical figures from present-day honors, Bullhead City residents should also think of the cost of signage. If we are to sanitize the naming of city buildings, we should attempt to replace the least number of letters to make sure we spend the least amount of tax dollars in the process. One way to do that is to find someone else with the same last name to honor.

Perhaps Bullhead City could adopt Oliver Hardy as the symbol of its political-historical karma. That way we wouldn't have to change the Hall's sign at all and (former Councilman) Damian Holther could still portray the character during Hardyville Days. Perhaps the mayor could join him by portraying Stan Laurel. On the other hand, Oliver Hardy was from the south. That could create another fine mess.

Although his personality might be a little too wooden, another possibility is to anoint Buffalo Bob Smith's old partner, Howdy Doody, to spruce up our image. It will take only two letters for Howdyville Hall and three for Doodyville. The City Council could then draft Public Information Specialist Toby Cotter to portray the character during Howdyville or Doodyville Days.

Then, of course, there's always Hootie of "... and the Blowfish," or the late Bluesman W.C. Handy. They are both black and Handyville or Hootieville could catch on nicely and lead to diverse music festivals. Unfortunately, I'm not sure if Hootie or Handy ever came to the Bullhead City area to shop, dine, bowl or inline skate.

Silliness aside, we really shouldn't be trying to rewrite history or blacklist anyone, living or dead, because their historical views on life don't live up to today's values. If we do, tomorrow's view of us may not be very kind either.

> *I just may have been alone in my judgment of such things back in October of 2001. Following the commissioner's hissy fit, Bullhead City's Hardyville Hall was renamed and the Hardyville Days celebration never happened again. And, I'm sure, if the city had already erected a William Harrison Hardy statue, it probably would have been vandalized and destroyed by "concerned citizens," much like statues of Robert E. Lee, Christopher Columbus and even Abraham Lincoln were in later years.*
>
> *Judging historic figures under a current politically correct point of view is almost as stupid as throwing out the history books and demanding people accept fictional accounts as facts. CRT is BS! It's head-in-the-sand history. To those morons who claim Lincoln didn't do anything for black Americans, be careful what you smoke.*
>
> *The abolitionist movement led to the creation of the Republican Party in 1854 as an attempt to end slavery. The Democrats of the era seceded from the Union because the first Republican, Lincoln, was elected President. The (election denier) Democrats created the Confederacy. Confederate President Jefferson Davis, like his followers, was a Democrat. Following the South's surrender at the end of the Civil War, the southern Democrat Party created the Ku Klux Klan as an enforcer-vigilante group to punish former slaves and northern carpetbaggers. For more than a century, the southern Democrats and the Ku Klux Klan were joined at the hip in controlling southern candidates, laws and elections.*
>
> *Today, left-wing Democrats have cheered at the cancelation of Confederate monuments, flags and just about everything that had to do with the Confederacy. That is, everything except the political party of slave owners, the Democrat Party.*
>
> *History can be fictionalized, but that won't change what took place in the past. We need to study accurate accounts of the old days and learn from them, not reinterpret them to destroy anything we want. Cancel culture has always been a weapon of small-minded people. Live and learn.*

3. Romantic Expertise

The next few annual tongue-in-cheek columns were, surprisingly, popular with women. Although completely silly, I believed they represented bits and pieces of their husbands. However, there were a couple of lady readers who took them seriously and were outraged. You can't please everyone.

I hope you interpret them as a bit of whimsy coming from a Vietnam veteran who enjoyed cold beer, lively discussions and smartass humor.

A reminder for men only

Feb. 8, 1996

This column is for men only. All you ladies should stop here and turn the page or read one of our other columnists.

Okay, guys. Now that we're alone: Warning! Valentine's Day is sneaking up on us. If we want to live through the rest of the year, we have to keep on our toes and be ready to deliver on February 14.

Of course I'm talking to married guys only. You single guys can always fall back on the old break-up-before-the-holiday routine. When you make up afterward, you will have saved quite a bit of money.

We husbands, however, have to be able to properly understand those blatantly subtle hints. For instance, if the little woman says something like "Roses are the most beautiful flowers in the world," it doesn't mean you should give her five bare-root plants and a bag of steer manure.

The same is true if she mentions how much she enjoys a little wine in front of the fireplace. Do not buy a new chainsaw so you can easily prepare wood for said fireplace.

I realize many wifely hints are very obscure. And it's easy to make the wrong gift decision by misreading those hints. But your happiness, and possibly your health, for the rest of the year may depend on your decision.

At this time of year, a man's first priority should be to make sure he discusses the level of his relationship with his other half. In other words, tell her how important she is to you. But do it in romantic terms. Do not tell her how much you appreciate her helping you change the oil in the truck. Tell her she is more important than the air you breathe.

Do not tell her how well she looks in cheap clothes, how the weight she has gained since marriage is hardly noticeable, or how sexy she looks cleaning the bathroom. Tell her you love her more every day and that you would be an empty shell without her. Then don't think about how much fun that empty shell might have.

Most importantly, don't forget to deliver that romantic gift on Valentine's Day. Your wife will appreciate your caring ability to understand her needs and her tips.

If we pull this off properly, our wives will appreciate us more than ever for remembering them with the right gifts. And we will leave our women with the impression we are compassionate, empathic, Phil-Donahue-type men ... not the complacent, pathetic, Homer-Simpson-type Bozos they usually consider us.

Good luck, guys. I, however, got lucky this year. I figured out my wife's hints weeks ago. All I have to give her is a bag of vegetables – fourteen carrots, to be exact.

Okay. You get the picture. I don't need to relate this 1996 column with anything going on today to make it relevant.
After all, I'm still the same Homer-Simpson-type Bozo that I was when I wrote this.

Valentine's Day can also bring nice gifts to men

Feb. 7, 1997

Well, men. It's that time of year again. Valentine's Day is slithering up on us. Be afraid. Be very afraid.

Each year at this time I try to prepare fellow married men for this special day. So you ladies please stop reading this column. The following information is classified for men only.

Okay, guys. The first question we have to deal with is, "Why should we do anything about Valentine's Day?"

The answer is simple. Because any man who doesn't make a big doo-dah about romance, linking his lovely lady with little flitty birds, pretty flowers and chewy chocolate goodies, will be doomed for the rest of the year.

It's genetic. Women see February 14 as an early spring day. They look at Bill and Hillary and see Bogey and Bacall. Mangy cats suddenly become cute little kittens. Pictures of a half-naked, bald-headed guy with a bow and arrow make them giggle. They watch "Love Story" without rooting for the McGraw woman to "Die already!" Go figure.

Most of all, women expect a romantic token of their spouse's undying love. And, of course, they reciprocate with a gift expressing their deep feelings as well.

Last year we discussed how to read those subtle hints from the little woman on what she wants for Valentine's Day. Be very careful to correctly identify what she wants from her obscure hints, and buy it.

This year I'd like to pass on a little wisdom on how *you* can get a useful gift out of your wife on this day. Usually a wife will buy her husband some fluffy little pink piece of nonsense that Richard Simmons would hide in his garage. So it will take a little bit of work to get her to purchase something useful, such as a chainsaw, weed chomper, a package of assorted gopher traps or an antique Falstaff Beer neon light for the bar. It's also a good idea to hint for something inexpensive. That way if she gets the wrong thing it still won't cost you much.

The first thing you have to do is to get her in a mood where she will be receptive to your gift hints. You can do that by showing your sensitive side. Watch a disease-of-the-week TV movie with her and do your best not to look disgusted. Wait until the Bozo with the disease is about to die for the fourth time and look into her eyes and see if she is weeping. Now for the hard part. Think real hard. Pretend, in your mind, that you are missing the

Holyfield, Tyson rematch. When a tear comes to your eye, make sure she sees it. She will think it is so sweet that you are sensitive enough to cry during an insipid movie.

Now that she is in a warm-fuzzy mood, she is primed for your subtle hints for that special Valentine's Day gift that will make your heart flutter. Now, be sure not to overplay the sensitive bit or you might end up getting a pile of pansies sent to your office where you will have to leave them on your desk until they die. (Or you die from all the embarrassing remarks made by your co-workers.)

When my wife and I reached that particular spot in a really awful TV movie about terminal scabies, I dabbed the tear from my eye and pined that I didn't have any way to record all of our wonderful, upcoming dates together, such as dinners out, plans to see a special Arnold movie, bowling, etc.

"Hey!" I said. "I could use a nice calendar."

Now, only a few days earlier, while in a local card shop, I had subtly shown her the 1997 Chuck Bronson Death Wish calendar. It is very well made and quite inexpensive. You guys will love March. It has Chuck lowering six gang members into a meat grinder. And June has Chuck, always the compassionate environmentalist, feeding a bunch of homeless ... to pool of rare sharks. I know it made in impression on her just by the size of her eyes when I showed her the December Christmas picture.

I'm sure that my plan will pay off on February 14 due to my brilliant yet subliminal preparation.

As for a gift for her, this year I've really aced it. I found out exactly what the little woman wants.

A couple of nights ago we were watching a cable variety show when Suzanne Somers performed a Marilyn Monroe version of "Diamonds Are A Girl's Best Friend." The wife just glowed while watching Sommers sing and dance in that red dress with all those shiny rocks on her fingers. I knew right then exactly what she wanted.

Now I can't wait for Valentine's Day just to see her face light up when she opens her gift box to find her very own ThighMaster.

I have to admit, this column is slightly outdated. It's been more than 20 years since I've seen a ThighMaster commercial.

Valentine's Day advice is free; worth every penny
Feb. 1, 1998

Each year at this time I attempt to have a little man-to-man talk with our male readers. In past columns regarding Valentine's Day I have urged all of our women readers to kindly go on to other stories as the information was confidential to men only. I understand, however, that many women did not accept my suggestion. They went ahead and read the men-only columns anyway.

Therefore, this year I am not going to ask the ladies to stop reading at this point. And I will not discuss anything that they shouldn't, or don't already, know. But, there is a big sale going on right now at the mall and I believe the cable has just started an All-Rosie-O'Donell-All-The-Time channel.

There. That should have gotten rid of them.

Now, guys, it's time to think about our futures. On February 14, G-Day (Gift Day), Valentine's Day, our futures will be sealed. You guys who have been married for a few years know what I'm talking about. You newlyweds, and soon-to-be weds, need to be warned.

We have all noticed the subtle change in attitude that our "little women" have gone through in the last month or so. Little things like: snuggling close and watching the Super Bowl with us; starting a sentence with "Sugar,.." before telling us to take that "stinky cigar" outside; returning that screwdriver to its proper place after using it to hammer a heel back on a shoe or to pry open a stuck curler-box-thingy; or attempting to discuss the state of professional boxing without suggesting Don King should see Richard Simmons' hair stylist.

In other words, they're being nice — too nice. And believe me, if we men do not come through with the right words and gifts on Valentine's Day, we will see personalities from the other side of the spectrum for quite some time. Our wives will make that woman who wanted those 101 Dalmatians for fur coats seem like Martha Stewart.

Now, as all of us men know, our ladies have been engaging in the fine art of subtle blatancy with their hints for desired Valentine's gifts. Most women, thinking we men are not as smart as we know we really are, will practically spell out what they want for Valentine's Day.

For example, a wife will point to an expensive clothing store and tell her husband how she spent hours recently looking at the merchandise there. Now a smart husband will simply go there later and find the good looking young sales lady and ask her if she has a dress available like the one that looks so good on her except in a much larger size. Buy it, and when the wife opens it on Valentine's Day, tell her she will look as good in it as the cute young saleslady did. She'll appreciate that.

If, in the last few months, the wife has said something like, "Wouldn't it be nice to hear the pitter-pat of little feet around the house?" — buy her a dog. Even young pit bulls look cute with red ribbons around their necks on Valentine's Day morning.

And if the last time you took her out to dinner she pointed to the dance floor and said, "That looks like fun," she probably would enjoy helping you put in a new wood kitchen floor. Sure, you would think she wouldn't want to put in the extra work to keep a wood floor cleaned and waxed in the kitchen. But if she said, "That looks like fun," why question her? As you guys know, sometimes women just don't make sense.

Luckily, my work is over this year. Once again I've figured out the exact gift that will make my wife's heart go pity pat, and keep her from complaining about poker night for at least a couple of months. For the last several weeks, every time we were in town walking by the shops, she stopped in front of the travel agencies and looked at all the pictures of people on cruises and foreign tours.

So this February 14th, my little kitchen dove will get the thrill of her life when she opens her very own specially packaged, complete collection of Chevy Chase Vacation movies.

Presentation is important

Feb. 7, 1999

A note to you guys: Do you remember the last weeks of school when you were cramming for finals? How about the stress of military basic training or perhaps your last couple of weeks in Vietnam?

Those were tough times. We had to struggle with a lot of problems knowing that, if we survived, things would get better. This month is always a reminder of those years – especially for us married men.

Valentine's Day is slithering ever closer.

In the past I have endeavored to share some of my personal expertise in finding out what our women would really like as Valentine's Day gifts. And although, like in politics, I'm always right, I've found that one can make a big mistake by not utilizing the best presentation. The act of giving the gift can be as important as the gift itself.

It won't matter, very much, what you get your little laundry flower as long as you package it properly and use some creativity in presenting it to her. Get some pink froofy paper, ribbon, some kind of tape other than duct and a small piece of heart-shaped paper. Wrap your gift with these goodies (eat your heart out Martha Stewart), steal a poem off a wine bottle and write it on the heart shape.

Pick your time for giving it to her very carefully. I suggest you wait until after she has finished the dinner dishes and has had time to relax. Turn on some romantic music — something by the Ink Spots or Ringo Starr. Now recite the poem, remembering to put her name in it somewhere instead of Red Mountain or Thunderbird (many poems don't rhyme), and present the froofy-wrapped gift to her. She will be delighted, and your life will be less of a hell on earth, for a while.

Another Valentine's Day land mine to avoid is to be too modern.

For instance, some gals are very emphatic about being treated as equals. As many of you know, I consider myself an enlightened '90s kind of guy who has always been considerate to chicks, especially the good lookin' ones. But equality gets drop kicked right out the window the minute you give your liberated lady a power saw on Valentine's Day.

February 14 is about the only day of the year that it is hard to find a feminist. Liberated wives hide their flannel shirts, avoid talking politics, pretend they can't think of any personal flaws to point out to their husbands and act enthused about fishing stories. They act sexy and claim they don't hate your hunting dog. It's scary. It's also a nice reminder of what it was like in the good old days (perhaps I should have said that differently).

Anyway, they all act as nice as they did before they were married and the key to your Valentine's Day success is to treat them the way you did then. Try to remember what that was like back before children, before debt, when you still had hair and she didn't need electrolysis. Yes, I know all the drive-in movies are gone. But if you think about it there were other nice things about those years. Mostly romance.

So, play the music, read the poem, present the froofy gift and perhaps dance a little in the living room ... with her. She will be overjoyed with the sentiment and you will enjoy the benefits of a lingering appreciation.

Then if she really isn't terribly thrilled about the actual gift, thanks to your unique presentation, she will still not go for the jugular. And perhaps you can use the gift yourself at some time so the expense isn't a complete waste. I suggest something to brighten up the house such as a nice colorful new duck decoy or an electric Lucky Lager waterfall bar sign.

Once again I'm ahead of the game. My romantic little oven angel will be all atwitter when she opens her froofy package. I'm surprising her with a collection of classic Randolph Scott westerns to watch while we snuggle together Valentine's Day evening.

Valentine's Day success takes special preparation

Feb. 7, 2000

I'm confused about Valentine's Day.

I was always under the impression that women considered this an extremely important day. I thought they believed that their relationships, and romance, could be rated on their partners' actions, words and, most importantly, gifts on that day.

Now, I have always made sure to show that I really do give a big flying doo-dah about my marriage on February 14. Just as soon as Super Bowl Sunday is over, I start planning my attack for this day. I listen for the little woman's subtly blatant hints so that I can purchase just the right heart-fluttery Valentine's Day gift and I plan the perfect moment for presentation so we will have each other's complete attention. Last February, during a commercial break on the ABC Valentine's Day showing of Terminator 2, I presented my little dust bunny with her special gift.

With this much brilliant planning and attention, why would I, of all people, be confused, you ask?

It seems that in the last few years my vacuum violet hasn't shown the enthusiasm she used to show on receiving my gift-wrapped Valentine's Day expressions of romance. Is this the first sign that the honeymoon is over?

Take last year, for instance. She came into the garage and told me she thought the project I was working on was "very interesting." "Ah-ha!" I thought. Always being a believer in sexual equality, knowing that a woman can do just about anything she puts her little mind to, I gave her a specially-packaged set of her very own pink metric wrenches.

She had also told me one evening that her favorite evening dress was getting a little tight but she didn't think she would have the energy to keep up with the younger crowd at a local fitness gym. So she would feel better about herself, I rushed out and bought her a set of those home workout videos that feature Richard Simmons with a lot of obese old people.

I tell you, the thrill is gone. What used to be enthusiastic expressions of gratitude have turned into a cocked eyebrow and a long sigh. Perhaps Valentine's Day just isn't that important to women anymore.

Ever the romantic, I shall not give up. This year I am working extra hard to find just the right gifts to express my inner feelings toward my precious pantry pixie.

I have decided to share more of my interests with her thus making her even more of my life.

First, I am getting a new "sissy bar" for my motorcycle just for her. This will make it more comfortable for her to join me on a "ride." (A law enforcement friend of mine told me that his new "sissy bar" had dramatically reduced the annoying whine coming from the rear of his bike.)

Second, I have purchased his and hers matching beer steins. Baseball season is just around the corner and auto racing is available on satellite. We can enjoy these events together in the privacy of our compound so much more if, every time she brings me a beer, she also brings one for herself.

And finally, since she has told me she likes nothing better than to go out and have a nice dinner and see one of those artsy-fartsy foreign films, I have planned a very special treat. I will take her to dinner at my favorite restaurant, Suds and Grub, followed by a trip to the movies to see a sneak preview of the new Jean-Claude Van Damme film, "Massive Contusions."

Ever the optimist, I believe romance will triumph this Valentine's Day.

Valentine's Day tips offered

Feb. 11, 2001

The 2000 presidential election was one for the record books. Election day stretched into election season. We had counts, recounts, contested counts and contested recounts. The anger, disgust, pain and jokes regarding the election have subsided now with the launching of the new administration.

Now we American men have to face a similar event where the stakes may even be higher than just choosing a leader of the free world: Valentine's Day.

The blatantly subtle campaigning has been taking place since Christmas. And believe me, if we men choose wrong on Valentine's Day, we may end up in the same shape as those final Americans and American supporters attempting to flee Saigon on overloaded helicopters as Charlie came to town.

Now, don't get me wrong. I'm known as a very romantic individual. Unlike many men, I understand the opposite sex. And I'm always the first to help interpret what they have to say to other men so that it makes a little sense. Therefore, I want to assist the rest of you guys to make sure we all don't wake up the day after Valentine's Day with demands for a recount.

So listen up, Pilgrims. We've got a rough couple of days to get through, and with a little of my specialty, sensitivity, we will survive.

Some of our women are going to expect to be taken to the movies. And we can do that, even though they will probably want to see something awful.

Valentine's tip No. 1. Prepare: The first thing we need to learn to do is to be able to sit through an insipid movie without incessantly sighing like Al Gore at a debate. You know the kind of films I'm talking about: just about any American film with Shirley MacLane or Oprah Winfrey, and every British film without James Bond or Benny Hill.

I've found the best way to prepare for one of these masochistic episodes is by watching a test pattern, skin-care infomercials or Richard Simmons workout tapes for a few hours. Once you've done this you can sit through just about anything.

Now that you have armed yourself for this portion of the "special" day, you need to move on to the next phase: She will expect to be taken out for dinner.

Valentine's tip No. 2. Although it's the best eatery in the area, don't take her to Suds and Grub (trust me on this one). She will expect to be taken to some flootsy tooey joint with ferns hanging all over the place and waiters who were probably picked on a lot in high school. And be very careful around the ferns. Believe me, if you just barely touch one of those crawly plants with your cigar, they will flame up like a Napalmed village. Come to think of it, so would those perfumed waiters.

Also at dinner, pretend you enjoy the table-hopping violinist. Tip him well and he will go away. And for God's sake, don't request that he play "Put Another Log On The Fire."

And for your final assault on the evening, give her a Valentine's Day gift right after the main course at dinner. If you have chosen the correct gift, she will be so excited she won't order dessert and you will have saved a few bucks.

Valentine's tip No. 3. Women don't like ferrets. Do not give her an animal of any kind on Valentine's Day. I know those little weasely characters are cute and a lot of fun as they hunt bugs, but I guarantee you that the little woman won't be impressed. And those fern restaurant guys have no sense of humor when a ferret escapes in the dining room. In fact, they get rather hissy.

Also, weapons and ammunition is not a good Valentine's Day gift. I've learned that women are not into guns. Believe me, this is a good thing.

Through countless hours, years actually, of standing in stores wondering what the heck my little Visa kitten is doing, I've discovered that women enjoy shopping most of all. Therefore, the ideal gift for a woman is not something tangible. It's gift certificates and coupons. They love those things. This allows a woman to waste as much time as she wants looking at every boring little item in a store before she chooses her own gift.

And if you are truly successful, as I usually am, and she really enjoyed the dinner and movie, your little toaster queen might just spend the gift certificate on you as a reward.

And there is a 20 percent off sale on mulch at a local fertilizer and soil treatment emporium for you guys who plan to create your own putting green this spring.... and guess what: They sell gift certificates.

Association wants to take a bite out of Valentine's Day shopping
January 25, 2004

We husbands are all winding down from the holiday season. We have stopped the madness.... I mean the shopping, started paying the bills and are now beginning to relax during the peaceful, except for the current political campaign, time of the year.... or so we thought.

Valentine's Day is coming up soon and entrepreneurs are already attempting to herd consumers into a gift-buying fervor — a Visa-bouncing lovefest.

Commercials, emails, print and junk mail ads are beginning to appear with little pink hearts, fluffy stuffed animals (not the taxidermy kind), bunches of flowers arranged in a manner that would offend *most* NFL players (and really of little use since florists remove the roots) and diamond and gold bracelets and rings which are not bad looking but could cause the amputation of a hand or finger if caught in heavy machinery. Women never seem to understand the latter.

One of the strangest press releases I have received at the *Daily News* recently is a listing of "helpful hints" on purchasing that special Valentine's Day gift.... for a household pet!

According to the particular pet product association responsible for the release, folks can show love for their favorite feathered, furry or scaled creature with a multitude of oddities. There are pink heart-shaped rawhide chew toys, flower-shaped, catnip-filled whacking toys and even dunkable fish-food hearts. One canine answer to animal crackers is a box of cat- and postman-shaped cookies. There are also "edible dog greeting cards." I wonder what the loving boa constrictor owner will bring home to fluffy on February 14.

Now, I love animals as much as anyone (especially beef, pork and chicken), and I have a good dog. But, as far as I know, Toby can't read greeting cards and doesn't have a calendar in his doghouse. So, I'm sure, he doesn't know that Valentine's Day is coming.

Toby, like any good dog, agrees with my politics, doesn't complain about cigar smoke and enjoys an occasional sip of Sam Adams. And he is also a good home security guard when he isn't curled up under the pool table polishing portions of his anatomy. If he could ask for a gift, I'm sure it wouldn't be a froofy, pink heart-shaped sow's ear. It would probably be a rabbit with a limp so it would be slow enough for old Toby to catch.

He does deserve a treat now and then, but not on a day that is already filled with the tension of presenting the "right" gift to the real household pet, the wife (she does have seniority).

I'm not going to be judgmental in that I know there are people who will be thrilled to present their dogs with loving gifts this year. And, in spite of what most of us think of their value, even some cats will get a chance to turn up their snotty little noses at some special Valentine's Day presents.

But, instead of worrying about canine confections, my pet project will be to make February 14th special for my little Laundry Lassie.

The little woman of the house has recently told me how she misses her family in California. So (call me Mr. Empathy), I thought about the old neighborhood and, walla, decided on the perfect Valentine's Day gift. On February 14, my little Kitchen Dove will unwrap a very special DVD of the first two seasons of COPS.

Holiday gifts for any occasion questioned

September 2017

There are only 34 more shopping days until Halloween.

That would have been a pretty ridiculous thing to say a few years ago. But, apparently, times have changed. Currently, many people consider every holiday and specially designated day as an opportunity to purchase gifts. Unlike me, my wife is one of *those* people.

Now don't get me wrong. When Christmas gets close, with all sincerity I paste a fake smile on my face, release the moths from my wallet and shop for "darling" items that I then wrap in frou-frou paper and stick under the smelly, shedding tree that continues to die in my living room. When my annual purchases are complete, I stand back and assure myself that the gifts are well chosen and will certainly warm my sweet kitchen dove's little heart.

And sometimes I'm even right. Yet who knew that amazing little Dust Buster specifically designed for messy cars, the steam iron that also makes hot tea, the Little Miss Sock Darning set, the package of five colorful toddler leashes designed to be used when her friends bring their little rug poopers over to try to yank on my pool-table pockets and break ashtrays, or the his and hers gun rack wouldn't result with squeals of Christmas morning delight?

Thankfully, Christmas only comes once a year, or so I thought. Now, there are birthdays, Valentine's Day, Easter, Mother's Day, Father's Day (my grown kids sure spend a lot of money on our former postman), Thanksgiving and, even, Halloween. Who has the time to choose amazing gifts for so many days? And what advertising genius was able to convince so many people – women – that gifts need to be given – and received – on all those days?

I didn't quite catch on last year when I noticed the little pantry pixie boxing up gifts to send to family members before Thanksgiving. I just thought she was getting her Christmas mailing done early. But no-ooo! She was sending stuff to her sister, nieces and nephews in celebration of Thanksgiving.

At the time, I shuddered to myself thinking that whatever it was she was sending might not be that Thanksgivingish by the time it arrives. After all, how long can candied yams last in the mail without becoming rancid? I didn't say anything to her, as she does get a little prickly about holiday situations. I've learned over the years to always keep my cigars away from her stuffing, never hang political buttons on a decorated tree and always laugh at her brother's jokes. I usually laugh when he starts them because I don't think the man understands where to put a punch line.

As an enlightened modern man, I have learned to adapt to change or, as my drill instructor used to say, roll with the battering. Surprisingly, I survived Valentine's Day this year. I had hoped for that fairy tale moment of excitement when my love dumpling opened her special Feb. 14 gift. I had to settle with a long sigh as, apparently, the spinning brush on the long pink extension handle for cleaning high windows wasn't exactly what she was hoping for.

With lessons understood, I stepped back and kept my mouth shut as she sent off not quite a C-130 load of Easter gifts to her family. After all, it's very important for her to send and receive enough stuffed bunnies each year to take up the space in the garage I would like to use for my truck.

I've begun to wonder how long it will be before we're required to send out roadmaps to relatives on Columbus Day; spend those stupid little quarter-sized dollars that came out at the end of the Carter Administration for Susan B. Anthony day; or just continue to do nothing on United Nations Day.

But now, Halloween is coming. The stores are filled with wonderfully sick items to send to all the in-laws for this, their appropriately special, holiday. And the All-Hallows wife has her eyes spinning like Linda Blair's head this year as she goes from store to store stocking up on pumpkin buckets, rubber spiders, monster-feet slippers, fangs and Billy-Bob teeth.

It's not the cost of the useless Chinese-made junk that I object to. It actually costs more to send it than to buy it. But what message is she passing on to the kids in the family with this never-ending supply of free stuff? Sooner or later, young people are going to be rioting in the street demanding that single-payer government-sponsored Mortal Kombat video games are a right, not a privilege.

But that's just me and I know enough to keep my mouth shut. Except for the other day when my sweet scrubbing bubbles was boxing up a set of Billy-Bob teeth to send to her sister. Without thinking, I told her I'd known her sister many years and that she already has a set of those.

Halloween's a month away and it's already pretty spooky at our house.

What's amazing to me after all these years is that my wife is still with me. She never objected to my columns, never told me my cartoons offended her and, usually, she laughed at my jokes. I've had a lot of coworkers over the years who surmised that Patricia must be the most tolerant woman in the world. Many have stated that she deserved sainthood. I didn't argue with them.

Monty Python made a 1971 film titled, "And Now For Something Completely Different." That title describes the next chapter, as well.

4. War and Remembrance

Earlier I did promise that "serious" topics would be dealt with. This is about as serious as they get. Sadly, the history of our country is punctuated with the history of our wars. America has changed dramatically over the last few decades. As I look at my work during that time period, I see opinions relevant only to their publication dates. America's current military and foreign policy issues are certainly more complex than those in the 1990s. Yet, how did we get to this point? Why do we continue to snatch defeat out of the jaws of victory? We used everything we had to earn VE (Victory in Europe) and VJ (Victory in Japan) days. Wouldn't it have been proper if we had simply used whatever it took to achieve Victory in Vietnam Day, Victory in the Mideast Day, Victory in downtown San Francisco Day? Like most veterans, I value our military and take attacks against this country personally. I only apologize for the lack of humor in this chapter.

Military stories prompt concerns

June 20, 2001

As a U.S. Army veteran, I have a few concerns regarding recent Associated Press stories on our military.

One story reports on statements made by Army Secretary Thomas E. White on military "modernization." According to White, plans are moving forward to make the Army into a lighter, more-mobile force... better suited to post-Cold War era conflicts.

Apparently White believes that now that Central Europe and the Soviet Union are no longer a threat, the Army needs to lighten up, including cutting down the number of fighting units.

Now, correct me if I'm wrong. But haven't we cut the military in size quite a bit over the last 10 years. We've cut Army forts and Navy bases in this country at the same time as sending American soldiers off to serve United Nations commanders in that apparently now non-threatening Central Europe.

I guess White thinks the Cold War is a thing of the past and that the U.S. Army will now probably never have to face a large enemy force like the Soviet Union. White didn't mention Communist China as a possible large enemy.

According to another AP story, the U.S. Army is willing to pay for a new look for its troops. Soldiers are adopting black berets as part of their uniform both stateside and overseas. Ranger units, formerly wearers of black berets, are adopting a beige beret while Green Berets will continue to wear their namesakes. Airborne units now wear maroon berets, leaving all other non-airborne outfits the new black beret.

When I was in the Airborne, (in the dinosaur age) our class-A headgear was the overseas cap with the "glider" patch. The name we had for it is, I am sure, not allowed to be mentioned in today's politically correct military. And, as in all things, times they are a changin'. Our trimmed-down military should have a more-modern look.

The sad thing is, Army Chief of Staff Gen. Eric Shinseki ordered the headgear last year... and to get enough of them by the June deadline, some had to be ordered from Communist China.

Not surprising — just sad.

It's a shame that now even our military uniforms are not American made. Perhaps this is why Mr. White doesn't think China should be considered a possible enemy. The Communists control so much of America's former products that perhaps he considers China as our new U.S. Army Quartermaster Corps.

According to another AP story, "A German corporation that is paying compensation for Nazi-era slave labor owns the Charlotte-based construction company hired to build the World War II Memorial in Washington D.C."

It won't be long before some of our American troops could wear their Communist Chinese-made uniforms when they go on leave from their United Nations commands and tour our German-made World War II Memorial.

Kind of makes you proud.... or not.

Communist China makes so many products these days that if they ever decide to go to war against us, our economy will come to a dead stop.
And our military will be caught flat-footed without certain necessities like vehicle parts, computer chips, titanium, uniforms and perhaps even ammunition. A lot of so-called Americans have become very wealthy by assisting Red China with the takeover of our industries. I would assume that, on the day that war begins, those same multi-national entrepreneurs will be charged as traitors, even if they are related to a President.

Looking back on Memorial Day

May 27, 1996

It was 1966. The Huey formation flew low over the Vietnam jungle.

"Anytime now," the sergeant hollered.

We prepared to exit the choppers quickly.

The helicopters stopped and hovered a few feet over the top of what looked like thick shrubs. I quickly stepped out on the strut, tossed the outer ring of a mortar into the air, grabbed the strut with one hand, swung down and dropped into the "shrubs."

About the same time, everyone realized those shrubs were the tops of some very thick, very tall jungle trees.

As I broke branches all the way to the ground I remember thinking in third person, "Holy ****, Purcell!" Dazed, bruised and embarrassed I heard the formation fly off to find a better LZ (landing zone).

I gathered my rifle and equipment. The outer ring is probably still up in one of those trees.

Within a couple of hours the platoon found me. Sarge was mad. My friend Speer thought the situation was hilarious. He chuckled through his description of my head vanishing into the foliage.

"Someday you'll look back on this and laugh," he said.

Speer used that line on me several times during my year in Vietnam. And though I usually failed to agree with him at the time, he was eventually right.

I think of the night at Pleiku Pass when Sergeant Moore taught me I wasn't a good poker player. It cost me every dollar I had, but the lesson was worth every cent, as I haven't played poker since.

I remember our platoon leader, Lt. Hayes. He was one officer, unlike most I had to deal with, who was well respected. He went on patrols with the rest of us. Other officers just sent out squads led by an E-5 (buck sergeant). Along with his M-16, he carried a captured Thompson, which he planned to somehow send back to the states so he could, jokingly, be "king of the block."

Hayes made me an RTO (PRC-26 radio carrier) and attached me to recon. That kept me in the field, on patrols, and away from other officers. He knew I had a tendency to get in trouble when I was around the brass.

I think of Carly, who was 17 when he came to Nam. When the rules changed that one had to be 18 to be sent into combat he was offered the chance to return to the states. He decided to stay out his tour.

Carly was a pretty good guitar player. When we were in base camp he would attempt to teach me the instrument. I had paid 800 dong (eight bucks) for a Vietnamese guitar. At the time I didn't know I had no musical ability. Anyone who listened in, however, knew.

Lt. Hayes, Sergeant Moore and other officers and NCOs tolerated privates like Speer, Carly and me. We were still kids. We did our jobs, made mistakes and always had a Bilko-like scheme going which usually rewarded us with KP or other extra duty whenever we returned to base camp.

As with all veterans, there were close calls, twists of fate, and just plain insane situations that we all would have a good laugh about, after the fact, over a few Beer LaRues.

Speer and I finished our tours and returned stateside. Lt. Hayes, Sergeant Moore and Carly, like so many more, came back in bags.

Speer was right, though. Sometimes I think back and laugh. But sometimes I just think back.

This column was published less than four months prior to 9-11. Things change.

There are reasons to remember

May 28, 2001

Today is Memorial Day, 2001.

It has been sixty years this coming December 7th since World War II got its explosive start with Japan's attack on Pearl Harbor. That's a long time ago. Just ask the survivors.

But the memories of the events and the participants of that war, and all the wars that have taken place since, are perhaps even more important today. Lessons learned in those days need to be passed on to future generations.

Memorial Day, Veterans Day and Pearl Harbor Day are all opportunities for everyone to reflect on life and death situations in which our people and our nation have been involved. Those who were never in combat are able to reflect on historical recounts of those terrible times. Those of us who participated can be more specific. (I was First Battalion, Airborne, Eighth Cavalry, First Cavalry Division in Vietnam— 1965-66.)

The final result of this reflection is to not only honor those who gave their lives, but to learn from our history and never again allow ourselves to be lulled into a situation where we can be attacked by an enemy like we were in 1941.

We must never allow foreign interests to pull us into another war where we will have our hands tied behind us either by bureaucrats with vested interests in keeping the conflict going, gutless politicians too fearful to win and too stupid to avoid prolonging a war, or those who openly support the enemy, such as some of our fearless leaders did during the Vietnam War.

American troops should never serve under foreign commanders. They have their priorities — we have ours. This is one mistake in which our country is presently engaged.

Memories need to be kept fresh. Ask a veteran.

War is not a game of paintball. It is not glorious, glamorous or cinematically idealized in any way. It is extremely confusing carnage where military bean counters fudge their body counts and luck is usually the difference between life and death. It is hot, cold, filthy, wet, frightening, boring, frantic, hateful, disgusting and sometimes necessary. Civilians do get killed. Villages are destroyed. It's an insane world where one either accepts the insanity or loses his mind.

No veteran would ever wish that today's youths will have to witness the horrors of the battlefield. In fact, most of us wish the world situations had not occurred that put us through our experiences. But although the past can't be changed, we hopefully can continue to learn from experiences and keep an American peace that is too strong to be challenged by any Hitler- or Stalin-wannabes.

War is a necessary evil that we must always militarily prepare for as our best defense against having to become involved in one.

Today is a day to remember and honor our friends and relatives who served and are no longer with us. As long as we remember them, they are still serving America. If they are ever forgotten, we are doomed to repeat the mistakes that led to the countless war deaths of the 20th century.

Today is Memorial Day, 2001.

September 11 happened later that year. American troops engaged in combat with our enemies over quite a few years. This country didn't demand unconditional surrender of the enemy. Our political leaders made every civilized mistake possible that allowed the enemy to again and again rebuild and assault our warriors. And, after two decades, President Biden abandoned weapons, equipment and allies to the enemy as he yanked our military out of Afghanistan with the flourish and dysfunctional BS of a senile dog with his tail tucked between his legs. History is supposed to teach us something. Most of us learned close to 50 years ago that you don't negotiate with rattlesnakes like we did at the Paris Peace Accords and you don't set yourself up for a fall-of-Saigon moment when the enemy breaks every agreement. But, sure as hell...

City to get more bang for their bucks with new fireworks display
April 20, 1997

The Bullhead City Council voted Thursday to fund a July 4 fireworks celebration. In (*Daily News* reporter) Dave Garvin's news story about the council action, he recorded one council member's comment that the cost of the fireworks was a small tribute to pay to Americans who lost their lives in combat to secure American freedoms.

Now, I'm not opposed to a fireworks display. There certainly seems to be a lot of people who enjoy seeing bombs bursting in air. I just really wonder, if the spirits of soldiers killed in combat were to visit Bullhead City on July 4, would they really want to see a bunch of explosions, or would they rather just toss down a couple of beers and shoot a couple of quick games of pool?

Having been an infantryman in Vietnam, I witnessed a lot of colorful explosive effects. Many of those explosions were a little too close for comfort. Some filled many of us with delight, such as when Sky Raiders would strafe, bomb, then Napalm an area that we were preparing to enter. The sounds and colors were uplifting in that we would think, "Nothing could live through such an attack." That gave us the confidence to advance into the charred area.

After dealing with that kind of activity over a period of time, one does become a little "sensitive" around popping, booming and various surprise noises. Surprise explosion sounds tend to make one a tad skittish.

I wonder if other living vets really enjoy seeing unnecessary explosions. Why would one want to see a bomb go off for no other reason than visual effect? I have yet to see a fireworks display that could match a Napalm strike in color and visual power. With no enemy, no enemy-held village and no threatening entity to destroy, why blow things up? The fireworks concept, to me, is like playing war ... playing with matches ... seeing pretty lights and making things go boom.

I'm sure there are many vets who see fireworks in a positive light, and certainly many non-vets who also get a patriotic thrill out of fireworks. And I don't want to pour cold water on their pyrotechnic thrills.

But for many of the guys who remember explosions – which contained people – fireworks are not a lot of fun. And I am of the belief that if the spirits of soldiers killed in battle did return, the last thing they would want to do is view a colorful display of explosions. What kind of an R&R would that be?

One friend from our recon platoon, Hatcher, lost his life in 1966. I can visualize his spirit returning this Fourth of July.

"Welcome back, Hatcher. You here for the fireworks?" I'd ask.

"#@%*&! no, Purcell!" He'd answer. "That mortar round was the last explosion for me. What happened to your hair?"

"It's a long story. Thirty years long. Whad'ya wanna do while you're here?"

"Well, I'd like to start by hitting a couple of go-go bars, have a few COLD Beer LaRues, and listen to some records of that new rock group ... the Monkeys," he'd say while lighting up an unfiltered, C-ration Camel.

"Sorry 'bout that, Hatch. The bad news is go-go bars, Beer LaRue, records and the Monkeys are history. The good news is Beer LaRue and the Monkeys are history," I'd explain. "But one can get a cold GOOD beer and listen to oldies rock in an air conditioned sports bar. That is if we can convince a bartender that you only look 18 and you were really born in 1947."

Anyway, Hatcher and all the guys whose names are on The Wall, and all the other guys killed in the other wars, are not coming back for the Fourth of July. And during their short, wartime lives, their priorities were not parades, fireworks and speeches. They were normal guys who longed for some of the basic, peaceful pleasures of home.

I truly hope this Fourth of July fireworks celebration is a success for all those who enjoy that kind of thing. As for me, I'll stay somewhere quiet and enjoy the peace.

No sour grapes on Veterans Day

Nov. 11, 1996

The voters have spoken. President Clinton has won a second term. A majority of voters have affirmed the President's history, character and vision. The loyal opposition must now accept their loss and, as Johnny Mercer said, "accentuate the positive."

Republicans can enjoy their majorities in Congress. Editorial cartoonists can rejoice because, in my opinion as an ex-political cartoonist, Bill and Hillary Clinton are easier to draw than Bob and Elizabeth Dole. And fast-food restaurants can be pleased they still have a friend in the White House.

As for veterans, some of us have to "just get over it."

The President's activities during the Vietnam War are well known by all. Those of us who served in wars, specifically Vietnam, have to finally realize the war is over. And, obviously, we lost. Many of us, especially me, are still bitter over the way the war was handled from the beginning, and the way it was ended. Too bad.

As the election results came in Tuesday night, the bitter me thought, maybe we should cancel Veterans Day this year and replace it with Draft Resisters Day. Maybe we should honor those service avoiders who used to say we didn't belong in Vietnam; that war was none of our business; the North Vietnamese Communists were not a threat to America; etc. After all, Clinton made that government a trade partner last year.

The reasoning me said it's time to move on.

We veterans know what we did and why we did it. We remember the faces of those who died around us. Most of the time we didn't know the guys' names, but their 18- and 19-year-old faces will always be with us, especially that first face, the first guy who looks you in the eye as his life foams red and white out of his chest. In the mass confusion of a firefight, all sound stops as his face changes color, maybe only in your mind, and you witness the metamorphosis of death.

But even if the country seems to be forgetting, veterans will never forget. This Veterans Day should be a time to remember both the living and dead we encountered during those years.

We can learn from the wars' 1960s and '70s opposition as well. Wars are created by politicians and fought by soldiers. Citizen Clinton didn't serve in the war he opposed. Let's hope President Clinton remembers his Vietnam-era beliefs and doesn't send any more Americans to die in any foreign political wars that have nothing to do with the United States.

Political and tribal elements have slaughtered each other in the Mid-East, Africa and Eastern Europe for thousands of years. There is no justification for adding American casualties to these areas.

Veterans Day is a good time to reflect on the past with the hope of not repeating our mistakes.

Then again, when an enemy attacks America, it's time to take out that enemy government, leaders, officers and infrastructure, immediately.
That's the only message an enemy will ever understand.

Wars' worst moments should be remembered
Monday, (Memorial Day) May 26, 1997

Should we really attempt to remember the horrors of war? Or should we let the death, and all the insanity surrounding it, fade into the past?

Vietnam veterans are now in their 40s and 50s. Surviving World War II and Korean vets are retired from the workplace.

Diversity and sensitivity training is now a big part of the military curriculum.

Germany and Japan have been rebuilt and are now successful economic trade partners with the United States. The Soviet Union has crumbled into a gaggle of struggling independent governments. China, still the same Communist dictatorship that was our enemy for so many years, is considered a friend and economic partner by our present political and corporate leaders. Companies that profited from the war with North Vietnam are now profiting from trade with the same enemy government. A Vietnam-era draft dodger is now commander in chief of our military.

A generation has grown up without having to deal with a major conflict or the threat of the military draft.

As Lyndon Johnson said *(lied)* during the 1964 election, "And we are at peace."

Veterans will always remember, until our time is up, the horrors of war. Non-veteran politicians, social engineers and corporate leaders need to be reminded. War is not fun. War is not a place for sensitivity and acceptance of diverse views. War is killing and destroying. The only way to prevent going through the horrors of war is to have a realistic attitude about, and be fully prepared to endure, war.

Every time this country has relaxed into believing there will be no more wars, it has been proven wrong the hard way.

Wartime soldiers quickly learn to hate the enemy. It makes killing and destroying easier. Sensitivity goes out the window when one is confronted with killing. It's a lot easier to slaughter the hated Japs, Nazis, Commies and Gooks than it is Oriental and Caucasian peoples with diverse viewpoints. The sensitivity training could come into play when wars are won and soldiers return to civilian life. Unfortunately, sometimes the hatred lingers. This is one of the horrors of war, which we need to remember. For some people, it ain't over when it's over.

Certainly we must remember our friends and family members who served in time of war. Some gave their lives. Many gave their health. And others gave their sanity.

But our political and corporate leaders also need to remember the brutal realities of our past conflicts to avoid repeating them. They need to remember Charley Company, First of the Eighth Cavalry (Death From Above) placing airborne-winged skull calling cards on bodies of the enemy; troops who looted enemy bodies for souvenir knives, pictures, trophies, ears, etc.; enemy POWs who were lined up and shot in reaction to the North Vietnamese refusal to follow Geneva Convention rules; and the constant body bags being flown back to the states. They also need to think before they aid and arm a potential enemy.

We needn't dwell on the horrors of war. But remembering gives us reason to be fully prepared to quickly destroy any enemy who may want to put us or our children through that again.

Currently I don't wonder about the ability of our SEALS, Green Berets and Rangers to engage against future enemies. I know those guys and the few gals that made the cut have more realistic attitudes about what they may face. Many of them are already combat vets. But I do wonder about the remaining infantry, artillery and support divisions. I've read about training classes where some recruits can hold up a sign and opt out of certain situations because of sensitivities. Those signs won't work in war. I worry about recruits who are being trained by drill instructors who are doing their best not to offend anyone. The enemy will offend you. The enemy will cut your head off! Let's face it. A woke Army will lose!

Has sleeping giant reawakened?

Sept. 12, 2001

September 11, 2001

We are at war.

There is a lot of tough talk coming from our political leaders. But talk doesn't do the job. We don't need flap-jawed congressmen telling us to "Wait," "Let calmer heads prevail," "Negotiate a peaceful resolution," and other clichés that allowed us to lose wars and be taken as a joke by fanatical terrorist regimes. We don't need to listen to any promises that the guilty ones will be found and brought to justice.

Our intelligence knows who these folks are and what countries harbor them.

We need to strike back quickly with whatever force it takes to eliminate the people and government(s) responsible.

Just shy of 60 years since Pearl Harbor, America has been attacked by an enemy force. The force is very capable and was extremely successful in their destruction. They must be sanctioned by one of our enemies or they wouldn't have a place in the world to hide.

We need to destroy any country that allows this element to exist within their borders. We need to use whatever military capability to achieve this result.

Our President should, with the support of Congress, declare war on every nation involved with supporting or harboring this enemy force or condoning their actions.

Our armed forces need to be placed on our border to stop all illegal immigration or suspected smuggling of drugs, weapons and people, all of which could be used for terrorists' ends. Legal immigration needs to be put on hold. All foreign aid needs to end, as we need every dollar to assist in, finally, strengthening our defenses and taking care of America first.

We need to defend our country with space technology and every other innovation we can devise, as our enemies will use every weakness we have to destroy us.

A drill instructor summed it up for me when I was in Army infantry training. He told us troops that our only job was "to infect the enemy with a terminal case of leaky body." We don't need to open our doors to our enemies; we don't need to negotiate, have dialogue or take meetings with them; we need to kill them.

Gun control fanatics need to be overruled by those of us who know the final defense of America is Americans. We need to stop allowing these extremists to disarm America.

The only way we can stop the type of maniacal devastation that took place Tuesday is to heap many times more destruction on the enemy. Japan learned this in 1945. The world must need a refresher course.

My thoughts haven't changed a bit on this one. When the U.S. is the victim of an act of war, the right thing to do to the enemy is to, as Curtis LeMay said, "Bomb them back to the Stone Age."

None dare call it 'collaboration'

September 16, 2001

Americans are revisiting terminology of the 1940s and '50s such as "sneak attack" and "saboteurs." One other very important word has been used for the first time since the United States was worried about fifth columnists, Japanese spies and Communist infiltrators. That word is "collaborators."

The F.B.I. and other law enforcement agencies are vigilantly seeking out "terrorist collaborators" who may have been involved with the recent murder of thousands of Americans in New York, Washington, D.C., and Pennsylvania.

During World War I and II, those who supported the enemy were known as collaborators. The pro-Nazi Americans changed their philosophy, went to jail or became silent for the duration. During the Korean War, Communist sympathizers were not tolerated while Americans were dying in battle.

During the Vietnam War, many Americans used their "First Amendment rights" to openly support the enemy. Many of those "collaborators" are now elected officials. So far this week, they seem to have learned their lesson and realized whose side they are on this time. (Has anyone heard any outrage out of Hanoi Jane or Vanessa Redgrave?)

We have all read various columnists who have debated their views on Israel vs. the Palestinians. My favorite columnist, Charley Reese, has defended the Palestinians and has been quite critical of Zionism. Certainly there is justification for his point of view. But, Charley, it wasn't the Israelis who were dancing in the street Tuesday in celebration of the killing of Americans.

Now that the country is cracking down on these murderous collaborators, the question is: how much "collaboration" have we all been guilty of over the last 40 years?

Was it really "jingoism" when Pat Buchanan said that we needed to start taking care of "America first"? Or was he one of the few who had a realist view of the way Washington was selling out our country?

Was it "collaboration" when so-called environmentalists would rather see Shiite-house sheiks become mega-wealthy through selling America oil rather than allow drilling in a small part of the largest state in the union or along our own coasts?

How much "collaboration" was involved in the dismantling of our intelligence capabilities? When our political "leaders" neutered our information gathering agencies during our pro-Contra, anti-Communist covert actions, were they really helping the American way of life or just opening a back door for anti-American terrorists?

Were the supporters of open borders really thinking of the best interests of the United States? Are the so-called American corporations that have left the United States to achieve higher profits with lower wages manufacturing products in third-world countries really patriotic or have they sold themselves, and their fellow working-class countrymen, for a few pieces of silver?

Certainly we all have the right to disagree. As one who writes columns and draws political cartoons, I know that our constitutional freedoms are the key to our society. I support everyone's right to express a viewpoint different than mine, even the really goofy ones.

At the same time, just as a person's right to swing his fist ends at my nose, the right to protest against the American way of life ends where the body bags begin.... this time by the thousands.

We all need to continue to debate the issues. But anyone, anywhere, for any reason, who supports the actions of the terrorists who murdered Americans in New York, Washington D.C. and Pennsylvania, is my enemy.

I think at that time most of us were angry and wanted revenge against the terrorists and anyone who attempted to justify their actions.
After 9-11, it took me a while before I was able to find humor with the world situation.

The Taliban enemy and fifth column must be destroyed

October 24, 2001

The American way of life is under attack from many directions. And, although there seems to be a growing support for defending our country and our freedoms, there is still a spreading disease of self-destruction among us.

For every triumph and every disaster there are people who crawl out from under rocks to either rip off victims, assist the enemy via copy-cat hoaxes and other terrorist acts, or to capitalize on tragedies by creating enemies who may not exist.

Since the 9-11 act of war against the United States, President George W. Bush has rightfully brought our military into action. The majority of America supports our military and whatever it has to do to destroy the murderous Taliban and its terrorist lackeys. Even most of the dreaded newspaper editors of this country, those who make a living writing editorials and columns questioning government officials and actions, have united to promote the common defense.

But, in this country where we all have the freedom to speak our minds, or lack of, the questions are beginning to appear.

One network talking head, (I won't print his name but it rhymes with "Bumble,") while recently interviewing the secretary of defense about bombing in Afghanistan, asked the question, "Are you sure you are not killing civilians?"

I would like to ask Bumble if he knew what uniforms the terrorists are wearing.

The way I see it, the Taliban controls Afghanistan. The Taliban terrorists wear dishtowels on their heads and bathrobes. Their support rallies in Afghanistan and other Mideastern countries show folks dressed the same way with rifles and pictures of their leader, the soon-to-be-late Osama bin Laden. Their "soldiers" came into this country wearing our version of street clothes.

Perhaps if Mr. Bumble could explain to all of us what the enemy's uniform looks like we could not only target their official military, but we could have spotted those folks before they got on the planes on September 11. That certainly would have saved more than 3,000 civilian lives.

Until that talking head can do this for us, our military needs to continue to kill the enemy and destroy enemy property until there is an unconditional surrender.

Now we have anthrax attacks and hoaxes. Some degenerate scumballs are sending the disease through the mail to high-profile targets: networks, large newspapers and political leaders. Our officials tell us there is no proof yet that bin Laden is behind this biological warfare. It doesn't matter if we ever prove it comes from him. What does matter is that the people responsible are allies of our enemy. They may be just fruitcakes of the Oklahoma City bombing kind or People For the Ethical Treatment of Viruses. Whoever they are, they should be treated as enemy saboteurs and should be executed for their acts. This includes those who engage in hoax threats intended to spread fear and cause economic disaster.

While we're on that topic, there are those who have plagued us for years with the spread of deadly white powder. These people have retroactively joined the enemy in the destruction of America. They are the folks, many in our area, who manufacture and sell methamphetamine. Like vampires, they spread their disease and create more of their own kind. You've seen their pictures in the newspaper: bug-eyed, bone-thin, brain-dead, toothless wastes of oxygen who, while they live, clog our court system and keep our law enforcement busy chasing them down for drug, theft and murder charges.

These unofficial fifth columnists should be brought to justice for their work in the destruction of America. Good Americans should no longer look the other way and consider these poisoners as part of the "victimless crimes" of the drug culture. If we citizens don't support justice right now by actively working to eliminate the manufacturing of methamphetamine, we will be forever victims of the terror of these homegrown saboteurs.

I have always believed in our freedoms and our capitalist system. Those who invest in our communities have a stake in their futures. Anyone who invests wisely, rightfully, should expect a profit. And sometimes they receive a loss. That's business. But investing in marketable ideas, products and skills is what has made our country great.

However, there are those engaged in spreading a divide-and-conquer philosophy. They attempt to manipulate people who have very little invested and have large amounts of bitterness against those who have achieved success. They infect us with a class-conscious extremism, which plays those who have not succeeded, because of lack of education or skills or just plain bad luck, against those who have bettered themselves over the years and gathered some form of economic success.

It's very simple to turn the "poor" against the "rich." (The definition of "rich" is unique to every individual.) Those instigators talk of constant conspiracies and always allege that certain people couldn't have achieved their positions without back-room criminal actions. Enough already! By dividing Americans we are helping to destroy America. If anyone has proof of criminal actions, they need to immediately inform law enforcement. But spreading rumors of conspiracies against those who have built our roads, homes and entertainment facilities is an evil, destructive pastime that plays into our enemies' hands.

Most of us work for a living. If companies and individuals don't invest in growth, we're out of work, and the economy crumbles. Instead of looking for a villain under every corporation, we need to support our local businesses and attempt to bring in new business to increase job opportunities and better our lifestyles.

If our communities prosper with positive growth over the next year, our enemies will have suffered one more loss.

And finally, an alleged politician, while appearing recently on a "talk show," referred to me as "to the right of Attila the Hun." And from the transcript of that program that I received, that statement was about the only truth he had to say about this newspaper and me personally. I am a skosh conservative. And I figure, as far as Attila is concerned, any military leader whose troops call him "Hun," can't be that far to the right.

The feelings I tried to convey in this column haven't changed much over the years. There are still poisoners among us selling their illegal drugs. Methamphetamine may still be a problem, but Fentanyl is the latest death-dealing opioid to send addicts to the morgue. That drug is shipped out from our 1949 until present-enemy, Red China, and shipped into our country across President Biden's open borders.

During the last two decades, Cyber terrorists have also plagued our American way of life. Some of them are homegrown traitors, thieves and saboteurs, while others fire their digital ammunition at us from around the world, including Red China and our recently revived enemy, Russia.

As for my remark about Attila the Hun, times have changed. Under the Pentagon's new woke focus, there are probably several military leaders serving who wouldn't have a problem being called "Hun," except they'd probably spell it with an O.

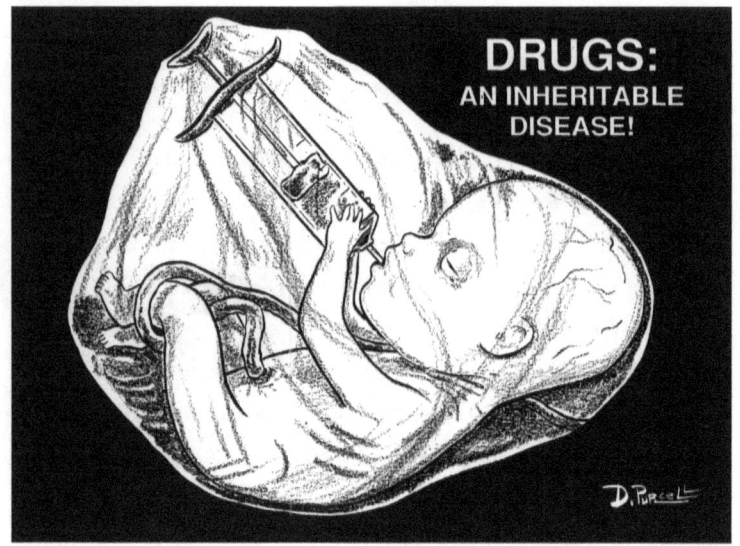

What makes celebrities' lives and politics so important?
February 16, 2003

I may be alone in this opinion, but I'm just sick of hearing about the lifestyles of the rich and insipid.

I have no interest in how many surgeries Michael Jackson has had to go from a black pop singer to a white nutcase who looks somewhat like a cross between his sister and a rat terrier. I'm tired of seeing television's so-called "news" reports on Penny Marshall defending her friend's rights to sleep with little boys or hang babies over balconies while she attacks the evil "press" because Jackson looked like a weirdo (what else?) in an interview.

First off, television is not the "press." Print media is the press. And most daily newspapers, editorial departments, do not give a rat's rear end if Michael Jackson dangled all of the Baldwin brothers off a balcony. If he actually dropped them, especially all of the brothers, you might read about it in a *Daily News* brief. With good news like that, this newsroom might even high-five all the way around.

Jackson was a talented performer, just as Marshall is certainly a talented slapstick comedienne and director. But, like most Hollywood celebrities, it ends there.

These folks spend a lot of money and time trying to get into the news to help their careers. Celebrity publicity has become a big-buck business with "Entertainment Tonight" and its TV clones, *People*-like magazines and supermarket tabloids. Obviously, there is a market for this material. But I find it sad that Americans will pay money to read about who's sleeping with whom in Tinseltown and which air-headed celeb is wearing which protest ribbon to what event.

I find successful entertainers entertaining when they perform, not when they share their immense expertise on the plight of the Lithuanian river carp or demand our military troops disarm and sing show tunes with subtitles for the hearing impaired.

Several years ago there was a popular television cop show that I liked very much. The top cop character was a tough, no-nonsense guy that John Wayne or Randolph Scott would have portrayed in an earlier era. Not long after that show finished its years on television, I was at a dinner honoring John Walsh. The actor who portrayed the tough cop was at my table. He had a purse.... and he didn't like to talk about the show I liked because... well, who cares?

Barbra Streisand, Jane Fonda, Sean Penn and Martin Sheen are talented people. These and other performers can do wonderful things portraying characters created by other talented people. And, like all of us, they have a right to offer their opinions to anyone who will listen. That doesn't make their political opinions, their military expertise, their social agendas or stories or denials concerning who they are sleeping with worth "press" coverage or television time.

In fact, the Hollywood elitists who are presently butting into the nightly news to spout enemy propaganda or attempt to revitalize their careers by being socially enlightened disgust me enough that I will probably have a hard time accepting them as characters in their next films.... unless they are all in a remake of The Greatest Show on Earth playing clowns.

Okay. Hanoi Jane and others left-wing activist/entertainers have the right to share their dumber-than-shit, alleged insights. And, in Arizona, Texas, Oklahoma and few other red states, we have the right and the ability to disagree.
And I'll drink to our God-given, Constitutional rights – just not with Bud Light.

Military troops are professional; Frisco nuts show their colors
March 26, 2003

I couldn't be prouder of America's Armed Forces.

And I couldn't be more disgusted by the wackaloons stopping traffic in Frisco and other big cities.

American and British forces are advancing at an unprecedented speed in capturing territory on their way to taking Baghdad.

As with all wars, we have taken casualties. But, thanks to a well-planned offensive, well-trained troops, proper supply lines and a nothing-less-than-victory goal, our military will keep those casualty numbers to a fraction of the Iraqi soldiers who will be captured or killed on this quest to eliminate the Saddam Hussein dictatorship.

All combat veterans know how horrible war can be. They also know that some battles are necessary. This one is not just to rid the world of Saddam Hussein, but to let all other nations that train, supply and support mass murdering terrorists learn that they had best change their ways — now! All governments that engage in gassing civilians in or out of their own countries, mass murdering those who have different religions or cultures, or funding wild-eyed nutcases to harm civilized people will find themselves the targets of future smart bombs. Osama's bankers had best pull the plug on his and other terrorists' fund and supply lines.

Thank God this time we have a President who won't settle for signed lies on a piece of paper to achieve the illusion of peace in our time. He won't call for a cease-fire to negotiate anything less than a complete surrender of the enemy.

Our country is rightly sending food and medicine to civilians in the occupied area. Other, not so lucky, Iraqi civilians are being used as human shields by the enemy in various locations including through the placement of government and military buildings next to hospitals and schools in Baghdad.

Hussein, who has already used Scud missiles he promised the United Nations he didn't have, may possibly kill many of his own people with other weapons during the siege of Baghdad.

Some so-called Americans in Frisco, Hollywood and other centers of the drug and nut culture are taking to the streets in support of Saddam and his actions. Older kooks who supported the North Vietnamese and blasted America during that war — the same folks who quietly smiled as the north broke every promise of the Paris Peace Accords in reinvading the South, imprisoning and executing pro-American South Vietnamese and engaging in the genocide of the mountain tribes — are now joined by the youthful illiterate, immoral and inexperienced experts of civilization as they engage in activities that, if they were in the country they are supporting, would get them gassed by Saddam.

These weirdoes do have a right to their often-treasonous opinions, as long as they don't break the law. Blocking freeways, trespassing "sit-ins" and vandalism are against the law. We shouldn't have a problem allowing these morons to make fools of themselves. But we also shouldn't tolerate the hijacking of our rights by allowing them to get away with criminal actions.

Along with our troops, I am also very proud of the journalists who have accompanied them to the front. These reporters are seeing first-hand how our military handles a war.... and they are reporting accurately to the American people. Television news may never be the same. Nothing cuts through anti-American biases like front-line experience.

The embedded war correspondents quickly learned that they were there to report facts, not salacious Hollywood lies. They also knew the American soldiers they were accompanying were the ones who kept them alive, as opposed to the Muslim enemy who would chop their heads off if given the chance like they did Daniel Pearl. They were the real journalists of that war, not the network talking heads that sat in plush chairs, had their television makeup applied while off air and read their copy from Teleprompters. I still salute the men and women journalists who report from the front.

Hollywood leftists must feel very impotent about now
April 10, 2003

American protesters are still parading through the streets of larger cities while demanding an end to the war. And now it looks like they are going to get their way. Unfortunately for them, it looks like their side has lost.

Certainly there are some dangerous days ahead for our troops. But anyone who watched the live toppling Wednesday of the Saddam Hussein statue in the heart of Baghdad now knows that the average Iraqi citizen is welcoming Americans and celebrating the end of the dictator's reign of torture and murder.

I'm sure that Sean Penn and Martin Sheen are wallowing in a Hollywood pity party bemoaning the fact that the live television images on the third week, to the day, of the war don't live up to their "Vietnam quagmire" predictions. Unfortunately for them, Lyndon Johnson is dead and Bill Clinton is out of office. President George W. Bush obviously finishes what he starts.

However, we have not seen the last of the leftist Hollywood crowd. It is quite possible that the two earlier-mentioned Bozos could join Babs Streisand, Hanoi Jane, Susan Sarandon and at least one of the Dixie Chicks to hold a fundraiser to rebuild Saddam's statue. Baghdad's version of Hanoi Hanna, Peter Arnett, could cover the event for the All-Terrorist, All-The-Time Network. Michael Moore could even film a documentary on the making of the fundraiser so Hollywood could give him another Benedict, I mean Oscar, award.

President Bush has led this nation into the 21st Century with honor. He didn't allow the coalition of dictators and fools, known as the United Nations, to get in freedom's way. Anyone with any brain cells at all has learned from Vietnam and the first Iraq war that one cannot negotiate with a snake.

This President sent our troops into harms way with full support, ammunition, technology and the goal of complete victory. What a refreshing idea. Let's hope the rest of the world has been watching the U.S. in action and the Iraqi civilians celebrating their new freedom from Saddam. The message is simple. Stop the seeds of terrorism before they take control. Terrorist states will pay a price.

If that message is received, we will have earned many years of peace in our world. And Sheen and Penn can go back to portraying American heroes in the movies and on television — if there is anyone left who will watch them.

Well, it's two decades later and Afghanistan is a mess again, Iran is still trying to start World War III, Russia wants to recreate the Soviet Union, China is spitting in Uncle Sam's face and the Hollywood Bozos, as well as a big chunk of Washington, D.C., do not seem to understand why many of us believe America needs to protect our borders, be energy self-sufficient and focus our attention on America First.

Defeatist politicians do not understand. War must be won!
November 11, 2003

The daily body count of American soldiers being killed in Iraq is a sobering reminder of the horrors of war.

We Americans want to know, we have the right to know, what is going on in Iraq, and Afghanistan as well. Every American death is a tragedy to us. We have empathy with the families of the slain warriors.

These feelings must be remembered when we are told we need to send soldiers to do battle. Some will always die. Many more will mourn.

Most of us, at the time, rightfully believed we should go after the terrorists in Afghanistan and, later, the mass-murdering dictator of Iraq. We prepared for the worst and hoped for the best. Our all-volunteer military has done a fantastic job.

The *best* came to pass with the victory in Afghanistan and the creation of a democratic government, and the end of bombing and major military action in three weeks in Iraq as well as the reconstruction of infrastructure and organization of a new free society there.

The *worst* seems to be the holdouts that want their dictator back and are engaging in a postwar sabotage campaign. These are people who hate Americans, freedom and anything else that gets in the way of their power to dominate, torture, rape, kill and all the other benefits of being a faithful Saddamite.

Should we listen to those who are using the recent American deaths as reason to put our tails between our legs and run away? Should we, once again, abandon the freedom-loving Iraqis to be tortured and killed by the dictator's brownshirts?

If we do, we will be spitting on the graves of those who died fighting our enemies and liberating the people of Iraq.

Wars are not won easily. Reconstruction has never been a smooth process.

The United States defeated Japan in 1945. Over 15 years later there were still a few Japanese soldiers found in the Pacific islands serving Premier Hideki Tojo, who was hanged in 1948, and the flag of the Rising Sun.

America defeated the Nazis in 1945 as well, and, in our truly free society, we will find members of the Nazi Party, as well as quite a few nutcakes who may not be members but who deny the Holocaust, today living, meeting and marching in the United States.

And, of course, the reconstruction of the south after the Civil War was met with the creation of a terrorist organization called the Ku Klux Klan.... and they still exist after almost 140 years.

We fought against the Communists in South Vietnam. But, at that time, we listened to those who believed we shouldn't attack into the enemy invaders' country, North Vietnam. Without leaders who believed in winning, defeating the enemy, we lost.

Those Democrats who want to reside in the White House should look back at the real Vietnam situation. They should look back at how Washington politicians limited our troops and eventually trusted our enemy during negotiations. They should remember the last days as the remaining Americans had to escape — leaving their south Vietnamese supporters to the hands of re-invading Communists who broke every promise on the "Peace Accords."

The voices of retreat and defeat have a right to express their opinions in our country. They have a right to pander to our enemies with their Chicken Little messages. But they insult our intelligence if they think we agree that we will achieve "peace in our time" by running away.

Americans need to realize that those who denounce a religious military general who called the enemy a bad name and supported his Commander in Chief, while using their freedom of speech to do the exact opposite, are nuts.

The terrorists declared war on us. They have attacked us. They will stop only when we are no longer alive. We have no choice but to do whatever it takes to defeat them.

To the presidential candidates, the Hollywood Left and other whiners, ordering soldiers to run away will not help.

In thinking back to this particular time in our history, I have say my hardline attitude was, and still is, based on my own experiences in Vietnam and the discussions I had with other family members who were veterans of prior wars.
That said, I would rather see an enemy city in ruins than see one American soldier return in a box.

Is National Guard a victim of candidate's friendly fire?

February 18, 2004

Sen. John Kerry is, like all candidates for office, on the offensive with attacks against the man he wants to replace. Unfortunately for Kerry, his remarks about the National Guard are offensive to many more people than just President George W. Bush.

Democrat candidate for President Kerry has likened service in the National Guard during war as to being equal with the efforts of a draft dodger. Of course, Kerry is trying to make that case against Republican Bush, not all the other voters in the country who volunteered to serve in the National Guard.

This is an old standby for some Democrats who successfully tarnished former Vice President Dan Quayle for his stateside service in the National Guard. They then went on to support former protester Bill Clinton who, coincidentally, left for Oxford about the time his draft notice was sent.

Guard members have been called to active duty in all of our wars. Many are presently serving in Iraq. NGs are among the casualties in our recent war against terrorism.

I find Kerry's slime of this branch of the military service typical of the hypocrite he is.

Sure, Kerry served in Vietnam like a lot of us. And, like many, he came back a bit disillusioned. But his collaboration with Hanoi Jane and the "Ho, Ho, Ho Chi Minh, we know you're going to win" crowd doesn't set him up as a credible critic of alleged draft dodgers.

Many active duty personnel during Vietnam and other wars did not see the eyes of the enemy, nor did they hear the whistle of bullets near their ears. But, like members of the National Guard who could be called to active duty at any time, they did support those who went into the firefights, flew the bombing missions or brought back the casualties. Will these vets be next on Kerry's attack list?

Any American man or woman who has served honorably in any branch of the armed forces, whether during peacetime or war, has performed an important service for this country. Strength is also necessary as a deterrent.

And anyone, whether disillusioned veteran or not, who supported the enemy in time of war, like Hanoi Jane and her then traitorous husband Tom Hayden and members of the Vietnam Veterans Against the War, should never be placed in a position of power over our fighting men and women of all branches of the service.

On a brighter side, it is nice that today even former Communist supporters are saying nice things about Vietnam veterans. However, it would be a tragic mistake to trust their motives or their honesty.

You're probably beginning to realize that I don't care much for Hanoi Jane. She was as big a traitor in time of war as Benedict Arnold, yet she never had to face the music. More than 50 years after her wartime criminal behavior, she is still making movies, television schlock and appearing on talk shows as an expert on just about everything. Just recently she was asked what should be done with those people who oppose her pro-abortion political view. Her answer was, "Murder."

Americans are just too darn nice

April 4, 2004

Last year I questioned whether American warfare had become too civilized to win.

Today I would have to answer that question with a yes. We are too nice to our enemies and too hard on ourselves. This puts us in a self-destructive alliance with the bad guys.

The saying that nice guys come in last is true in war as well. To beat the dedicated Imperial Japanese and maniacal mass-murdering Nazis, America had to use every deadly trick in the book. We flattened complete cities. We showed no weakness to the enemy. And in losing, the enemy understood and accepted its fate.

Sure, there were holdouts in the Pacific and a few in Europe. But we didn't see anti-America protests in the streets of Tokyo or what was left of Dresden. If we had, they would have been put down quickly.

During our recent wars in Afghanistan and Iraq, America precisely bombed enemy targets without bombing enemy held cities or villages. We did this to avoid "civilian" casualties. We immediately released thousands of surrendered prisoners of war to return to their homes and families with the hope they would then see us as compassionate liberators. Captured non-uniformed terrorists have been treated as prisoners of war instead of being shot, as they should have been.

This compassion on our side has led to the recent stories coming out of Fallujah, Iraq. The "civilians" of that rathole seem to think they can continue their war against us without reprisals.

Perhaps it is time to rethink whether the war is over. Perhaps we should give those enemy activists what they want.

Smart bombs aren't needed in destroying a stupid enemy. Good old fashioned Napalm, artillery and strafing runs would be a nice way to send a message that attacks against Americans will lead to much bigger attacks against morons.

In Vietnam, the South Vietnamese took care of the Communist prisoners of war. It was their country and that was a good way to share the decision-making processes and intelligence gathering of war.

We could do the same in Iraq. The Kurds would probably be glad to take over handling the POW situation in their country for us and we would be accepting foreign culture and sharing the war load, something our leftist critics have been whining about for some time.

America is sacrificing to bring democracy to Iraq. That country could have complete freedom to argue issues and settle them with ballot boxes. But we are not there to give them the freedom to attack us. Those who continue violence against America should be put down like rabid dogs.

As for those Americans who want to blame everyone except the terrorists for the Sept. 11 murders, back off.

A lot of folks have warned this country of terrorism throughout the last century. They warned against bomb throwing Bolsheviks; the rise of the American Nazi Party and fifth columnists before World War II; and the infiltration of Communists in America and their willingness to oppose our side throughout the Cold War, not to mention what they would do to our entertainment and news media if they ever got a foothold (wink, wink, nudge, nudge). They were all right and maybe we didn't act as strongly as we should have at the time.

And then there is still the open borders situation — an easy access for terrorists of any wacko cause.

Let's end the second guessing of whether Bush was watching his crystal ball close enough prior to the enemy attack on 9/11 or whether Clinton's zipper got in the way of his decision-making process.

The future is shaky. The terrorist enemy is out there and he wants to kill all of us. We have to defeat the enemy, kill the fanatics and make sure their supporters are impressed enough with our military to join us.

We must not care what others call us for doing what it takes to win. As we learned in Vietnam, the alternative to winning is not a negotiated peace. It's losing.

There is a reason the military doesn't award nice guy ribbons. So let's stop being so darned nice.

I personally have that same problem. I'm just too darn nice of a guy. I'm hoping these next few chapters will lighten the mood.

5. Frightening Conspiracies

SERIOUSLY FOLKS. LET'S GET back to normal sarcasm. We all know there are a lot of things that are funnier than war – such as diseases, air quality and lobbyists.

Mad cow cover-up exposed

April 4, 1996

Today's column deals with a very serious problem concerning the future of all Americans: Mad Cow Disease (MCD). This tragic sickness has struck without mercy throughout England. It now threatens all of Europe and may have infected portions of the United States.

We must not panic. This country has to deal with the disease with common sense. First of all, the populace must be educated about the disease. We do not need vigilantes destroying every cow that staggers or slurs its moo.

We also have to stress the right to privacy. We must deal with cows as individuals. We cannot allow all cows to be branded as carriers just because they have known or been seen with an infected creature. And what one does in the privacy of their farm is their own business.

All school-age children should be taught not to fear infected cows. They may be clumsy but they are still bovine, and should be treated with compassion.

It's said that some farmers are wearing rubber gloves while milking "Old Bossy." Scientists have proven Mad Cow Disease cannot be contracted while milking the creatures. I'll go into the reasons why at an udder time.

My confidential informant, Willard, tells me Dr. Kavorkian has set up a special stall at his London Outpatient Clinic. Apparently, he herds those with MCD into the stalls and hits them in the forehead with a hammer. Willard claims the doctor is being extradited to England next month in the world's first case involving the charge of "Doctor-assisted butchering."

Knowledge is the tool we must use to defeat this savage disease. We all should take the time to become more aware of how to deal with those who have become infected. Enlightened people are wearing black-and-white, Holstein-design ribbons on their lapels indicating Mad Cow Disease Awareness. The wearing of this ribbon says, "I care. I feel your pain." The ribbon should be worn at all awards ceremonies and cheese-tasting parties.

All known MCD cases have been reported in Europe. Why should Americans care? Yesterday Willard gave me a copy of a top-secret report from the prestigious Reseda Institute of Bovine Studies and Outcall Massage that claims the infection has struck in

America. The study says President Bill Clinton, who grazed at a London burger barn last summer, brought the insidious disease to the White House.

Clinton is only now showing the telltale signs of MCD. The report says it was first noticed in February when the President staggered toward the salad bar at a well-known Washington eatery and callously trampled George Will. Apparently Clinton felt threatened as Will was horning in on his alfalfa sprouts. The networks sat on the story.

The report points out that Hillary Clinton and Teddy Kennedy have taken on the job of keeping the President from falling during photo ops. It's said Hillary keeps a carrot in her pocket to lure Bill in front of the cameras. She gives him gum, and while his mouth opens and closes to chew the gum, Rich Little does his voice while Kennedy holds the President from behind to keep him from falling. Of course there are two other aides involved in keeping Kennedy from falling.

If this report is true, we all understand the necessity of quickly finding a cure for this dreaded disease. One unnamed source claims the White House is in turmoil until a cure can be found. On the brighter side, however, they're enjoying the milk.

It's a good thing Dr. Anthony Fauci wasn't America's Disease Fuhrer in the 1990s. I'd hate to think what kind of restrictions he would have placed on us for MCD. Perhaps he would have closed the schools, forced cowboys to wear helmets, made parents replace their baby bottle formulas with Bud Light and banned all teams from kneeling during the playing of "Cow Cow Boogie" at stadiums. And I'm surprised that then-Vice President Al Gore didn't demand an end to cattle ranching to protect the population. Of course, his fellow "environmentalists" hadn't decided yet that cow farts were destroying the ozone. Personally, I think it is more liable that vegan farts are doing the damage.

White House cover-up continues

March 22, 1998

Are there any women left in Washington D.C. that Bill Clinton hasn't groped, flashed or ... well ... given a helping hand in their careers?

Clinton has given new meaning to his tired old cliché "I feel your pain."

It was in this column a couple of years ago that rumors of a presidential cover-up were exposed. At that time, my confidential informant, Willard, turned over a top-secret report from the prestigious Reseda Institute of Bovine Studies and Outcall Massage that President Bill Clinton was suffering from Mad Cow Disease (MCD). And although the President continued to show the telltale signs of this insidious infection, the mainstream media avoided the story completely.

Well, thanks to Willard, I am in possession of a report that claims the President is now in the latter stages of full-blown MCD. The report, from a scientific study by Prof. Wineburger of the Oprah Asylum of Meat Deformities, claims that, in late term MCD, the virus mutates from bovine characteristics to the crazed weasel stage. This explains the President's present predicament. Prof. Wineburger believes, however, that Clinton can still carry out the duties of President with the right therapy and assistance.

According to the professor, it's not Clinton's fault. He is a victim of the disease and should be treated with as much compassion as any infected creature. (Rabid dogs come to mind.) Wineburger believes the President can complete his second term honorably if the Secret Service and White House staff assist him with specific actions. Hillary is reportedly working very closely with Wineburger. She has instituted several procedural changes in the way White House personnel perform their activities.

• All female White House interns have been issued new uniforms consisting of overalls, painter caps, fake noses and glasses with bristly mustaches and special paint to black out a couple of teeth.

• Fire hoses have been placed in all rooms used by the President just in case he needs to be separated from a female intern, staffer or White House visitor.

• All copies of *Playboy, Hustler, Ms., cosmopolitan, Arkansas Dairy Farmer* and any other magazine that might arouse MCD side effects in the President have been removed from the White House.

• Chickens and salt licks are not allowed on the White House grounds.

• To avoid an outbreak of crazed weasel activity, the only females allowed to be alone in a room with the President are Madelein Albright, Janet Reno and, of course, Hillary.

Professor Wineburger claimed that a cure for the disease was developed just last year. Unfortunately the scientist put the serum and all of his papers in a briefcase and asked Ted Kennedy to drive him to the White House. Thirteen hours later, a dripping wet Kennedy was found at a local sports bar. The cure and the scientist were, according to government files, officially "lost at sea."

It may now take years for science to conquer this terrible disease.

The Democratic National Committee is hoping Clinton's problems can be contained for the next two years. And just in case, according to Willard, Hillary carries the pager number of the veterinarian who neutered Buddy.

Come to think of it, a new strain of MCD may be the actual reason that President Biden has trouble with Teleprompters, goes off script to talk about children stroking the hairs on his legs, staggers up the mobile stairs when boarding airplanes, and walks around attempting to shake hands with people who aren't there. And maybe his strange habit of sniffing women and little girls' hair is because they've visited a Burger King prior to coming to the White House.

Beware of the gum lobby

Oct. 30, 1996

This has been a highly charged election season. Candidates for national offices have traversed the countryside swearing their loyalty to the voters, all the while accepting campaign contributions from powerful special interest organizations. Lobbyists have given various campaigns economic boosts with injections of politically tainted dollars.

Such an injection gives a candidate a rush of political power, which can spin him or her into a euphoric election-day victory, only to wake up the next morning to find oneself no longer alone in bed. Lobbyists appear immediately to demand the victor give the devils their due.

An obvious assessment is, "There is no free lunch." Political contributions always have strings no matter if they are from the tobacco companies, the beef, sheep or milk industry, gun enthusiast, gay and lesbian organizations, "artist" organizations supporting the NEA, Christian fundamentalists or the remaining members of the Jack Benny Fan Club. Every special interest would like favorable treatment by government.

The only alternative would be for the taxpayers to fund all campaigns. We taxpayers pay for enough in this country. I certainly would not like to increase my taxes to fund the goofball candidates who don't agree with me *(or even the ones who do)*.

Therefore, lobbyists should continue their campaign funding toward candidates who share some of their views. Good candidates, and there have been many, will say thank you for the support, and do their jobs fairly and consistent with their own views and those of their constituents. So even if jaded companies think they are purchasing a candidate's support, the ethical politician knows better.

Now, a lot has been made of the lobbying efforts of the tobacco companies, the National Rifle Association and a variety of foreign interests. We are well aware of their attempts to purchase political favors. Since we know so much about them, they are obviously not that successful. A friend, and self-proclaimed investigative journalist, Willard, says it's the lobbyists we don't hear about who are really successful.

For instance, how many of you have heard of the Korean AIDS Ribbon Lobby? This group, known as KARL, is an underground Marxist-terrorist organization, which is attempting to pin its evil little red flags on every tuxedo-clad Bozo in the world, according to Willard. He claims to have unraveled this red ribbon ring and is attempting to present the evidence to Congress.

KARL produces its red cloth in a political prison sweatshop in North Korea. The material is then shipped to an Italian cummerbund factory, which packages the product for export around the world. Willard says, red cummerbunds are shipped by the thousands to operatives in the United States. Those operatives, under direct orders from General B. Streisand, slice the garments into their evil little red flags, which are then sold at a tremendous profit to award nominees who would be banished from their fern bars if they appeared at a ceremony without their red ribbons.

"The profits go to supporting politicians who have no morals and play the saxophone," Willard claims.

Willard has uncovered another sticky group that attempts to control our politicians. They are the dreaded gum lobby. We all know that sugar-filled gum is bad for our teeth. What we don't know, according to Willard's report, is that gum chewing is addictive. And, thanks to the continuing television commercials, this habit starts at an early age. Unfortunately it is extra destructive to twins: double the damage.

"Some politicians have put the bite on gum companies for contributions only to find out they are then stuck to defending the industry line. For several generations, children have been sold out to these gum pushers because Washington won't get off the stick and do something about the spread of gum addicts. From bobby soxers and bubble-gummer baby boomers to today's hip-hop, funny hat generation, America's youth has fallen victim to chewing gum addiction," Willard said.

Willard claims the first thing he will do is to ask Congress to ban Bazooka Joe from commercials, billboards and comic-strip wrappers. Bazooka Joe should ride off into the sunset on Joe Camel. He would like to see baseball cards sold with something less addictive than gum – perhaps breath mints or athlete's foot spray.

According to Willard, the gum lobby has already started its offensive against the anti-gum forces. They are distributing bumper stickers with the message: "They'll take my gum away when they pry it from my cold, dead teeth."

"These insidious organizations, KARL and the gum lobby, must be stopped before they control the complete American political system. Contact your legislators and warn them against these groups. Do this before you find yourself at a political fund raiser and you see your congressman is not only wearing a red ribbon but chewing gum as well," Willard said.

Now I don't know how factual Willard's claims are, but I definitely would rather have lobbyist dollars funding campaigns than tax dollars. And I, ever the optimist, believe some politicians are honest public servants. While I'm at it, I would like to see the Jack Benny Fan Club persuade Arizona politicians to make the comedian's birthday a state holiday.

As I reread these conspiracy columns, I'm beginning to wonder if, at the time of writing, I was suffering from a case of Mad Cow Disease.

The great dust conspiracy

June 9, 1995

Bullhead City, Ariz., has finally achieved the status of a "great city." We have worked hard to grow and become what we are today. Now we take our place on the same level as Los Angeles, Phoenix, Houston, Washington, D.C., and Irwindale. What milestone have we passed? What great achievement have we attained to equalize our status with these other megalopolitan super cities? Air pollution! Dust in the air, to be precise.

Apparently our city was in violation of the Clean Air Act during two instances in 1989 due to high measures of dust. Thank God we have a government bureaucracy to tell this Mojave Desert city that dust sometimes gets blown into our air. Some of us might have just gone on thinking Los Angeles smog is air pollution and dust is a natural part of living in a windy rural desert. We're very lucky to have our Arizona Department of Environmental Quality step in to help our elected officials correct this terrible problem.

My first reaction is to ask who is to blame for this problem? Where does the majority of the dust come from? Well, since the federal government owns most of Arizona, and our little chunk of paradise is surrounded by Bureau of Land Management (BLM) land, I'd have to guess the majority of the dust blown across us is airborne federal government land. One would wonder why the feds are not attempting to keep their dirt out of our private sector air.

I decided to contact a friend who considers himself an unrecognized expert on environmental problems. Code-name "Willard" has a theory on just about everything. And surprisingly enough, he claims black helicopters have something to do with the mighty dust clouds, which have cursed our environment. He believes the slight breezes we get are certainly not powerful enough to cause that great a problem. Therefore, something must be disturbing the ground, thus lifting the particles skyward.

"Over the last several years environmentalists and the federal government have protected many species of animals which they considered endangered," Willard recently told me over a glass of cold beer. "The feds have attempted to make BLM land a breeding ground for desert tortoises. Apparently they have been too successful. I believe massive numbers of breeding tortoises are kicking large amounts of BLM dirt into the air which then darkens our fine city's sky."

He claims the problem is only going to get worse as the feds continue to protect these prurient beasts. "The government is engaged in a conspiracy to have Bullhead City create a tax to pay for a large carpet which will cover all exposed dirt areas in the city limits. This won't solve our dust problem, but a certain carpet-making foreign power will make a fortune, as will those New-World-Order lackeys in Washington D.C."

"What do the black helicopters have to do with dust-kicking tortoises?" I asked.

"I have reliable information the world-order choppers have been seen flying in low formations over the tortoise breeding grounds and blasting German marching songs over their loud speakers. That kind of music drives tortoises wild!"

Willard believes the people need to act first before the multi-national carpet lobby takes charge.

"The only real way to end the dust assault," he says, "is to have every city resident line up along the BLM area border. Armed with deadly tortoise clubs, residents then should make a night sweep of the government land, beating, crunching, stomping every one of those four-legged, half-shelled, lascivious polluters into the dust they so love to thrash into our air."

Now, I don't think Willard's solution will put us in compliance with federal clean air standards. But I believe he makes about as much sense as any government agency attempting to crack down on desert cities, which get a little dusty now and then.

6. An Arizonan's View of Modern Science

KEEPING AN EAR TO new technology

Nov. 3, 1995

This week's *Time Magazine* has an interesting article titled "An Eary Tale," which is accompanied by a photo of a rat with a human ear growing under the skin of its back. The photo looks quite gross, like something from a science fiction film, but the possible application of such experimentation is wondrous. The bottom line is that scientists are coming closer to being able to regenerate missing body parts.

This is quite a breakthrough for people who have lost an ear or a nose to disease or accident. Possibly in the near future scientists will be able to genetically reconstruct just about any body part that needs replacement.

All the great possibilities with this new technology will also lead to many dilemmas. For instance: I'm sure people won't need to have their new noses grown on rats' backs. They will probably grow their own, which would help avoid rejection from transplantation. But how far will plastic surgeons carry this capability? Will prospective movie stars grow a better looking nose on their left cheek so that when it is ready the plastic surgeon will simply remove their old nose and slide the new one over?

A few years ago it became possible, and legal in some states, for a woman to be a surrogate mother. Many a woman has carried another couple's fetus to term. Will this new tissue engineering open the door to parts surrogates? Will some bizarre entrepreneur saddle his/her back with 50 movie-star noses, or any other body parts, to be transplanted at growth completion? ... or sold to the highest bidders?

Will freak shows return with living Medusas and monkeys with human heads?

Will some unsavory dictatorship with a free-trade agreement with the United States create human parts factories in its political prisons?

Every great scientific discovery creates new legal and moral questions. Our society must handle the future possibly more carefully than we have earlier technological breakthroughs. As we become more capable of altering the human condition we have a chance of helping millions of people. But we also have a chance of doing unalterable damage to the future of our own species.

Hopefully, our scientific community, and our government, will proceed with positive experimentation toward altruistic goals. It is, however, just a little worrisome to think of some of our present lawmakers overseeing the future scientific possibilities. Senator John Glenn would be pleased to have science regrow hair (as would I); and Senator Ted Kennedy could use a smaller nose with less blood veins showing; but it's a little frightening to think what former Senator Bob Packwood or Congressman Barney Frank might want changed.

When I think of the Washington "insiders," I wonder if this technology is as new as proclaimed. It seems some of our political leaders may have already received sci-tech transplants. Those are the ones who probably got their morals from rats.

If written today, I would probably have to inject Congressman Eric Swalwell at the end. His morals might have been grown on U.S. Rep. Adam Schiff's back.

What's wrong with traditional rats?

June 6, 1997

I've found it odd that, while scientists can clone a sheep, they can't develop a cure for the common politician.

As the years edge toward the millennium, the advanced technological breakthroughs have been amazing. But what is really amazing is the direction that science seems to be heading.

Automobiles, for instance, have all kinds of computer bells and whistles such as satellite tracking devices, warnings in English when a door is left open (and voice messages for everything except a surgeon general's warning on the cigarette lighter), super sound systems and industrial strength air bags added to their capabilities. But the engines are still based on gas-fed technology of 70 years ago.

Electric-run vehicles are still pretty much rich men's toys. They are expensive, pretty things with the capabilities of a nine-hole golf cart. Science needs to extend the time periods electric vehicles can operate between recharges.

But instead, scientists seem to be fighting over who will be the first to call himself "God."

Genetic engineering is the experimentation of choice. Developing cows that produce more meat and milk; tomatoes that can be machine picked and packed without bruising; bacteria that eats oil spills (keep it away from Sam Donaldson's hairpiece); chickens that can lay more than one egg per day; and, for some reason, new kinds of mice.

Now, although I consider old-fashioned cows and tomatoes preferable, I can understand the thought process, which would justify creating bigger corporate profits with less investment: pigs that bring home more bacon.

But what is it about the creation of new kinds of mice?

One company recently patented a new mouse. Why? Are humans getting so overpopulated that this company feels there will soon be a need for an International House of Mice that specializes in rodent sushi for the masses? Is some fanatic cat lover attempting to make a tastier treat for Morris?

The company that developed the new mouse claims it is better for experiments than the traditional mouse. This gives me an uneasy feeling. Scientists have experimented on mice for years and now those experiments have culminated in the creation of a "better mouse" for more experiments.

What are they going to do now? Create a bride for it?

Just this week, Japanese scientists have announced success in transplanting vast stretches of human DNA into mice. They claim that some of the mice have a "complete human chromosome with about 50 times the amount of DNA that scientists had been able to deliver before." Some of the mice "were able to pass it on to their offspring."

It's frightening to think that if scientists continue to experiment in this direction, it is possible they may create a new half-human half-rat species. Think of the poor creatures: four inches tall; wearing ill-fitting suits; eternally running for political office while attempting to sell aluminum siding. Of course, if these creatures are brought into this country, legally or otherwise, we will eventually have to give them citizenship and benefits. Hollywood stars will, to show their politically correct compassion, have to add plague awareness ribbons to their award ceremony uniforms.

And poor Paula Jones will have to hire the Orkin Man as a bodyguard.

Anyway, technology can be a wonderful and amazing thing. But, in my opinion, some of it isn't worth a rat's ***.

Even a quarter of a century later, articles about new technologies and scientific discoveries still scare the hell out of me. The facts that there are Fauci-like scientists trying to clone mastodons, the military is experimenting with artificial intelligence-controlled robot dogs and American-funded laboratories exist in Red China where Commies dabble with strengthening bat diseases are enough to really mess with my dreams.

Trekking down information on the Phoenix UFO sightings

June 22, 1997

There has been a lot of high-flying rhetoric lately regarding unidentified flying objects (UFOs).

Apparently some folks down in the Phoenix area have reported seeing V-shaped lights quietly swooping through the night sky. UFOphiles have been pestering their government officials for some kind of X-files investigation to take place.

Governor Fife Symington called the press together Thursday to give them some extraterrestrial answers. He then presented an aide in a space-alien suit. "This just goes to show you guys are entirely too serious," Symington told the reporters.

A few people didn't take the gov's humor lightly. They wanted real answers for the surreal questions.

I decided to contact noted space-case investigator Prof. Ann Dromeda of the Fort Mojave Institute of Parapsychology and Outcall Massage. She has been investigating reports of a variety of bizarre experiences for more than 30 years.

"Prof. Dromeda," I said. "Do aliens and flying saucers really exist?"

"Positively," she answered. "They are here among us. I have personally met many aliens in the Southwest region of the United State."

"How do you react to the governor's attempt at levity?"

"It was a very sneaky maneuver to divert attention from what is really going on."

"You mean the governor's trial?"

"No, of course not. The governor was deliberately drawing attention to the guy in the funny alien costume, when I know the real alien was standing right there on the stage. Have you ever noticed how light skinned the governor is? Have you ever held a Klieg light up to Governor Symington? If you do, you will see right into him. His two hearts will expose him as a real alien!"

I was a little skeptical at this point. After all, Fife Symington is a Republican. No way could he have two hearts.

"And he isn't alone," she added. "I have identified several aliens in our society.

"Princess Diana is an alien. Right now she is trying to gain sympathy against the use of land mines. Why is she doing that? How could we have a decent war without land mines? Is she afraid her insect-like species could be hurt as their landing crafts hit land mines?

"... and those daytime talkshow hosts. Where else could they come from?

"David Brinkley. Have you noticed how his face is puckering almost inside out? He's slowly reverting to his original form. Then there is Madeleine Albright, Larry of the Stooges, at least two council members of each Colorado River city, Eddy Murphy — of course a Klieg light won't work on him — the O.J. jury, and..."

"What about flying saucers?" I said, hoping she wouldn't become violent.

"There are many shapes and sizes of space vehicles zipping around our planet. Many of them are the traditional saucer style. But we also have the cigar-shaped vehicles, sometimes described in Central America as the bat-guano-shaped vehicles. There are also sightings of saucers which look like large silver basketballs, 1977 Toyotas and fluffy white clouds."

"Do you have any idea what kind of spacecraft it was that was seen over Phoenix?"

"Those lights were not spacecrafts. They were geese. Arizona Game and Fish Department has been tagging geese to follow their migration paths," she answered. "They started with simple leg tags. Then they went to radio-signal tags. But now they are strapping special tracking lights with computer-chip batteries to the geese.

"The geese will space their lighted comrades approximately by every third goose to cut down the glare while night flying in their V-formations...."

Prof. Dromeda went on for quite some time about her theories, some of which I thought might be plausible, until she made the mistake of saying how much she enjoyed a very-humorous speech made by Al Gore. It was then that I knew she was funny-farm fodder.

Maybe more information will be available someday. Anyway, I wanted you folks to know just how seriously I take the subject of UFO sightings.

You know, in the Mojave Desert, a lot of folks took this UFO column more seriously than they did my war columns.
One local radio flap-mouth considered my tongue-in-cheek words to be blasphemy.

Let's not send in the clones

Jan. 15, 1998

A self-described "eccentric or brilliant or near genius" physicist named, appropriately, Dr. Seed, has announced he will soon clone a human being.

As a result of the doctor's statement, President Clinton and others have called for a worldwide ban on human cloning as a misuse of science. Seed, however, has said that if the United States forbids him his human experiments, he will simply go to that Mecca of medical science, Tijuana, Mexico.

Several scientists have stated that they believe Seed's plans to be unethical, unprofessional and all-around nutty. I concur. Perhaps I have seen too many Frankenstein movies, but the whole idea of duplicating people by transplanting their DNA scares me right out of my genes.

Apparently, many members of the scientific community have a rather low opinion of Dr. Seed. In one televised interview with the good doctor that I saw, he showed a personality that suggests he may have already injected himself with the DNA of Joe Isuzu and Wile E. Coyote.

Dr. Seed seems to think he will be quickly successful in his quest. Other scientists point to the fact that it took 277 sheep failures before the first mammal success, known as Dolly, came along. Cloning experiments with animals other than mammals, such as amphibians, have had some pretty frightening looking mistakes.

Let's assume Seed is as successful as the Scottish team of scientists that "created" Dolly. What will he do with the 277 failures? If they live, what will they be? Could we end up with a few 200-pound iguana women with poisonous stingers? Will he have to lock up several eight-foot-tall, six-armed canaries that wear jackboots and sound like Henry Kissinger? Will he attempt to pawn off his mistakes onto society as professional wrestlers and rock groups?

And most of all, why? Why should we duplicate people? The natural way of reproduction has been pretty popular for, oh, say, since the beginning of mankind. And science has assisted people to be fertile, but only to reproduce normally. Who would be so egotistical as to want to raise a copy of him or herself or someone else who has already existed?

The answer is, there are a lot of weird people out there. Celebrity stalkers could keep off their targets' lawns, stay home and raise their own David Lettermans, Cindy Crawfords or Ernest Borgnines. Political nutcakes could make the plot of "The Boys From Brazil" come true by raising copies of their favorite world leaders or maniacal dictators. Motion picture and record companies could clone their superstars so when the originals begin to wrinkle and sag, they could be replaced. Think tanks could create a team of Einsteins, Oppenheimers or von Brauns while France could put a Jerry Lewis on every block.

In other words, nothing good could come of this frightening scientific scenario. This is one of the times I agree with President Clinton. Let's keep our world populated with individuals with "distinguishing characteristics."

That last "Clinton" reference is a bit dated. But, after having grown up with all those outlandish 1950s horror films, I believe scientists need to be very careful of what they are trying to create, and why. If they aren't and science goes out of control, we could wake up one morning and step out into a Roger Corman-like world of giant grasshoppers, Studebaker-size spiders, electrified teenage werewolves and a battalion of Kamala Harris clones, all announcing their campaigns for the presidency.

7. The Culture War

HAS HANOI JANE SEEN the light?

Jan. 12, 2000

According to various news stories, Jane Fonda has not only left her husband Ted Turner but has "embraced 'born-again' evangelical Christianity."

I can't wait to start hearing the Gospel according to Hanoi Jane.

Fonda's conversion is about as believable to me as an imprisoned Manson family member's, Watergate burglar's, child molester's or murderer's. No matter what the crime is, all some convicted criminals have to do is to claim to be "born again" and some people will forgive ... and be foolish enough to help them get out. I believe 100 percent of jailhouse conversions are just con games to fool fools into giving slimeballs another chance.

Then again, Fonda is no jailed slimeball. She is an award-winning actress with a lot of money. Sure, she has a questionable past, but the majority of America doesn't really care — or she would have been dealt with 30 years ago. Perhaps she really is serious and is looking for peace in her own mind — or maybe it's just another radical political trick.

Will the new "spiritual" Fonda merge the Christian Coalition with the Hollywood Left? Can Barbra Streisand be far behind? I guess if Warren Beatty can attempt to be presidential, Fonda can pretend to be Martin Luther King. Of course, if she says, "I had a dream," everyone will wonder what she was smoking.

Fonda's conversion has probably left Ted Turner without a prayer of reconciliation. And, considering her cutthroat past and coziness with the ACLU, old Ted will be lucky to walk away with his TV stations and a tomahawk chop.

Perhaps Fonda could take Turner Classic Movies station and convert it to the Reverend Jane's 666 Club, which would host programs such as Praise The Lord And Pass The Marijuana and Makeup Solutions With Jane And Tammy Faye. She could probably hock a lot of dated workout tapes if she would only sit on her Commie-lovin' butt and cry that God wants everyone to buy them. I don't believe she's above that.

Perhaps she could also become a television healer. I can picture her now, wearing a long flowing white robe and leg warmers over her sacred calves, seated on top of a golden North Vietnamese anti-aircraft gun with her arms stretched out toward the camera as if to say, "Come, let me heal all of America of its sinful, evil ways." She could lay her hands on Senator John McCain and ask the Lord to heal him of his terrible temper; gun owners could be cured of their paranoia; Tom Selleck could be repaired to agree with Rosie O'Donnell; and the working middle class could lose their biases and accept those who won't work for a living as equals with whom to share all earnings and property. (This would surely take a large tax load off of those earning as much as sweet Jane.)

And most important of all, she could heal all of us Vietnam vets of our hatred for her due to her traitorous acts during the war.... yeah, and Hell could freeze over, too.

It's now more than twenty years since this column appeared. In looking back and thinking of how I characterized Jane Fonda in 2000, I've come to the conclusion that I was, once again, just too darn nice. And Hanoi Jane is still a traitor.

Humor is a serious topic

May 2017

Having grown up reading the classics – *Mad, Help, Cracked, National Lampoon* magazines – I do appreciate satire. The storylines and illustrations were only funny to people who kept up with the news. So I credited the very savvy artists and writers of those publications for their twisted, yet intellectual (for lack of another word), minds that kept us readers on our toes.

Since television news was only 15 minutes a day in 1950s and early '60s, I read a lot of newspapers to keep informed on the characters the humor magazines were ridiculing. Just like now, there were wacky politicos making silly speeches about some very serious issues. Real news, however, has always been of value. It is a wonderful cornucopia of material, which cartoonists, writers and comics can harvest to prepare feasts of silliness.

My youthful interest in satirical literature led me to a few trouble spots during my high school years when teachers would confiscate cartoons that I drew concerning President Kennedy and then LBJ. Apparently, they must have thought I was offending delicate sensibilities in their "safe spaces." Their negative reactions solidified my desire to, eventually, become an editorial cartoonist. And, believe it or not, I did complete high school – just in time for the Vietnam War. Even Fate has a sense of humor (which is more than I can say about some of the sergeants I had to deal with).

One thing about *Mad* and other humor magazines of the mid-20th Century, the staffs never let political correctness get in the way of a good laugh. If they could wring chuckles out of readers concerning President Eisenhower, Vice President Nixon and Sen. McCarthy, they could also stir up a brew of guffaws over Senator-then-President Kennedy, Attorney General Kennedy, Vice President-then-President Johnson, Senator-then-Vice President Humphrey, De Gaulle, Churchill, and little shoe-banging Khrushchev, as well as Elvis, Sinatra, Pinky Lee and Marilyn Monroe.

And I know that, in later years, there was no restriction against drawing JFK's little-brother Teddy making a few bucks on the side from his swimming schools (I seldom drew the senator without heart-decorated trunks and swim fins). But that's another story and I'll cross that bridge when I come to it.

Flash-forward to 2017, we have Saturday Night Live. And although many of the skits are very funny, there are subjects that are favored for ridicule and subjects that are not allowed to be touched. That show is an illustration of what political correctness has done to America. The gags are written and performed by an elite gaggle of enlightened Leftists who only see humor in going after Republicans. Of course, that doesn't make their work any less funny. It just makes things one-sided.

Alec Baldwin does an impressive impression of President Trump. Melissa McCarthy is hilarious in her skits as White House Press Secretary Sean Spicer. And just like the baggy-pants burlesque comics of an earlier era, SNL's slapstick attacks on the Trump Administration garner tons of laughs and, thanks to modern technology, Tweets, Facebook likes and YouTube replays.

But what if Sean Spicer went on television and, in a wig, fat suit and dress, did a slapstick impression of Melissa McCarthy? It wouldn't matter how funny it was, he would be attacked as an anti-feminist male chauvinist, a body shamer and someone not qualified to perform – anywhere. And I'm sure the LGBLT (or whatever letters are in that acronym these days) would denounce him for Cross Dressing Without Conviction. (Which reminds me. Why haven't polygamists added their P to the LGBLT consortium? Shouldn't they get a parade? It would only take a few of their families to put one on, anyway. But I digress.)

I don't believe SNL ever had a skit where President Obama curtsied to a long line of Sheikhs just to get on a golf course or Michelle Obama forced pre-teen child laborers to produce moonshine from her "vegetable garden."

Perhaps Kate McKinnon could do Hillary again, only this time she could be arriving in Benghazi "under sniper fire" to hand out "I'm with her" buttons to survivors. Baldwin could portray Senator Blumenthal, wearing his "Nam" fatigues, running in to save the day. Oh, well. "What difference does it make?" Anything but anti-Republican humor has about as much chance of being on SNL as Achmed the Dead Terrorist has in teaming up with Sen. Pocahontas Warren on Dancing With the Stars.

Today's censorship demanded by political correctness makes the Motion Picture Production Code of the early 1930s look quite laissez-faire and Will Hays (of the Hays Office) as being very Jeffersonian in his restrictions. Life has become a lot more complicated than it was during the golden era of humor magazines. Be careful what you laugh at.

The latest Hollywood political correctness insanity is the new Academy Awards mandates that, to be eligible for nominations, motion pictures must include specific percentages of actors and crewmembers from a variety of racial and ethnic groups. Now that is a more Draconian dictate against artists than either Pope Julius II or Leo X had for Michelangelo. Any future historical films about World War II will probably have to show the invasion of Normandy looking more like a Broadway musical. Casting directors will be forced to find an Obama-look-alike to play Gen. Eisenhower, Nathan Lane will have a crack at Patton, and RuPaul will be the appropriate choice as FDR.

Wrestlers get a grip on politics

Dec. 4, 1998

Who would have thought it would take professional wrestlers to improve the image of American politics?

First came Jesse "The Body" Ventura to body slam both Republican and Democratic opponents to become Minnesota governor. Now "Hollywood" Hulk Hogan is running for President. And presently the two of them have better credibility than any of the prospective "legitimate" candidates.

The average American knows that professional wrestling is faked — or I guess I should say, "choreographed." Wrestling depicts good guys and bad guys engaging in mock battles of good vs. evil. Wrestling fans enjoy booing the villains and cheering the heroes during performances, which are really on the same scale as ballet dancing – except these dancers are usually fat and violent. Not unlike a political campaign.

Where wrestlers wear fake military costumes, feathers, fur and funny masks; politicians don military unit caps, Indian feathers, yarmulkes, cowboy hats and hard hats to appeal to their specific audiences and campaign donors.

Professional wrestling and politics are the only two careers where the participants spend most of their time telling the rest of us just exactly how great they are, what they promise to do for us and to their opponents and why we should applaud and support them.

Wrestling fans buy their tickets, enjoy the show and go home entertained. Voters elect their champions and then spend the next several years trying to keep the politicians' hands out of their pockets. Wrestlers finish their matches and go for beers with their opponents. Once politicians get a stranglehold on taxpayers, they never let loose.

So far Hulk Hogan hasn't released his platform. But when he announced his intention to run he said, "We need an honest American to take over and make all the decisions that come across the desk ... and think of America first." What a radical concept! That's almost as radical as expecting a President to tell the truth.

Both Republican and Democratic politicians should be worried. If Ventura and the Hulkster can continue to convey a message of common sense, even while wearing feathers, bandannas and a chain or two, they may rightfully steal the populist vote.

Perhaps our elected leaders could learn a few things from Ventura and the Hulkster — for instance, nicknames.

Traditionally politicians have had dull nicknames: John "Jack" Kennedy, Robert "Bob" Packwood, Ted "Teddy" Kennedy, Ronald "Ronnie" Reagan, etc. Ted Kennedy could change his moniker to Ted "The Bawdy" Kennedy. Others could imitate wrestlers by using body part nicknames like Jesse "The Body" now "The Mind" Ventura. This tact might give Newt "The Mouth" Gingrich the possibility of a comeback in the presidential race, but would not be appropriate for Bill "?" Clinton or Barney "?" Frank – both already too closely associated with body parts.

It may be a little early to predict the presidential election, but it is refreshing to think of what a "Hollywood" Hulk Hogan presidency would be like. Would he replace the Secret Service with Roller Derby queens? He probably could send a strong message by naming Sgt. Slaughter to be secretary of defense and sending Ambassador The Undertaker to the U.N. And Janet Reno could stay on as Attorney General. She's not worth much in action, but she looks like she would fit in with the Hulkster's cabinet. Then again, maybe she should have to fight Xena Warrior Princess for the position.

Now if only Dick "Leatherbritches" Lane were still alive. He would make one heck of a White House press secretary.

Coming up with appropriate nicknames for today's politicos might be a tad risky, in that Kamala "the orator" Harris wouldn't work. Every time she opens her mouth I think of Porky Pig's alleged communication skills. From his political track record, Adam Schiff already has a nickname. However, I'm sure he doesn't approve being called "Pinocchio." And although Joe Biden might support a unique middle moniker, Joe "Exotic" has already been taken. Now that the President is running for reelection, he'll probably create a backstory that will give him a heroic nickname – something from his mythically historic battle against that "bad dude," "Corn Pop." And speaking of his reelection campaign, I'll bet even Democrats will shy away from letting him kiss their babies.

Today's Americans need to start giving a 'Hoot'

Jan. 3, 1996

Just what has gone wrong with this country and why?

That's quite a question. I think all of us could come up with a different answer depending on the time of day. Here are a few related questions.

How can this country tolerate lawbreakers such as illegal immigrants and welfare cheats at the same time chastising as "uncaring" anyone who doesn't tolerate them?

When did our political leaders begin selling their offices by promising to give bigger and bigger shares of working Americans' earnings to foreign interests and to those in our country who WON'T work?

Why do we allow the government to take more and more of our self-reliance away by creating more federally controlled, tax-funded programs to supposedly help us?

When did we become so jaded as to elect a President who dodged the draft during a war against our Communist enemies, has questionable morals, and now sends a volunteer military into harm's way in a no-win situation with an undefined enemy and no known benefit to America?

We are in a mess of our own making. Our country has had a loss of focus since "diversity" pushed "American dream" aside. We have lost our unifying beliefs that built this country and made us strong. And we lost Hoot Gibson.

Americans no longer believe in the truths that were taught to us in Saturday matinees.

From the 1920s through the mid-50s great teachers passed on the American beliefs of self reliance, honesty and fair play every Saturday afternoon in many theaters and daily on early television. You ask who were some of these great American philosophers? Hoot Gibson, Ken Maynard, "Lash" LaRue, Tom Mix, Gene Autry, Roy Rogers, Buster Crabbe, Hopalong Cassidy, Buck Jones, Col. Tim McCoy, and ... oh, yes ... John Wayne.

In those days, every American boy had a favorite cowboy. And every leading cowboy was a "straight shooter" who always told the truth, paid his debts, was kind to animals and courteous to the ladies. Only bad guys lied, stole, cursed, back-shot, and mistreated horses, women and children.

Good guys always fought fair, no matter what sleazy tricks the bad guys used. In the long run, bad guys were always brought to justice. Honesty and fair play was always a reward in itself.

Several generations grew up living by the codes taught by Hoot, Lash, Hoppy and the others. We believed in our country and ourselves.

Then the traditional western morality plays ended. John Wayne continued to portray the "just American" for several years after the others hung up their spurs.

But by then society was changing. Draft dodgers were given amnesty. Entertainers became more popular with each of their trips to the Betty Ford Clinic. Ball players were given one chance after another to choose baseball over cocaine. Celebrities became excused for their bad-guy activities — whether it was just an extra couple of kids by someone other than their wives, or the killing of a wife. Patriotism became known as "jingoism" and "isolationism." "The New World Order" took the place of "God Bless America." And people began to be told they were not responsible for their actions. Society was to blame.

Well, folks, we ARE society. We ARE responsible for our own actions. To believe in our country again we must first believe in ourselves. And to believe in ourselves we must relearn the code of the matinee cowboy: Straight shooters always win. Good guys fight fair, tell the truth, are courteous to others, self reliant, kind to animals and expect the same from others.

The New Year is an election year. We should all resolve to give a Hoot about our country. We need to Lash out at politicians who are selling our independence to the highest bidders, be it multi-national interests or voting blocks who demand chunks of someone else's hard-earned income. We must Buck the trend to accept mediocrity in leadership. Then America can once again stand tall wearing the good guy's white hat.

And who knows? After the election, Hoppy days may be here again.

And although I didn't celebrate the election results that year, the great old cowboy movies of the 1930s, '40s and '50s continue to be an influence on my world today, as I write and illustrate Hollywood Cowboy Detectives neo-pulps as a way to cope with the pressures of the modern world. I have included a complete chapter – Chapter 10 – concerning the therapeutic value of B-westerns.

HELL TO HUMOR

It's obvious that I think highly of the real cowboys and cowgirls who grew up in the saddle, made their names in the rodeo circuits and became the B-movie stars and stunt performers of the first half of the 20th Century. But, I also appreciate the great cartoonists who pioneered the American art of newspaper comic strips.

Beetle bugs Hillaryists
May 8, 1997

During the early 1950s, those who were politically correct branded anyone who disagreed with them as Communists. They soon earned a brand of their own: McCarthyists, after their spiritual leader, Sen. Joe McCarthy.

Today's politically correct folks like to brand anyone they disagree with as fascists, racists, sexists, homophobes, gun nuts and a few other selected slams. Unfortunately, these folks don't seem to have a moniker of their own. Therefore I respectfully suggest the label of Hillaryists.

Hillaryists, named after guess who, are liberals who are very open minded about anything that's a little wacky. And they believe anyone who is not as open minded as them should be silenced, beheaded or somehow neutralized.

Case in point, "Beetle Bailey."

Mort Walker's very popular comic strip, "Beetle Bailey," has been around for almost 50 years. And during that time, Walker has always aimed for the laughs. Beetle doesn't try to preach any anti-establishment, pro-drug or anti-tobacco societal statements like "Doonesbury" has. The strip just makes fun of Army life.

Now, one would think Hillaryists, many of whom are aging draft dodgers of the Vietnam era, wouldn't have a problem with making fun of Army life. But they do.

Apparently they have a little problem with the strip's characters not having enough 1990s sensitivity. For instance, General Halftrack is a bumbling old fool who lusts after his sexy (formerly WAC, now Regular Army) secretary Miss Buxley. Beetle is a mess-up private who not only can't do anything right, but also doesn't seem to care that much. Killer, Beetle's buddy, has a one-track mind set on gorgeous young ladies. And Sergeant Snorkel is an overweight aging non-com who likes beer, cigars and his ugly dog. Snorkel gets fed up with Beetle's incompetence and beats him to a pulp on a regular basis.

So what's the problem? That sounds just like the Army I was in. All of the characters in "Beetle Bailey" were just like all of us. In fact, I can remember when, just after I returned from Vietnam, I made Beetle Bailey look like a spit-shined lifer. And any paratrooper in my outfit who didn't have the same attitude toward good looking young ladies as Killer does in the Bailey comic strip would have been removed from the barracks, and the Army, permanently.

But normal isn't normal anymore. And King Features Syndicate has received complaints from Hillaryists who would like to see the "Beetle Bailey" characters modernized, diversified, sensitized, and thoroughly liberalized so as not to shock any "open-minded" women, minorities, handicapped people and dabblers in alternative lifestyles.

I wonder how many of the over 1,800 newspapers now printing Beetle would continue the strip if the Hillaryists are successful? How funny would the comic be if General Halftrack kept his mind on his business instead of his secretary? Maybe Ms. Buxley could be drawn to look a little more like Janet Reno. That would make the general less interested and still give the readers something to laugh at.

Possibly Killer could stop chasing babes, win the Nobel Peace Prize and come out of the closet. Of course his character could never act in any stereotypical manner. He could possibly have a sensitive relationship with Zero, the really stupid guy. But then Zero wouldn't be allowed to act stupid anymore.

Sergeant Snorkel would have to lose the cigar, go on the wagon, change his ugly dog in for a nice poodle, and behave more civilized in his dealings with Beetle. Instead of pummeling Beetle for messing up, he would have to properly counsel the private in a tactful and sensitive manner.

And, of course, more strong women officers who make wise decisions for a modern military would have to be written into the storyline.

Political correctness isn't funny. Mort Walker's classic comic strip wouldn't be funny anymore either if the Hillaryists succeed in forcing changes. And, if that happens, I believe Beetle Bailey's final thoughts on the matter would be, "How do I get out of this chicken outfit?"

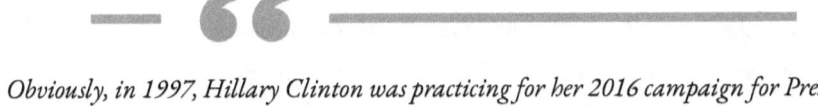

Obviously, in 1997, Hillary Clinton was practicing for her 2016 campaign for President. And, as I remember, her campaign really belonged on the funny pages.

This looks like a job for...

Feb. 14, 1996

February 1996 brings down the curtain on America's innocence.

True, we have been sliding into moral decadence for many years. Americans wouldn't bat an eye these days if the President got charged with extra-marital affairs with an ex-secretary who can't type, a rodeo clown and Mr. Ed, the retired movie horse. (Which makes me wonder why the White House was so shocked recently when a convention of sailors got out of hand.)

But all that is chickenfeed compared to the startling shock we are to face this month. DC Comics has announced that Lois Lane, after 58 years of standing by Superman, will drop the Man of Steel for another guy. The fickle female reporter, according to the comic book publishers, will catch Clark Kent (Superman's other personality, as if you didn't know) making out with a mermaid. What's worse, Marvel Comics' Peter Parker, a.k.a. Spiderman, will begin courting Miss Lane.

What ever happened to loyalty? I realize 58 years is a long time to wait for Superman to say, "I do." And it does look incriminating for Kent to be smooching with a mermaid. But who knows what reasons he had for lip-locking with her. Perhaps she choked on some calamari and he was using his super tongue to remove the blockage. (Everyone knows that if Superman ever gave someone the Heimlich maneuver he would rip the person in half.) Or perhaps the two of them were just commiserating over working for scale at DC all those years.

Whatever the reason, Lois just threw in the towel and hit the comic book singles bars. She gave the big S less benefit of the doubt than Steve Forbes would give the IRS (or vice versa). Then she takes up with Spiderman, which makes one wonder if her hang-up is guys who like to parade around in loud-colored underwear. I don't know if Connie Chung has asked the question yet, but I'll bet Newt Gingrich's mother would have a word for Lois.

After all, who has saved America more than Superman? Yes, Ronald Reagan comes to mind, but Gorbachev and his Evil Empire was only one villainous adversary. Over the years, the man with the big red S has battled Hitler, Lex Luthor and the mole men, among others. And all he asked for in return was a little Truth, Justice and the American Way from his one true love, Lois Lane.

Well, it looks like Miss Lane has kept up with the times. She obviously learned her versions of the truth from the Clinton Administration, justice from the O.J. jury, and the American Way from foreign lobbyists in Washington.

In other words, the honeymoon is over before it began. Peter Parker could be the real loser. Male spiders are usually devoured by their mates.

Superman may be better off in the long run. He is single, has a stable career, and able to leap tall buildings in a single bound. (While he's single he'll probably play down the "faster than a speeding bullet" stuff.)

And who knows? If DC and Marvel Comics can come together for this immoral social travesty, perhaps they can get King Features Syndicate to allow Blondie to drop her inept husband and take up with Clark Kent on the rebound.

Of course, the way things have been going in this country I wouldn't be surprised if DC moves their comic book company to Vietnam for cheaper labor, Clark Kent becomes a foreign correspondent for *The People's Weekly* and Superman trades in his red S for a United Nations patch.

Talk about spot-on prophecies... The brain trust at DC has messed with Superman's image so many times that one wonders if why the comic-book Border Patrol hasn't deported the cape and tights-wearing alien by now. Recently the big S has even been depicted with questionable sexual tastes. What's being peddled as graphic stories for children these days is making me rethink my opinion of Dr. Wertham's 1954 book, "Seduction of the Innocent." Perhaps that picky German psychiatrist was on to something. Of course, I'm kidding. Wertham was the godfather of cancel culture. I'll leave it to the marketplace to see if the new woke bastardizations of comic characters will survive.

Where have all the heroes gone?

Aug. 27, 1995

There have been several articles written since Mickey Mantle's death about how he showed heroism in his final days by renouncing the lifestyle that destroyed his health. I wouldn't expect anything less from him.

Mantle was a hero to nearly every baseball fan of the 1950s. His athletic accomplishments have been well documented. And in spite of his late words, he was a role model ... and a good one at that.

He and many others of earlier generations found alcohol as one way to escape the pressures of the limelight. Although it ruined his health, it was legal. Just like cigarettes were part of the American persona of the first two-thirds of the 20th century, alcohol was, and to some extent still is, an acceptable part of our national subculture. To somehow demote Mantle's stature as a sports legend/hero by using a 1990's politically correct measuring stick is wrong.

He was a hero. And his own retrospective during his final days was a continuation of that kind of heroism. He took responsibility for his faults. Something many of today's over-paid, coke-sniffing sports superstars wouldn't think of doing.

I think of other heroes of Mantle's era who may not have made the list in today's world. Audie Murphy was the most decorated soldier of World War II — a real combat hero who became an author and movie actor. Not many combat soldiers have been treated as heroes, or even fairly, since Hanoi Jane straddled a Charlie anti-aircraft gun.

Joe Louis and Rocky Marciano fought the top contenders of their day. They were civil to the public and seemed to care about the human condition. Don King, on the other hand, is looking for another big-hype, big-purse challenger for Mike Tyson. Perhaps he should select Shannon Faulkner. She lasted at the Citadel about as long as Peter McNeeley did against Tyson.

Which brings me to my point. In the past, achievement was celebrated. The best fighters fought each other to ascertain who was the real world champion. Soldiers killed the enemy to WIN a war. The more enemy killed, the sooner the war would be over. Baseball players played to win. They loved the game. Many a ballplayer spent his whole career with one team.

The Tyson fight was not a duel of titans. It was a big-money event ... a well-choreographed overture of breast beating with no payoff. Like many recent heavyweight fights,

Tyson vs. McNeeley was a deal of dollars over sport. The baseball strike showed America that today's players have joined owners in rating dollars over sport. No heroes here.

Soldiers today are still asked to risk their lives for their country. However, they are asked to go into combat situations with limited equipment and limited backing from our gutless politicians, some of whom were draft dodgers. They are placed in harm's way and told not to shoot unless shot at in areas such as Somalia or Bosnia which have no value to the United States and no concept of our system of government. Audie Murphy would not appreciate what our leaders have been doing with the military.

Heroism of the stature of Mantle, Murphy and Marciano is hard to find today. Society has obviously become jaded. However, we can find our own individual living heroes: family members who fought in this country's various wars; parents who work extra jobs to keep a roof over their family; teachers who give extra effort to children; cops who risk their lives daily.

Society may not be creating heroes for the masses anymore, but if we look close we may find a few in our own families.

Television offers weird worlds

Jan. 19, 1997

A lot of us question the strange world of daytime television. We wonder where Oprah, Sally, and all those other first-name hosts find their "unique" guests: women confronting bisexual ex-boyfriends who leave them for their fathers; ebonic-speaking 16-year-old men in baggy pants with funny hats and the 40-year-old high school teachers who love them; overweight albino twins in rhinestone-studded jump suits who minister the Church of the Sacred Spirit of Elvis; etc.

I believe there is a small town somewhere in Nebraska where all daytime talk show guests live. The government, rightfully, doesn't allow the town to be put on any maps. And only weird TV hosts and political pollsters have access to the residents.

I visualize a town of brightly colored tenements, trailers and Quonset huts. The central park surrounds a statue of Ed Wood; the hospital is fronted by a 15-mile-per-hour drive-by shooting zone; the city council dais is made up of seven Snoop Doggie Dog TV trays; the average citizen thinks William Buckley does the voice of either Beavis or Butthead and the Oakland school board is too conservative; and the community sport is a fingernail length competition.

Hey, it's only a theory. But then maybe you readers who write letters to the editor could come up with better explanations of where these "unique" individuals are found. Anyway, daytime TV is a strange world.

Television also offers another whole dimension of strangeness to people awake in the early morning hours. Between 1 and 4 a.m. one may channel surf a weird world of infomercials. I am amazed at the bizarre selections of videos, tapes and CDs available to anyone with a phone and a Visa card. Also one can learn the marvelous secrets of a variety of skin-care, makeup and focused-itch lotions.

Being follically challenged, I recently found myself watching a variety of "hair restoration" product shows. Some are simply gunks that one is supposed to put on the scalp regularly. The infomercial host will show a picture of a man as he appeared before using the product. He usually is a pinheaded geek with about as many hairs on his head as Clarence Thomas really would find in a Coke can. The host would then introduce the man, who, after using the product for a short time, looks like an adult version of Herman and Lilly Munster's son, Eddy – an amazing transformation at three in the morning.

Another scalper company shows a photo of a different, chrome-domed before-geek with an unhappy look on his face, followed by film of him with what looks like a large dead cat on his head as he golfs, swims and winks at 20-year-old babes on a windy day. How does he keep his road kill in place? He has patented process snaps planted in his head. He simply snaps his new hair into place.

Early morning viewers can also learn a lot about geezer rock 'n' roll. That's the music I enjoyed in my youth unaware that it would become classic 30 to 40 years later. One can spend $29.95 and receive a set of videos, tapes and/or CDs containing such classic memories as Splish Splash, Flying Purple People Eaters, Short Shorts, and warnings against leaving one's chewing gum on the bedpost over night.

Other musical packages offer rerecordings of famous popular music such as the hits of Glenn Miller, Tommy Dorsey and Artie Shaw performed by Cecilia Wentraub and her seven-piece jug band. Tribute recordings are also big in the morning, such as "A Tribute To..." albums for only $19.95 plus postage and handling. One can get "A Tribute To Dino, Desi and Billy" performed by Dino O'Hara, Desi Washington and Billy Fine (alleged to be the original replacement for the original Billy in the original group).

Now I'm not saying anything against our American capitalist system. If businesses can make a profit selling snap-down rugs and recordings of today's celebrities singing the oldies, such as "Chris Farley Sings The Hits of Russ Columbo," then I say more power to them. And ditto to the people who enjoy watching both the infomercials and/or interviews of "women who date dwarfs and the witches who hate them."

But as for me, I'm just not interested in all that weirdness. I do wonder, though, if Sam Donaldson's road-kill rug is held on with snaps.

Since online downloads have replaced records and discs, late-night television commercials have found other offensive products to hawk. And I have to apologize to Nebraska for my belief that weird daytime television guests might have come from a small town there. I now know that those particular people were all from Portland, Chicago and Frisco (Seattle residents will probably be offended I left them out). And since there are less Jerry Springer-like programs needing wacky guests these days, most of the former guests and their alleged families have all found positions on the big city councils and in the mayors' offices.

When the chips hit the fan
March 15, 1996

Will the V-chip, which may soon be on the market, solve America's television problems? Maybe.

Everyone seems to have an opinion on the values of the self-censorship technology. I'll share a few of my thoughts on the subject, and let the chips fall....

The V-chip, which is supposed to be placed in every television sold in the United States, will be able to block certain programs from viewing. Everyone who says there is too much violence on TV will have the ability to program out the offending shows, thus allowing their children to be free from Rambo, Terminator, Die Hard and Teenage Mutant Ninja Turtle movies.

Whatever you think of those films, the chip does give parents one more control on their children's environment. But what's specifically in it for us adults?

If the chip can program out violence, it can also program out insipid claptrap. I would like my TV to go blank whenever Oprah, Donahue, Ricky Lake, Jenny Jones or any other daytime talk show host opens his or her mouth. I'd also program it to black out Bryant Bumble's post-interview, political remarks; any situation comedy with canned laughter; any awards program where people wear red ribbons; all rip-offs of Friends; any movie of the week about a disease; every program which starts off with the "Entertainment Tonight" jingle; O.J.; every news feature titled "the swimsuits of..."; and every night talk show hosted by a guy with a big jaw, a cigar or fake-looking hair. These blocks alone would get the V-chip two thumbs up from me.

That pretty well wipes out all television programs except those with Angela Landsbury and Barney (who may be teaming up for a series titled "Extinction, She Wrote").

Now we get to commercials. We should be able to block all TV commercials that insult our intelligence.

This is where the V-chip may get into trouble. Those anti-Hollywood, anti-violence politicians, whose campaign chests are fed by Madison Avenue, may suddenly discover hidden satanic messages attached to the V-chip. Congress would then have to create a long-term select committee to study whether Americans should be allowed self-censorship.

We can leave this debate up to our great political leaders, or we can cut out the middleman and solve the problem ourselves with a simple flick of the off switch.

Offensive programming has changed over the years. The few scripted dramas and comedies are different than they were in the 1990s. And talk shows today have younger, hipper hosts who allegedly have senses of humor (could have fooled me) while reality TV is a whole new problem. Television offerings may have changed, but they are all still very offensive. And, fortunately, we the viewers still have our one most powerful tool in dealing with disgusting TV images. We still have the off switch.

Screamers have short shelf life

Sept. 8, 1995

Is there anything more sad than a 50+-year-old rock 'n' roller singing about a counterculture which has not only been off the counter for years, but has been removed from the shelf?

Last week I watched portions of the rock 'n' roll concert for the new Rock Hall of Fame in Cleveland, Ohio. I took it in small doses because, one, I'm not a masochist, and, two, the concert ran not quite as long as the Vietnam War.

In my youth, I enjoyed rock 'n' roll during the '50s and '60s. During that time I also enjoyed the sounds of other popular artists. It seemed very natural to see Frank Sinatra, Bing Crosby and various big bands continue to entertain in their styles as time progressed and their hairlines receded. Crosby was able to sing ballads in the 1970s, which he made popular in the late 1920s. Big bands continue to entertain today.

Some of the rock entertainers of the '50s and '60s have evolved with the years to, not only show their versatility, but to continue to present a fresh and exciting sound. Johnny Cash went with his roots in country to continue to grow into a musical legend. Jerry Lee Lewis, one of the "bad boys" of 1950's rock, has had a bumpy road of successes and failures. But his rhythm and blues and country and popular ballads are enjoyed today because of his talent, not his image.

Some rockers haven't been as lucky. Some of them, in my opinion, were embarrassing. One guy, I believe his name was Iggy something-or-other, came bouncing onto the Hall of Fame stage shirtless, with thinning long hair, screaming incoherent babble which may have made sense 28 years ago at the Whiskey on Sunset Strip. At a distance he looked almost young. Close up he looked like HBO's Tales From The Crypt host, the Crypt Keeper.

Time has been about as kind as the IRS to many rockers ... mostly those whose hits were made up of screams and drug references but very little range or talent. There may still be quite a few Bob Dylan fans roaming around. But I wonder, with all the money he's made, don't you think he could afford to get his sinuses fixed, not to mention wrinkle cream and someone other than Don King to style his hair? And Crosby, Stills and Nash... They sound just about like they did almost 30 years ago, but they look like Hardy, Hardy and Laurel.

I guess it's the style, based on angry youth, that doesn't transfer well to middle age. The ballads of Roy Orbison, Dinah Shore, Dean Martin and the Mills Brothers and others are timeless because of the talent of the songwriters and performers. The screams of heavy-metal rockers are of the moment, with a short shelf life.

My views are obviously part of my own aging process. But the subject does make me wonder what today's rap-music (a contradiction in terms) performers will be doing in 30 years. Will they be touring the "oldies" circuit bringing back fond memories of monotone racist sermons that would make Detective Mark Fuhrman blush? Will M.C. Hammer's baggy pants look as funny then as they do now? Will Snoop Doggie Dog, Ice-T and Ice-Cube (no relation) appear in K-Tel Records' TV commercials featuring music of the nasty '90s?

I don't know what the future will bring, but not all music of the past or present deserves to become classic.

Popular music of the 2020s is a mixed bag of computer-tweaked offerings from obnoxious rappers, squeaky voiced little men, almost identical pop princesses, and a few surviving geezers who need walkers when they pretend to hop around the stage while shouting archaic drug references. Fortunately, the television, radio and computer device off switches work very well on them. But thanks to modern technology, I can still enjoy Bing Crosby, Louis Armstrong, The Platters, The McGuire Sisters, Patsy Cline, Carolina Cotton and the ever-popular Russ Columbo.

March mania is latest 'happening'
Nov. 2, 1997

Washington D.C., the murder capital of the country, and W.C. Fields' alternative to death, Philadelphia, have become popular visiting places for large numbers of people.

The Million Woman March recently filled the streets of Philadelphia to listen to Winnie Mandela speak her political philosophy for black women. The event was a feminine version of Louis Farrakhan's Million Man March on Washington D.C. of a couple of years ago.

Then there was the Promise Keepers' D.C. march, which filled the streets with men vowing to be good. A couple of months earlier, 500 virgins had converged in front of the White House urging young people to "honk for purity." I believe Hillary sent Bill out of town that week.

I'm not sure these gatherings are beneficial to anyone other than restaurants and motels in the D.C. area and a few network television news crews, which may receive a little overtime pay. But, their short-term effect on the American culture seems to be a kind of '90s happening.... like a Woodstock with clothes on.

I suppose we Americans seem to want to always be part of some kind of movement — showing some massive sense of hipness. We apparently enjoy looking around and seeing large numbers of people nodding their heads in communal agreement. Why else would we have invented the baseball stadium wave?

We can probably expect another year or two of massive marches before the concept becomes uncool.

It's a shame we can't cash in on the "March Mania" here in Bullhead City, Arizona. Perhaps our chamber of commerce could urge various political factions to come show their unity by converging on Ramar and Highway 95. It would be great for business. Our fast-food restaurants, for instance, would be in cheeseburger heaven.

We could see, for example, a Million Man Country Beer Bar Patrons March converging on our city to urge motorists to "horn if you're honky."

We could also fill the streets with Promise Breakers. This group of people would not only spend a lot of money in our bars and motels, but they could legally raise a lot of political donations because they would be away from the White House.

In fact, we could have quite a turnout if we only invite potential Arizona governor candidates.

Well, it's an idea. Until we can come up with something, D.C. and Philadelphia will get the crowds.

I understand the next Million March will be made up of nonconformists, followed by the Loyal Order of Organized Anarchists. I may even join the nonconformists if I receive my uniform in time.

Apparently massive marches in D.C. haven't gone out of style. Enormous gatherings of whiners periodically continue to block traffic and trample lawns. The protesters that broke the law and entered the Capitol building on Jan. 6, 2021, have been going through various stages of the justice system for more than two years. Angry politicos and newspapers called that event an "insurrection," and an act of "sedition." Whatever your opinion of that day's events is, the folks who broke in broke the law.

Since then, a large number of protesters vandalized the Arizona Capitol building to show their outrage over a Supreme Court ruling on Roe vs. Wade. That violent behavior was not labeled "sedition" or "insurrection." And, pro-gun-control protesters recently swarmed into the Tennessee Capitol to shout down the legislature, accompanied by three state representatives. No arrests were made during this "insurrection," but the state House voted to expel two of the three offending representatives. A few days later the expulsion was overturned and now the offending lawmakers are honored guests at Biden's pro-gun-control, pro-abortion White House.

Personally, I don't care what protesters are whining about. If they break into or vandalize a building (government or not), burn a business, assault lawmakers, Supreme Court Justices or homemakers (or anyone), block traffic, or break any law during their tantrums, they need to be arrested by law enforcement officers and punished for their offenses.

Teen fashions continue to grate

May 24, 1996

If (as Shakespeare claimed) "all the world's a stage," then today's teenagers deserve a generational Oscar award for costuming.

Every generation develops its own special "style" during its teenage years, which usually consists of unique musical tastes, a special deviation on the English language, and noticeable clothing. All of this is brought to its fullest strength in the obligatory generation gap. Teens show their differences as part of their rites of adulthood. They use these "differences" to break loose from childhood and parental authority.

We can expect a new look and a new rebellious culture every decade or so: Masses of teenagers wearing the same outfit, talking the same way, and listening to the same "music" will be declaring their individuality and demanding our attention.

Many can remember their parents groaning over loud swing records only to become groaners themselves when sons and daughters played that Presley fellow. Those parents surely thought the leather-clad, side-burned youths were fighting to get good seats in handbaskets for one-way trips to the fiery place.

I can remember the comments adults made about long hair (back when I had hair) in the early sixties. Long hair at that time was anything other than a flattop.

The early sixties differed from the late sixties dramatically. In the early sixties surfing bands played songs about pretty girls and big waves. In the late sixties surfers were too stoned to find the beach. When Uncle Sam sent me overseas in 1965, the Beatles were singing about holding hands. When I came back, they were doing Lucy In The Sky With Diamonds and the cocker-spaniel hairstyle was the latest look.

The hippie clown suits of the late sixties became the nightmare leisure suits of the seventies. In looking back, it's hard to believe clothing and music fads could become any funnier than they did in the seventies.

Well, I was wrong. Today we have rap music and teenage clothing designed for anthropomorphic walruses. Call me old fashioned, but does anyone ever sing along with rap music?

And those giant pants ... Teenagers could hide a fifty caliber machine gun, a boom box, two badgers and a year's supply of Wheaties in them. I guess that's the idea. They are designed so gang-types can hide weapons and stolen items. In fact, they could hide just about anything but their socks.

Backward baseball caps are part of the nineties look. The only logical reason to wear them that way that I can come up with is that having the plastic strap in the front must cover up the lobotomy scar. Of course some of the guys I've seen wearing their caps backward don't really need the bill to shade their eyes. Their brows stick out far enough to not only shade them but to allow them to smoke cigarettes in the rain.

Whoever was the first to wear today's teen look must have been a real salesman. I can picture him telling other teenagers, "Hey. The whole idea is to look as inconspicuous as a gorilla in a maternity ward. If you wanna be cool, you got to look really stupid."

The other teens obviously answered, "Cool," and adopted the generational uniform.

The good news is, like all other generational fads, in a few years this style will be old hat. A new generation of teens will be expressing their individuality with a new mass-produced clothing style and some other form of irritating "music." And then the aging ex-rappers will gaze into their closets at their mothballed baggy pants and pine for the good old days.

It's the 2020s and the backward hat, baggy pants-wearing, goofy teens of the 1990s are adults with jobs, mortgages, vehicle loans, in-laws and children of their own. And I'm sure several of those former rebels are slapping their own foreheads and gasping as they see their teenage children expressing their individuality with today's mass-culture clothing choices. In fact, some are probably speechless when they first notice their sons come down the stairs to breakfast while wearing dresses.

Men, women and movies and the right to choose
Jan. 14, 1997

Tim Burton's latest motion picture, "Mars Attacks!" is showing throughout the country. As always, Burton has given us another look at his uniquely bizarre imagination. The special effects were great, the storyline was childish, and the characters were caricatures. My sons and I loved the film.

My wife, whose favorite films always seem to have Shirley MacLaine and five other actresses of various ages and social backgrounds droning on for hours about their childhoods and relationships, hated the film.

This illustrates, I believe, how movie choice is a prime example of the difference in the sexes. Being able to enjoy seeing 1950s-style Martian heads explode to the sound of Slim Whitman yodels is definitely a guy thing. So is getting a good laugh out of seeing Arnold Schwarzenegger accidentally slug a midget Santa Claus during a Christmas brawl.

On the other hand, tearing up during a coffee commercial is a woman thing. Women also seem to have cornered the market on watching disease-of-the-week movies. How in the world can they enjoy watching an actor or actress die for two hours when they know there is no hope before the titles vanish? I have a mental picture of the typical couple viewing one of these ghastly films as the woman having wet makeup streaked down her face and the man either asleep, disregarding the lady's makeup problem as he makes an evening suggestion, or glowering at the TV character and thinking "Die already!" because there is a good western on another channel. (When I say western, I'm thinking Randolph Scott, not Dr. Quinn.)

Now before I get attacked for being sexist, I must say that the differences I'm pointing out have nothing to do with job capabilities. A man who enjoys the Three Stooges and a woman who watches the two stooges, Regis and Kathy Lee, can both handle being journalists, city council members, crop dusters, chefs, chicken pluckers and CEOs of major motion picture companies.

Women have known there was a sexual difference in entertainment choice for a long time. Wives have never understood how their husbands could listen to Rush Limbaugh with his table-tapping, snippy remarks. Now women have their own Rush Limbaugh in Rosie O'Donnell. Go figure.

Fortunately for women, most men are patient and always pleased to take the time to explain the intricacies of our beliefs. For instance, I explained to my wife the deep philosophical moral of Mars Attacks! – Never smile at a crocodile. Never negotiate with an enemy.

Every time the movie's government characters attempt to negotiate with the Martians the outcome is about the same as the United States' negotiations with other governments. We negotiated with the Soviets at the end of World War II and all of Eastern Europe was enslaved. We negotiated an end to the Korean conflict, which put us back to square one for the next 45 years. And we negotiated peace with North Vietnam, which resulted in the total loss of that war.

It's funny. My wife didn't catch that moral at all.

Anyway, when it comes to men, women and movies, I'm pro-choice. I don't expect the little woman to understand the deep intellectual teachings of Chuck Bronson's classic Death Wish series. And I'm sure she doesn't expect me to suffer through the mind-numbing boredom of Now Voyager. How fair can one get?

I don't think my point has changed one bit over the last 26 years. I still enjoy watching the subtle acting and amazing storytelling of Dolph Lundgren and the little woman seems to be addicted to the Hallmark Channel.

Television sitcom character controversy is ratings hype

April 18, 1997

How important is television in our daily lives?

My quick response is that it is not that important. TV is merely a bit of light entertainment, something to occupy a portion of our leisure time between large doses of real life. We catch up on world and national events with news broadcasts; get a shot of nostalgia by watching an old movie we enjoyed umpteen years ago in a theater; and relax with a few laughs from one of the better sitcoms.

Although there have been many dire predictions, television has not replaced man's desire to attend live theater, sporting events and first-run motion picture theaters.

Accepting this premise, then why is there such a flap over the upcoming exit from the closet of a lead sitcom character?

Ellen DeGeneres is about to become the first openly homosexual TV sitcom star and it seems the whole country is flapping its wings in preparation for a falling sky. Is this change in a half-hour program going to destroy life as we know it?

Heck no.

This is just another who-shot-J.R. move. All television shows get stale after a while. Therefore, changes must be made to give viewers a need to watch. All the controversy, magazine articles, talk-show gossip and moral outrage concerning this character's outing, including this column, has become marvelous publicity to help tweak the ratings for ABC.

Do you remember "Rhoda?" That show was beginning to hurt for ratings. It was decided the main character would marry her TV suitor. The wedding was a ratings bonanza. Then every sitcom started having weddings in attempt to gain watchers. Fred Allen was right when he said, "Imitation is the sincerest form of television." (He originally made the remark in reference to radio.)

After the big wedding Rhoda became stale again and was canceled.

I'm sure, thanks to the publicity, the outing-episode of "Ellen" will be watched by fans, the morally outraged, and even a few people who have never watched the show. Then what?

The event will be over. The show will go on with fans continuing to watch while those who find "Ellen" offensive will not watch. I, however, doubt the show will be as funny as it has been in the past. After all, if TV is anything, it is politically correct. I don't think

Ellen will begin to behave like a reverse of Nathan Lane from The Birdcage. She won't suddenly become a cigar-smoking John Wayne with breasts. That might be funny, but would definitely be politically incorrect.

And, unlike "Rhoda," I doubt many other sitcom characters will follow Ellen's lead. "Columbo" will not trade in his rumpled raincoat for an Elton-John-style evening gown; a popular western will not be retitled Dr. Quinn, Medicine Gay; Homer Simpson will not leave his wife for Barney; and Dan Rather will probably not anchor the CBS Evening News in lipstick, false eyelashes and rouge.

Whether the "Ellen" show stays popular enough to continue or not is yet to be seen. The upcoming episode is a ratings blip and nothing more. Sitcoms, after all, are only make-believe. They exist as long as their viewer ratings stay up.

When people take things, especially television, too seriously, there is always someone to say, "Get a life." The fact is, we all have real lives which are, hopefully, much more interesting than television escapism. We need to make the best of our real lives, appreciate our real families, and not get lost in placing too much credence on television's Wonderland. We only have so much prime time. Unlike "Ellen" and "Rhoda," we won't be around in syndicated reruns to bore people forever.

The "Ellen" show led to "Will and Grace," which begat "Modern Family," and eventually led to every television show, commercial, movie and cartoon to include gay characters. And, of course, Broadway was way ahead of "Ellen." It seems to be part of the modern entertainment world. But since everyone seems to be okay with that these days, why are some blue noses still upset with Pepé Le Pew? Is a relationship between a cat and skunk considered miscegenation to these people? Those who are okay with Ellen DeGeneres, Elton John, Dylan Mulvaney and Richard Simmons need to cut Pepé a break!

Girl Scout cookie sales crumble in New Jersey
Jan. 24, 1997

An Associated Press news story out of New Jersey tells of a group of Girl Scout troops who have organized a protest against their governing council.

Apparently the scouts requested a ten-cent increase in their share of each box of cookies they sell. When the scout's governing council declined the increase, the girls organized a "slow down" of cookie sales.

The story says, "Currently, the bakery gets 81 cents per ($3) box, troops get 50 cents, and the council spends the remaining $1.69 on maintaining three scout camps and other properties, recruiting and training troop leaders, fund raising and administration." The scouts' share had increased from 40 cents per box the prior year.

The protest "slow down" means the girls will only sell the minimum number of boxes allowed.

The only conclusion that I can gather from this story is that Jimmy Hoffa is alive and well and disguised as a Girl Scout leader.

All of the scout organizations across the country, whether they are Boy, Girl, Cub, Brownie, etc., are designed to help children grow into honest, resourceful, caring and capable adults who believe in truth and justice as the American way.

Once in a while adults involved in the organizations have misplaced their priorities and guided the children in the wrong direction. Involving children in an economic protest, collective bargaining effort, or whatever one would like to call this instance, is certainly not a positive learning experience for the kids.

On the other hand, these Jersey scouts may be on to something. Their attitude mirrors the behavior of a lot of adults today. Why shouldn't they attempt to force their organization to slice them a bigger piece of the pie? It works for athletes, movie stars, rock singers and just about anyone with a lawyer. These scouts could probably increase their percent of the cookie take by simply making an offer their governing council can't refuse. Maybe after a few den mothers wake up to find Shetland pony heads in their beds...

They could also, for a small monthly fee, offer insurance against broken windows to anyone wise enough to buy their cookies. Who knows? Within a few years the troops could be raking in enough dough from betting on rigged soapbox derbies that they could drop the whole cookie thing.

Okay. So I exaggerated a little. But I do believe scouting is one aspect of life that needs to hold on to its tradition of wholesome, all-American goodness.... all the things that childhood should stand for. And strikes, boycotts, sit-ins and other forms of protest should be something reserved for unhappy adults.

As I remember my time as a Cub Scout, it was very outside oriented and made us feel like we were six-year-old members of a really fun ROTC program. I still have my old scout knife. But I recently did a little research and found that times have changed with scouting organizations as well. The Cub Scouts and Boy Scouts no longer exist as I remembered them. Today, Scouts BSA is for both boys and girls. Whereas the Girl Scouts are still around and boys aren't allowed. But apparently most of their cookie sales are handled online.

Attorney General Grant Woods takes aim at frivolous lawsuits

Aug. 4, 1995

Arizona Attorney General Grant Woods released his list of "top 10 most frivolous inmate lawsuits" earlier this week. Attorneys general of 23 other states also released top-10 lists in an effort to persuade U.S. Senate Judiciary Committee Chairman Orrin Hatch to back congressional legislation that would help curtail frivolous inmate lawsuits.

Woods said, "This office spends well over a million (tax) dollars a year processing and defending these frivolous filings, lawsuits that serve no purpose except to clog up the courts. Why should convicted criminals be allowed to file such ridiculous suits when a law-abiding Arizonan waits years to get his claims heard?"

Why indeed? The following is a boiled-down version of the list:

10. A convicted murderer on death row sued correction officials for taking away his Gameboy. (I wonder if he tried holding his breath until he turned blue.)

9. An inmate sued for $110,000 over a delayed dental appointment for a toothache. (Prisoners' dental care is free, and should be worth every penny.)

8. A convicted murderer, who also attempted to escape, sued because he was denied dental floss. (If I had my way, convicted murderers would be denied teeth.... No, make that air.)

7. An inmate brought suit for damages to his typewriter and fan because he was denied a surge protector in his cell. (The only prisoner-access electricity I would allow would be to "the chair.")

6. An inmate alleged his freedom of religion was trampled because he was not allowed conjugal visits. (Anyone know what church services he's talking about?)

5. An inmate alleged he was libeled and slandered by a female prison official who referred him to disciplinary action after he continually walked into the restroom she was using.

4. A convicted murderer sued because he was not allowed to reside with his convicted kidnapper wife who he married in prison.

3. An inmate alleged the Department of Corrections failed to properly rehabilitate him. Therefore, when he was released on parole he was arrested and convicted of another crime. (I guess this one would make sense to those people who claim criminal acts are society's fault.)

2. A male inmate sued alleging his Constitutional rights were violated by the refusal of prison officials to allow him to wear a brassiere.

1. An inmate alleged correction officials retaliated against him by not inviting him to a pizza party for a departing DOC employee. (Even if he were invited, this guy would have probably sued because he didn't get a photo opportunity with Chuck E. Cheese.)

After reading Woods' list, one wonders what prison inmates might NOT consider a right. The sad part is that we taxpayers struggle to pay bills, send our children to school, follow the rules of society and attempt to get ahead, while our tax dollars pay for idiotic lawsuits filed by convicted criminals. Such actions allow prisoners to victimize the rest of us again and again.

Woods announced that our own U.S. Senator Jon Kyl and Senator Bob Dole will soon introduce a proposal which demands inmates "pay filing fees and court costs, prohibit inmates from suing when there is no serious physical injury, and remove good-time credits for inmates who file frivolous suits."

Let's hope Congress looks favorably on the proposal. Otherwise we can look forward to Susan Smith's lawsuit for being traumatized by having to use a seatbelt in the prison bus.

> *I wrote this one 28 years ago. And, if someone were to waterboard Susan Smith every day since that time, she still wouldn't be punished enough for her crime! (Unfortunately, that child murderer is up for parole in 2024.) As for the silly court cases, they continue to waste time and money. And today's prisoners seem to have more rights than the average, honest working American. On the other hand, with all the George Soros-backed attorney generals and DAs we now have littering up our legal system, more and more violent thieves, rapists and molesters will not be able to launch frivolous lawsuits from within prisons. They'll be kept out on the streets doing what they do best – stealing, raping and molesting.*

Are news stories indicative of times?
Jan. 12, 1997

Some of the first news stories of 1997 may give a hint as to what to expect for the rest of the year.

For instance, both major political parties are engaged in charges of misconduct and calls for reform. Senator Barbara Boxer of California is calling for more anti-handgun legislation. Hollywood's latest hyped motion picture, produced by Oliver Stone, features a sleazy pornographer as a crusader for free speech. Nothing is new there.

One story we all noticed was about the Continental Airlines pilot who was fired for failing a drug test and then rehired when his ex-wife admitted secretly putting marijuana in homemade bread she baked for him. The airline is now suing the former wife to compensate for the expenses incurred fighting her ex-husband's appeals.

This story is only newsworthy because a commercial pilot is responsible for the lives of his/her passengers. And one doesn't want to be on a flight to Chicago and find out the pilots are Cheech and Chong.

What the former wife did was criminal and could have led to tragic consequences. On the other hand, I'm not sure the pilot should have been rehired. A man of normal intelligence would have the common sense to react to an ex-wife handing him something to eat about the way he would if the witch from Snow White offered him an apple.

Another story tells us that the widow of Fred Astaire will allow his image to be used in a commercial.

Now the late Fred Astaire was the type of on-screen, and off-screen, personality who not only was extremely talented but was the personification of "class." When I visualize Astaire, I see him in a tuxedo with cane, white tie and tails.

Wives and husbands of famous personalities often find it difficult earning a living once they are widowed. And many will continue to live off the names and images of their former meal tickets. But the line should have been drawn with Fred Astaire. Mrs. Astaire didn't sign for Fred to represent some rare vintage of fine wine. She set him up to computer dance with a Dirt Devil vacuum! Why not dub his voice arguing with the late Billy Martin whether a beer tastes great or is less filling?

I assume if this marketing ploy is successful we will see a lot of dead celebrities' careers revived. Perhaps we will see Dwight Eisenhower asking some kid to leggo his Eggo Waffle;

Cary Grant extol the virtues of scented kitty litter; and Eleanor Roosevelt demonstrate the ThighMaster. Let's hope not.

Another ominous story for 1997 is that DC Comics is going to redesign Superman. We remember a couple of years ago the publishing company killed off the Man of Steel. Within a few issues, after tremendous profits, they brought him back. Last year they had Lois Lane drop the big guy and start fooling around with Peter Parker (a.k.a. Spiderman). That affair also ended after a circulation coup.

Now the company is not only giving Superman a new look, but he's also getting new powers and a new storyline. He will drop his blue tights and red cape and replace them with a new blue and white outfit.

Some things are meant to be sacred. John Wayne should never be depicted in a ballet dress with a feathered boa; the Star Spangled Banner should not be sung with a rap, polka or Tiny Tim beat; and Superman should not be redesigned to wear a milkman's uniform.

One other story worth mentioning tells of environmentalists being upset with the 1974 book, "Joy of Cooking." Apparently the book contains a recipe for green sea turtle soup. The turtle is on the endangered species list. Many so-called environmentalists believe the recipe must be removed from further editions to keep American mothers from massing to the sea to slaughter the beasts for their children's hot lunches. Or perhaps they think Campbell's Soup will release a new offering of Cream of Sea Turtle.

So-called environmentalists are always thinking the worst. I don't know of anyone who would take the time to butcher a turtle for dinner. I also know the stuff tastes a lot worse than spotted owl in dumplings with eagle grease.

All of these stories tell us that America is changing, not necessarily for the best. Certainly 1997 will be remembered for many reasons. Let's hope not all of those reasons will leave us crying in our turtle soup.

The Fred Astaire situation was a preview of what may come in the next few years. Now that CGI (computer-generated imagery) is perfected to the point that A-list film makers don't have to spend a dime on stuntmen, we can probably expect to see Humphrey Bogart make a successful comeback in a delightful, multi-gendered NBC sitcom; Victor McLaglen show off his dance skills in a Netflix musical production of "Mr. Belvedere;" and Angela Lansbury return to compete on 21st Century Bowling With the Late Stars.

Holiday fun approaches

October 2017

The most celebrated holiday of the year is coming up quickly and shoppers are struggling with their annual decisions – what costumes to purchase for Halloween.

The stores are filled with very elaborate versions of traditional Frankenstein, Dracula, Wolfman, Hillary, Darth Vader and the Creature From the Black Lagoon costumes. The quality of these outfits has improved so much in recent years that Roger Corman has been forbidden to purchase them for fear he will use them without authorization in an upcoming film.

But every year, new more-relevant costumes are sold to politically motivated celebrants. Almost 60 years ago, many adults were mortified when they opened their doors on Halloween to a sea of children wearing Kennedy and Nixon masks. For several years, the cheaply made Nixon masks enjoyed a fairly long shelf life, as opposed to the short-lived popularity of the Spiro Agnew masks.

Today, not only has the quality of "relevant" Halloween costumes improved, but also the selection has increased dramatically. I'm sure this year we will see many three-foot-tall Donald Trumps delightfully squealing "Trick or Treat." And, I'll bet, there will be quite a few Kim Dung-Un impersonators wearing recycled Mao jackets and carrying toy rockets under their arms as they ask for candy. Some youngsters will probably disguise themselves as Vlad Putin in warmer areas of the country, as it will be too cold in a lot of places to go out at night without a shirt. As for Obama, I've heard all of his masks have been recalled, melted down and recycled into Dr. Ben Carson masks. Such is fame.

There's a rumor that Jane Fonda costumes are coming back this Halloween. Only this time, instead of a Hanoi Hilton bandana and workout leggings, she comes complete with a child-sized walker and a "North Korea forever" shawl. Perhaps Fonda costumes could be sold with Bernie Sanders outfits as a geriatric Trick or Treat team theme, as long as the wearers redistribute all milk duds with less-fortunate costumed kids.

Some regional costumes will work for a good laugh. For instance, Gov. Chris Christie dressed for his private beach will probably be popular in New Jersey while Madonna (not the religious figure) will certainly infest many front porches in Frisco and Hollywood.

Some older kids will be wearing congressmen outfits. They won't actually ask for treats. They'll just let the other children gather the candy and then they will demand their "fair share."

Many creative parents will work hard on adapting fun and unique costumes for their children. "Star Wars" characters are always popular as are ghosts, pirates, vampires, mummies, Ninja Turtles, Batmen and SpongeBobs. And, I hope, there will be soldiers, police officers, fire fighters, doctors and nurses. I doubt there will be any kids dressed as football players.

I hope all children will have fun and stay safe.

Seeing little kids in fun Halloween costumes is certainly delightful for adults, even us old Boomers. Three to 12-year-old "Star Wars" characters with light sabers crack me up. And funny monster outfits are just so cute on little kids. As I think about it, life is already confusing enough for children. Perhaps we should completely avoid the politician masks as one more way to protect children's innocence.

Another American icon falls to foreign interests

September 28, 2003

Milestones come and go. We all hear "It is the end of an era" every time a well-loved entertainer or political leader dies, a fine example of earlier architecture is demolished to make room for a soulless glass and metal tower or the Ninth Circuit Court of Appeals makes a logical decision (the latter can't come soon enough).

My generation has witnessed the passing parade as the "pop" music of our youth became first "golden oldies," then "blasts from the past" and finally, according to our neo-adult children, "geezer rock."

Well, another major milestone was announced Thursday. Levi Strauss will close its last two U.S. plants by the end of the year. The company also plans to close its last three plants in Canada early next year. This means Levis will not be manufactured in North America.

If a southern baseball franchise can be labeled America's team, the 150-year-old Levi Strauss & Company could surely have been known for producing America's pants.

Finding out Levis will be made in another country is like seeing Clint Eastwood fired from a western movie set and replaced with Roberto Benigni or hearing that Harley-Davidson has been sold to a French car manufacturer and will be imported and available in 15 feisty pastel colors. It's about as American as apple-sushi.

Apparently the company has fallen on hard times in recent years. One cartoonist pointed out that the loss of profit in Levi sales was equal to the increase in size of baby boomer butts. For whatever the reason, western-style jeans are pullin' up stakes and headin' for greener pastures – most probably in cheap-labor plants throughout the third world.

Seriously, enemy countries, as well as formerly friendly countries, have been sucking the life out of America for many years. Their diplomats have smiled while shaking hands in peaceful negotiations with the United States that always seem to end with us giving them what we have earned. Very few of these countries have come to the aid of America during our times of need. Other than Britain and sometimes Australia, the United States has fairly few real friends in the world. The others all seem to require to be paid for their statements of support.

When America started bestowing special trade status on Communist and Fascist dictatorships and garden-variety third world nations, we gave away the farm. As our manufacturing companies left us to seek the benefits of slave labor, our leaders pontificated on how we were improving our relationships with the rest of the world — even if we are now dependent on foreign countries for some of the materials we would need to go to war with those same countries.

The recent lack of support from the United Nations for America's war on terror should be a sign that, as always, in the long run, America has to take care of "number one." When we go to war, we must stay the course that benefits America. When we aid other countries, we must make sure they are not backstabbing, corrupt, smiling enemies. We must appreciate our true friends in Britain and elsewhere, and cut off all other parasites.

We need to rethink all of our trade agreements so, like a good business, we truly benefit.

The loss of Levi Strauss manufacturing is only the latest example of this country trading away its ability to stand strong and independent.

Unfortunately, non-American Levis is *truly* the end of an era. Let's just hope we can turn this trend around before we are really caught with our pants down.

Obviously, international, national and local issues haven't changed that much in the last 20-some years.
I'll bet that today even "Made in the USA" stickers are probably mass-produced in Beijing.

8. The Home Front

SORTING OUT THE BLAME

April 3, 1996

It has recently been brought to my attention (by an un-named publisher who signs my check) that I should explain the difference between an editorial and a column.

An editorial will appear on the opinion page right under the mast (that top left informational box). An "editorial" logo will appear above the copy. The opinion expressed in an editorial is the official opinion of the newspaper as approved by the editorial board and the publisher. An endorsement is also considered the opinion of the publication.

A column, such as this one, will have a "columns sig" logo with the picture of the author on it. A column is the opinion of the author and not necessarily the newspaper, the publisher, or even the columnist's wife.

Another difference between the two forms of writing, for this paper anyway, is the tone of the piece. Our editorials, whether they are critical or congratulatory, are straight to the point. My columns, I'm told, have been known to be a skosh facetious. Now I don't know how someone could come to that conclusion. I've always bent over backward to be fair. Most of the time my columns even treat liberal politicians and advocates such as Bill and Hillary, Janet Reno, the ACLU and Hanoi Jane, among others, just as if they were decent honest human beings. Talk about a stretch.

Other folks have pointed out that my columns might be a tad lacking in compassion for convicted criminals. Perhaps they are correct. Certainly any lack of compassion would be my own and not that of any other employee of this publication. It is a problem I've had for many years. I am one of those unfortunates who are unable to shed a tear over the plight of convicted murderers, molesters, rapists and Dahmer-like predators who dine on their victims. Call me heartless.

Apparently I have also said a few unkind things about the New World Order people. Sorry 'bout that. I must have been over reacting to the fact that "nationalism" and "patriotism" have become bad words. I guess I should be a little kinder to a group that might goose-step into town at any time.

While I'm baring my soul, I have to admit to not being very accepting to the beliefs of "environmentalists." In particular, I might have been a wee harsh on Secretary of the Interior Bruce Babbitt. He has claimed for many years to be an environmentalist. I always thought he was just anti-private property. Then I saw a tabloid picture purported to be Babbitt hugging a desert tortoise. The emotionalism of the shot brought a tear to my jaded eye. I felt I had grossly misjudged the man. (But then on the next page, a snapshot appeared to show him trying to put net stockings on the little beast.)

The bottom line is: This publication stands behind all its editorials. A columnist, however, stands alone (out on a desert willow limb).

This particular column was done at the request of a publisher who was, at that time, stinging a bit from the words of an unhappy elected official.
He was relatively new at his job and learned after a few years not to take angry words personal from people
who would like to dictate every move one makes.

ET was to call home, not call the Daily News

Sept. 13, 1996

It's not even a full moon.

Every now and then I receive calls critical of our news stories. Many times the caller will have legitimate issues to discuss. Sometimes they have information, which will allow us to follow the particular story with another. And sometimes I wonder if the caller has a direct line to Neptune.

For instance, I believe some of the people who are arrested for crimes have never read a newspaper before. They seem rather shocked that their names appear along with an account of their felony arrests. Many think newspapers don't have the right to print their personal arrest stories. Usually they start off with, "A friend told me my name is in the paper and I'm going to sue you, you (bleep, bleep bleep)."

Although a few of my friends will admit I am somewhat of a (bleep), I usually attempt to explain what makes a news story, how we gather the information, and why we follow crime stories from initial arrests through the justice system. Usually I get about 15 seconds into my presentation when the individual tells me to (beep my honkin' a-ooo-ga) and hangs up.

One of the more often used remarks thrown at me is, "You people are ruining my life! You're embarrassing me and my family." This usually comes from someone who is going through the justice system and our court reporter has quoted the prosecutor or judge regarding evidence and/or prior convictions.

Once in a while individuals call because they are "outraged" over our coverage of a particular alleged or convicted molester. Sometimes it's the molester him or herself. Sometimes it's just some reader who would like our paper to act like there are no molesters out there and only print the "good news." Well, we do print the good news. We print stories about the community helping an abandoned dog, charity events, victim assistance programs, scholarships, and molesters who are sentenced to endure jailhouse justice for the rest of their worthless lives.

I have to agree with most callers that molester stories are disgusting. The fact that molesters exist and breathe our oxygen is also disgusting. The *Daily News* will not ignore (another word for cover up) news stories because they are disgusting. (Otherwise we would ignore politics as well.) People have a right to know when someone is arrested for such an outrageous crime, in what neighborhood the crime took place, whether the person is found guilty or innocent, and, if guilty, what punishment is given. This paper also will not ignore other crime/court stories, local politics, local sports, education stories, or community events – all topics various callers (full moon or not) have demanded we not publish.

A recent caller was upset with a story regarding a female molester who, shall I say, doesn't deserve the title "mother." The facts of the case are disgustingly gross. But, in my opinion, the grossest thing about the story is the judge can only sentence the woman to no more than six months in jail. Residents who are not made aware of these stories will never find the outrage to strengthen the law and lengthen the sentences of these creatures.

Without our coverage, readers would never have learned of Bobbie Jo Dunlap who pled guilty to second-degree murder in the shooting of her husband. She was charged with killing the old boy and leaving him to be eaten by her dogs. Disgusting! But we don't make 'em up. These kinds of people are out there and readers have a right to know.

A lot of questions arise from a story like this. Personally, I wonder about the thought processes a person goes through before committing such a crime. Was the husband an abusive person? Or was the woman just out of dog food? And what happens to the dogs? Are they able to go back to Purina?

Hey. The world is getting nuttier than a fruitcake. We can't hide from it. The only way we can do anything about it is to be aware of it.

It's not a full moon. Perhaps we should check the drinking water.

> *This was a very factual column, even if it was written in a snidely manner.*

Oops! We dood it again

Sept. 5, 1997

One of our local radio stations has decided to play the fun game of "find the error in the *Daily News*."

This isn't a new radio game in the Tri-state area. When I began working at this paper in April 1993, several stations were having fun with the *Daily News*.

I used to enjoy one radio talk show that would refer to us as the "Daily Snooze." A gaggle of about five people would call the host each day with a variety of interesting conspiracy theories. This newspaper was sometimes accused of being involved in some of those great conspiracies.

In an effort to clean up our image, one of my first moves as editor was to give up my personal black helicopter. (My U.N. pilot wanted to move back to Bavaria, anyway.)

The host of that radio show has since moved on to bigger and better things. It is rumored that he assisted Mel Gibson as a secret technical advisor on a recent film. In fact, I'm told, Mel learned enough from him that the actor's life may now be in danger.

Another radio station used to play the find-the-error game around 1993. A couple of disc jockeys who claimed to have a comedy show would give away T-shirts and other grand prizes to people who called in to say, "Yup. They messed up in calling the Denver Broncos the Azusa Broncos." And everyone had a good laugh.

As I remember, these same disc jokeys, I mean jockeys, made it a quest to get on the front page of the *Daily News*. They went so far as to have one of our ad reps of that era present an offer to the then-publisher that if we put the guys' picture, riding a donkey backwards, on our front page they would trade out some advertising. My reaction was, if two disc jockeys riding a donkey are hit by a car, it's newsworthy. Other than that, livestock fun is more fit to radio than publication.

Let me just say, we do make mistakes. Every day. Anyone who strings as many thousands of words together everyday, as we do, will make mistakes. We work very hard to fix both Associated Press and local copy errors. Sometimes we are given incorrect information. Sometimes we use an incorrect word. When a mistake reaches print, and it is not just a typo, we run a correction as soon as we can gather the correct information.

And our readers are not shy about calling in to let us know when we need to make a correction. There are a lot of grammarians out there who are very good proof readers.

I've always wondered if some of those same readers call radio personalities when they use incorrect words or incomplete sentences while introducing a rap song, telling an elephant joke or rewording *Daily News* stories when they present the news.

The latest version of the find-the-error game appeared on a station that I enjoy listening to once in a while. After all, I still get a kick out of hearing a Los Angeles-raised entertainer sing with an Alabama accent about leaving his momma and best old dawg waitin' for the train in the rain.

The DJ, so nobody will know who he is, I'll just call him Al Gerbil (*editor's note: The real DJ was Al Lama, who is presently serving time for murder in California*), gave away a T-shirt to the person who found the mistake in Thursday's paper (the word "today" appeared rather than "Friday"). I congratulate the reader who won the shirt. And I congratulate all of our readers who call us with information and keep us on our toes.

We at the *Mohave Valley Daily News* will continue to work as hard as we can to produce a quality newspaper. But just like when I clean my windshield, one of my kids can always point out the remains of a river gnat splattered in a corner. Of course I probably missed it because I was paying too much attention to my radio.

There were several small radio stations in the area in the 1990s, and most of them had local DJs and call-in political shows.
I knew a few of the DJs and found they were basically fun people. Some of the political call-in "pontificators" weren't.

Radio criticism offered free is worth every cent

June 3, 2001

I have been told, more and more often recently, that there is quite a bit of criticism being thrown at the *Daily News* each weekday morning from an alleged local radio station. Like most of us, I have a job and cannot spend time listening to the pontifications of radio gurus during working hours. I also have a life, therefore I avoid that activity during my family hours as well.

The policy of this newspaper over the last few years has been to ignore much of the sillier remarks made about it by those who think they should be in charge of everything. We have attempted to gather the news, no matter what the news is, and present it to our readership – mostly people who know the meaning of the word "attribution."

But there are those who don't understand clauses like, "according to the police department," or, "the councilman said." They believe anything written on a news page is a reporter's opinion as opposed to a news report. Of course there are also people who know better but will continue to make that charge, as it is the easiest way to manipulate those who are not very bright. One radio program offers these folks not only a chance to voice their views, but the benefit of the expertise of like-minded hosts.

Apparently the aforementioned radio show (so I won't offend the actual disc-less jockeys, let's just call it "Don't Start Us Whining" on KTOXIC) "personalities" read the *Mohave Valley Daily News* each morning before they go on the air. (Either that or one of them reads it and draws a picture for the other one.) They then spend the next few hours telling everyone that the stories that appeared in the paper should not have been there; the rumors they discuss are the real stories that should have been printed (in their words); their opinions are the legitimate news; and they are the true Edward R. Murrow and Dan Rather of low-power AM radio. (I see them more as Sesame Street's Ernie and Bert presenting "news" from a Hee Haw cornfield.)

But that is the nature of small-town radio talk shows. It's a free country, and, just as those who cannot draw are capable of critiquing a political cartoonist, those who cannot write and know nothing of journalism, ethics, deadlines or production processes are free to give their biases on newspapering. Those without knowledge and talent have every right to call a radio program and pontificate on anything they want to anyone foolish enough to listen to them.

And let's face it. Every time Beavis mentions the *Mohave Valley Daily News* to Butthead, even if he does so in a negative manner, we are getting a free plug. That means that the seven to twelve listeners of that station will be hearing our names — over and over. And perhaps someday one or two of those folks will want to learn to read and may even subscribe.

And, up until just recently, I was glad the *Daily News* could be of service to these two guys. Without us, they wouldn't have a show. Every hero needs a villain. Every Rush Limbaugh needs a Bill Clinton and every Bill Press needs a George W. Bush. These guys need us so they can create a big wind patting themselves on their backs and telling everyone what legends they are.

But, from what I have been told, these two self-proclaimed geniuses have recently launched a continual attack on *Daily News* political reporter Howard Decker. And I can understand their resentment. After all, Howard is different than the KTOXIC boys. He has 45 years of experience. He started in the mid 1950s in the newsroom of the *Los Angeles Examiner*. He has advanced his abilities and earned his living over the interim as a reporter, photographer and editor at a variety of publications.

When it comes to newspapering, Howard is the wise man (sometimes wise guy) on the mountain. His talents are many. He can do it all. His picture should be in Webster's Dictionary next to the word "professional."

On the other hand, the "Don't Start Us Whining" boys are rebels who may or may not find a cause some day. One of them even wears leathers and looks a bit like Brando (not from "The Wild One," but more like Brando today) on his Leader of the Pack Honda with the basket and squeeze horn on the handlebars. They have shown their knowledge of world and local events is not quite as large as the musical range of a Gregorian chant.

Anyway, in spite of their remarks, I wish them the best. I hope they continue to show up for work at least three out the five days they are supposed to be there, and practice their craft (they have already made an art form out of dead air), and keep enough gerbils on hand to generate the station's power. We will continue to assist them by providing factual coverage of real issues that they can then distort as they see fit.

Little word skirmishes like this can really be fun. The key is to always keep a smile on your face and, hopefully, readers will get a laugh at your attacker's expense.

Lawsuit is first shot in City Council's war to operate government in secret
April 21, 2000

The City of Bullhead City has launched a new assault against the people's right to know. Our Council has, during one of their many secret meetings, approved City Attorney J. Edgar Lenkowsky's double-O License To Sue those who seek information.

The *Mohave Valley Daily News*, *Bullhead City Bee* and Police Chief Glenn Walp each filled out the necessary paperwork to view the Maricopa County Sheriff's Office (MCSO) investigation report on the city police handling of Robbie the dog. When the report was given to the City, Lenkowsky viewed the material and decided "the people" should not be allowed to see it. With the secret approval of Council, Lenkowsky filed a lawsuit against the *Daily News* to, one, delay anyone seeing it, and, two, get the material before a judge who just may agree with him and clamp down on us nosy citizens.

Lenkowsky obviously didn't sue the police chief because that would be the city suing the city — a rather silly situation even for Bullhead City. Nor did he sue the *Bullhead City Bee*, which, coincidentally, broke the story of the lawsuit. He chose to use the *Daily News* as his legal opposition.... simply because the *Daily News* filled out a request to view the MCSO material and the *Daily News* has an obligation to report the information to the people.

The message Lenkowsky (and the Council) is sending to the people of Bullhead City is: Don't try to find out what your government is up to because it will sue you and cost you a bundle. Lawyers aren't cheap. Ask Lenkowsky.

The *Daily News* will have to pay its legal fees to fight for the rights of all of us. Bullhead City's fees will be paid for by Bullhead City's taxpayers.

This assault against the people begins a new era in Bullhead City. Our new Secret Society Council, city attorney and new city manager have adopted a Don't Ask, Don't Tell policy: If anyone asks, sue him (or her). If anyone tells, discredit him (or her).

Our fearless council members have been given orders to refer all questions regarding the suit to City Attorney J. Edgar Lenkowsky.

I wonder how much Dan Dible, our new city manager, has to do with this new belief in Supply Side Information (the City bureaucrats give the info to the important people, themselves, and let small bits of it leak downward to the little people). If he buys into this scenario, and he hasn't openly opposed it, Supply Side Information could locally become known as the Dible Down Theory.

Perhaps City officials should purchase a multi-headed, Maxwell Smart-style Cone of Silence to lower over themselves at Council meetings to keep all of their top-secret thoughts out of the hands of the us, the enemy. They could then televise the council meetings with pre-written subtitles which would have been approved by the vice mayor's ministry of propaganda. Viewers would see Councilman Sullivan's mouth move and read a subtitle such as, "... and the okra is to die for." While Mayor Vick and Councilwoman Downs-Vollbracht may look like they are arguing but the subtitles would show them comparing cute puppy stories.

Seriously, secret government can be made to look very benign. But it is really a malignancy that we do not want to allow to grow in Bullhead City.

I have already given my opinion that I believe the MCSO material will turn out to be a gaggle of worthless accusations. There will probably be very little substance tucked away in hundreds of pages of claptrap equal to the allegations shared in this newspaper from the credit card investigation. Many of our officials will probably come off very foolish. However, we are quite used to seeing that in Bullhead City.

The only thing that will make our officials look any more foolish than their own documented words in some of these reports is their present actions to hide public information and run a secret government by the people, for the people, in spite of the people.

Whether it's a small, rural city council action or an alleged investigation of the assassination of President Kennedy, American citizens have the right to know the truth. And, unfortunately, government officials don't always support that right.

Who's in charge here?

April 26, 2000

An interesting Bullhead City press release was faxed to the *Daily News* Friday. The key remark in that release, headlined "City clarifies legal action," was "The City Council would like to make it very clear that it is not withholding information from the public."

If that remark was true, then why was there no attribution on the release? Nowhere throughout the release were there any quotes or paraphrases attributed to any single person: not the mayor, not the city attorney, not the city manager, and not a single council member.

It was what I call a "dummy" release. That is one where many opinionated statements are made but the sources are unclear. Any publication that printed it verbatim would seem to be making the statements itself. The *Daily News* is always pleased to print statements made by officials, even if the statements are claptrap, as long as those statements are attributed to individuals. When the newspaper makes a statement, such as this, it will be on the Opinion page. And the closest we can come to the above statement is "The City Council most assuredly is withholding information from the public."

Monday, City Public Information Officer Toby Cotter was asked by a *Daily News* reporter, "Who made the statements?"

His answers started with "Technically, it came from my office, through the city manager, so however you want to attribute it." Great! Maybe I can blame this one on Janet Reno too.

Although no known Council meeting took place, "The city manager did talk with each council member," he said, "alerting them of the issue, and talking with them, basically alerting them of the situation. Through these conversations, I'm sure a couple of council members may have given some input." Clear enough? "... I guess you can say it was authored by me, which is true. I was given that information from the city manager," he concluded.

So, basically, Toby wrote it. The "information" came from the city manager and, possibly, a council member or two or "... however you want to attribute it."

Whatever happened to the idea of city leaders speaking up for themselves? Of course the next election is quite a way off, so why should any of them tell the public anything?

Reporter Howard Decker's question to Toby Cotter was like Costello to Abbott:

Decker: Who made the statements?

Cotter: Yes.

Decker: I mean the official's name.

Cotter: Who.

Decker: The one who made the statements.

Cotter: Exactly.

Decker: Exactly who made the statements?

Cotter: Yes.

Decker: Well go ahead and tell me.

Cotter: That's it.

Decker: That's who?

Cotter: Yes.

The next time that Cotter organizes a Bullhead City softball team, I'm definitely going to check out who's on first base.

The point is that the city is not only withholding public information, it is presently withholding who is really calling the shots at city hall. Who is meeting without the public's knowledge and coming up with policy and assurances that nothing is being hidden? If no Council is meeting, then who is assuring the public that the Council thinks everything is peachy keen?

I picture a hologram of a giant head with flames behind it hovering over the burnt umber (not emerald) city administration building telling us all to "go away" and "never mind the man behind the curtain."

The *Daily News* wants to tear down the curtain and expose the activities of our governing officials to the light of day. The more light shined on government, the less likely government will engage in embarrassing activities, allegations and expenses.

Individual councilmembers could have made all kinds of statements concerning whether individuals were withholding the truth or whatever they were attempting to put out to the public. But not one did. The members could have released a meeting agenda to the public, then held an official meeting and discussed the issues. But they didn't. The public information officer simply put out a release that was just about as clear as a Kamala Harris speech without attributing any of the statements to anyone. Clear. Oh, yeah. And the Hunter Biden laptop is Russian misinformation – wink, wink.

I figure by now you all understand that I just don't like or trust Communists. And, if you have read up on the behavior of the Bolsheviks, Mensheviks, Soviet Socialists, German National Socialists, Venezuelan Socialists, Cuban Communists, Vietnamese Communists and the bloody trail of Red China's Communist government, then you understand that Democratic Republics that value freedom should stay completely away from them. Trying to do business with the Commies is like ripping off your collar and holding your neck close to Count Dracula. Commies lie and they bite!

Should 'moderates' be embraced?
Nov. 30, 1997

Mayor Norm Hicks announced Wednesday that Bullhead City will be, if the Council says "yes," a sister city to Weinan City, China.

The *Mohave Valley Daily News* story, which appeared Thursday, claimed the two cities will "share in economic development endeavors and share cultural heritages." Weinan City boasts of an agricultural, mineral-producing and industrial economy.

I will be the first to admit that I'm somewhat of a dinosaur when it comes to international relations in the 1990s. After all, weren't the Communist countries our enemies for a lot of years?

Oh, yeah, I know we made a deal with Joe Stalin during World War II. But after the war, "Good Old Joe" enslaved Eastern Europe and exterminated at least as many people as did Hitler. And while I was learning to duck and cover under my school desk, apparently to keep from being killed by a Commie nuke, American and Red Chinese soldiers were killing each other in the Korean War.

And when I went to Vietnam in late 1965, it was to "stop Communist expansion before we had to fight on our own shores." While we were in South Vietnam fighting against the Communist invaders from North Vietnam, another young man was dodging the draft and protesting America's involvement in the war by, among other things, going to the Soviet Union to share his beliefs. Well, times have changed. That young protester is now our President. We lost Vietnam, and, son of a gun, the Communists are on our shores ... and we gave them the key to the city.

Now, before you get upset with me and accuse me of being closed minded and against the economic growth of the area, let me explain that I am attempting to understand and accept the philosophy that is bringing about this international partnership.

The present Chinese Communist government, I'm told, is not populated with the same "hard-liner" guys that we went to war with in the early '50s and who held POWs for decades. These Communists are more "moderate." Well maybe they do have a rather extreme policy concerning birth control; and their labor force does work relatively cheap; and they did exterminate dissidents in Tiananmen Square; and ... well ... they're still being referred to as "moderates."

The more I think about it, the more I realize that I'm the old-time "hard liner." I should be more forgiving and accepting to the modern way of doing business. It's a new world order and I just better get used to it.

Perhaps if things had worked out differently in World War II we would still be faced with the same decisions:

Let's say the ailing President Roosevelt had decided that once we cleared the Nazis from France we should negotiate a conditional Peace Accord with Germany. He might have been worried about destabilizing the German economy a lot like President Bush was worried about the Iraqi economy after purging Sadam's troops from Kuwait.

So, Hypothetically, British and American forces stop at the German border and Stalin stops at his own border without "liberating" Eastern Europe. The Allies and Germany sign a peace treaty and, after a few months, Hitler allows Red Cross inspectors to visit his empty concentration camps. Everyone is happy.

Sure, we knew his "final solution" exterminated the European Jews, but then again, we knew the Communist North Vietnamese, after our "peace" agreement and rather clumsy retreat, engaged in genocide of the Montagnard people of Vietnam. After a couple of years, in a more "moderate" move, the Communist government did allow the less than 200 remaining Montagnards to come to America.

After a few years, Hitler dies and "moderate" Nazis (now there's an interesting coupling of words) *reach out to the international community. Forgive and forget.*

By 1997, I would assume, the mayor of Bullhead City could fly into Hermann Goering International Airport, drive past Dr. Mengele Memorial Hospital and be warmly greeted in our sister city of Dachau.

Anyway, I'm ashamed that I'm so old fashioned and that I have such a hard time understanding modern alliances. I'm sure our political leaders are doing their best for our economic growth and that this Communist, Capitalist merger will work well for the future of Bullhead City.

I can just picture how grand the Communist Chinese flag will look flying high over Bullhead City Tiananmen Square Administration Complex while Mayor Norm Hicks, standing bravely with his hands on his hips in front of a Communist tank, states loudly to the commander, "Did you bring Visa or American Express?"

This column didn't thrill the mayor that much. And, following 26 more years of U.S. foreign policy, it looks like old Norm was a pioneer whose ideas would fit very comfortably with those of the Biden Administration.

You know you're a redneck if...

Dec. 7, 1997

You know you're a redneck if you disagree with the mayor.

Jeff Foxworthy could get a laugh out of that line only if he used it in Bullhead City.

In a recent column I attempted to understand the logic of Bullhead City Mayor Norm Hicks' proposal to name Weinan City in the People's Republic of China as a sister city. True to the political dinosaur that I am, I was unable to grasp the mayor's reasoning. And from the calls that I have received, I'm not alone.

Apparently the mayor didn't care for the reaction he received to his announcement. At Tuesday's Bullhead City Council meeting, Hicks blasted his critics for engaging in "redneckism." He labeled the criticism as the result of "small-town mentality" from a small but vocal group of people who don't know the facts. He pointed to the hurt caused by remarks about certain ethnic groups.

I've heard from several people, including many veterans who fought with and for the Chinese people in World War II, and the South Vietnamese and South Korean people in our later wars. And I haven't heard any ethnic remarks at all. The common theme of all the criticism of his sister-city proposal is not against the people of China, but against the government of the People's Republic of China.

Hicks pointed out that the United States has accepted other former enemies, such as Japan, into our society. Now stop me if I'm wrong, but didn't Japan have to sign an unconditional surrender before acceptance?

The mayor also credits the transformation of the former Soviet Union to Washington's leadership rather than bullets or sarcastic remarks. Score one for the mayor on that issue. I will be the first to admit that my sarcastic remarks concerning the Soviet Union had nothing to do with its political collapse (although I do remember some readers of my political cartoons of that era remarking that I should have been silenced). The failure of the Communist system led to the demise of that particular brutally oppressive government labeled by our Washington leadership as the "Evil Empire."

Do the mayor's remarks about the Soviet Union mean that he plans to use his leadership to topple the Red Chinese government? Will his Bullhead City foreign policy become the liberator of many millions of Asians from their murderous masters? Should we look forward to seeing Norm Hicks standing in front of the Great Wall of China yelling, "Mr. Zemin! Tear down this wall!"? If so, I'm sure the Pentagon, not to mention a few doctors at the Happy Dale Funny Farm, will be interested in his plans.

Once again, I want to point out that it just may be my lack of culture that is keeping me from getting on the mayor's bandrickshaw. After all, he seems to be acting in complete harmony with President Clinton and Vice President Gore.

However, until I fully understand the mayor's motives, I personally oppose any economic deals with Communist governments (as I always have no matter who was at the helm in Washington). I will be looking forward to the informational meeting that Hicks promised would enlighten those of us who need to "broaden our horizons."

So, Norm, if you see me and my old yeller dawg ridin' around in my 1986 Dodge pickup truck with the shotgun in the window, y'all just holler, now hear?

It always amazed me that some folks think that "redneck" is a bad word they can use to label someone they think is less enlightened than them. While growing up on a farm, I soon learned that those of us who worked outside had red necks. The term really refers to hard-working people, folks who are self-reliant and blessed with common sense, unlike the "enlightened" ivory-tower types who look down on us.

Sister city stopped; City secrets snitch sought

Dec. 18, 1997

Bullhead City Mayor Norm Hicks deserves congratulations for hearing and responding to the will of the people.

Hicks withdrew his proposal for a sister-city relationship with Weinan City, China, Tuesday after hearing and reading a variety of negative reactions over the last few weeks. Most of that reaction, including my own, was against forming an alliance with a city governed by a Communist dictatorship, and then later against statements made labeling opponents to his proposal as engaging in "redneckism."

Hicks apologized, sort of, by saying, "As to other comments I supposedly made, many of which were presented inaccurately, I can only say that if I said anything to hurt anyone's feelings, I am sorry and it wasn't my intention."

This statement sounds suspiciously like the traditional political remark of "I didn't say that and I'll never say it again." But whatever the intention, the outcome was a victory for the pro-democracy crowd. Many people used their constitutional right to speak their minds on the proposal and the mayor responded.

Just think. If we lived in the People's Republic of China, those of us who disagreed would have been eliminated. Of course, on the other hand, that may have created an increase in organs made available for transplant throughout the world.

As for having given the key to the city to Chinese "businessmen" from Weinan City, that's all in the past. We can't ask them to return it. Let's just change the locks.

At the same Council meeting, Councilman Damian Holther discussed the recent controversy of information "leaks" concerning the city. In particular, he mentioned stories concerning recent city firings and resignations (such as the one written by reporter Heidi Wissler that appeared in the Nov. 23 edition of the *Mohave Valley Daily News*). Holther went on to say that he understood the right of the media to protect sources, but putting out information considered to be confidential is in effect "aiding and abetting" an unlawful act. Holther suggests anyone who receives such information should be willing to step forward.

I'd just bet the farm that Richard Nixon would have agreed with Damian Holther on this issue. If Nixon was on the Bullhead City Council, I'm sure, once he read Wissler's story, he probably would have **also** had some of his cohorts, such as John Dean, John

Ehrlichman and H.R. Haldeman, conference call and attempt to get the reporter to reveal her sources.

I also wonder if Holther is suggesting the *Washington Post* was "aiding and abetting" an unlawful act by utilizing tips which led to the linking of the Nixon White House to the Watergate Hotel burglary.

As to the subject of sources, all newspapers rely on off-the-record tips to get on-the-record stories. I suggest those people with questions reread Wissler's story "City personnel turnover called 'little more than average.'" Every statement reported is attributed to an on-the-record source. Bullhead City Personnel Manager Mike Callahan is quoted; then Councilman Damian Holther (wasn't it Pogo who said "We have met the enemy and he is us"?) makes a statement; City Clerk Pat Nichols went on the record, as did Assistant City Manager Robert Schaumleffel.

Every councilman, every politician, has said things to the press that they ask be kept off the record. Sometimes it's only something like "(name deleted) is an idiot, but that's off the record," or they call and ask to be kept off the record before blasting a certain editor or reporter or attempt to persuade the press not to cover a certain issue. Does Holther suggest that anytime someone talks to the press off the record that we step forward and expose the person and his/her statements? And does he mean that we should step forward publicly or go to the city politicos behind closed doors to expose evil tipsters? Do our city leaders really want a "report on the city, go to jail" law?

Politicos and bureaucrats usually only like news coverage that makes them look like a combination of Douglas MacArthur and Mother Teresa. Anything less is suspect. The press really doesn't care whether a councilmember's quote makes him/her look wise or stupid. If we cared, we'd be city public relations people. We only care that we get the quote or story as accurate as possible. Readers will make the value judgments.

The present "problem" the city has with keeping secrets seems to be an exercise in paranoia. The city government works for the people. What is it they don't want the boss to know?

Although the mayor publically backed off from his pro-Commie foreign policy, he privately told me he should have replaced the word "redneck" with "bigot!" I laughed at him, knowing full well he still felt he had been justified in being a "collaborator."

As for the Nixon reference, like a lot of us, I complained about President Nixon back in the late 1960s and early '70s. My complaints were all about his lack of blowing Hanoi off the map, his Administration's horrible mistake of negotiating with North Vietnam and his unforgivable act of making friends with Red China.

Biker ticketing not a federal case

September 19, 2003

Who overreacted? Bullhead City police who pulled over a large number of bikers or the bikers themselves in claiming they are being picked on?

We have all seen large groups of motorcyclists (usually during the annual Laughlin River Run) continue to go through a red light as if they were soldiers marching with road guards posted. This is a crime. No matter how many bikers ride in a group, they must individually obey the traffic signals.

Did the officer who allegedly armed himself with an M-16 do the right thing? Maybe – maybe not.

It is interesting to me that so many bikers who belong to groups have adopted images right out of Hollywood Central Casting. Many have expressed their individuality by conforming to movie bad-guy stereotypes. As Americans, they certainly have the right to look like anyone or anything they like.

What is confusing is when a 250-pound, pony-tailed, bearded man with skulls all over his leathers and a spider tattooed on his neck complains that he is being picked on. Peter Fonda would not be pleased.

If one looks, walks and squawks like a duck, one shouldn't be surprised if a duck hunter thinks one is a duck.

Now, if I was the lone cop who pulled over 50 patch-wearing tattooed mountains on Harleys, I probably would want to be armed with an M-16, an M-79 grenade launcher, four white-phosphorus grenades and a radio to call in a Napalm strike if one of them looked cross eyed. (Of course, I have said the same thing about dealing with panhandlers, graffiti sprayers and attorneys.)

As for the many light-running traffic tickets given out, the bikers can simply go to court and deny breaking the law. It really is up to the judge, not the Bullhead City Council, whether the ticketing was legitimate or not.

Of course, it would certainly be nice if all of the bikers who did run the light would take responsibility and tell the judge the truth. With mass honesty like that, I'm sure the judge would dismiss charges against the innocent.

I ride a Harley, probably a little more cautiously these days than a deer in lion country. That is because I hit the ground a few too many times in the 1960s. I was also pulled over by cops in the South and in California during those years not quite as many times as

Freddy has appeared in Nightmare movies. I have to admit that every one of those cops treated me better than I deserved at the time. That's because they were just doing their jobs and upholding the law. I was the one who was going too fast or doing some other stupid thing.

Police officers are just doing their jobs today when they pull us over or write tickets. As well as the occasional honest driver who makes a mistake, they deal with meth users, drunks, thieves and bums every day. Cops died saving lives on 9/11. Cops risk their lives daily to protect the rest of us.

They have a rough job with a lot of difficult in-the-field decisions to make. They deserve our support.

Another thing I remember about the sixties is a saying that "if you don't like the cops, next time you need help, call a hippie!" That goes for bikers as well.

There has always been a lot of anti-police rhetoric bubbling forth from individuals and groups for a variety of reasons. Sometimes complete law enforcement agencies have been the target of attacks from politicians, activists, college professors, reverends, transients, fruitcakes, rock groups and rappers. But now, in the 2020s, we've seen what it is like to be without law enforcement. The combination of Defund the Police movements and Soros DAs have turned once beautiful cities into crime-ridden hobo jungles. Back the Blue.

Does Pacific northwesterner have a future in Bullhead City politics?

November 21, 2002

Many major celebrity sightings have been reported in Bullhead City over recent years — Pamela Anderson, Tiny Tim, Robert Blake — but none have had the impact of the recent report that Bigfoot was seen crossing Highway 95.

A short article that appeared a few weeks ago in the *Daily News* reports the alleged incident. Another edition of the newspaper had a picture of two Bigfoot trackers, Will Wicklund and Brad Mortensen, who stopped by the Bullhead City Police Department to check on any other Bigfoot information available. (Would the creature have a rap sheet?) One of these guys, appropriately, looked a little like Indiana Jones.... if Wilfred Brimley was portraying that character.

I grew up near what was a small farming and logging town in Northern California (Redding) during the 1950s and early '60s. And during that time it was quite common to read the latest Bigfoot report in the local daily newspaper. Usually a logger, who may have spent too much time in the Cascades singing about the bottles of beer on the wall, would report a big, hairy ape-like monster had crossed the firebreak or logging road in front of him. The descriptions ranged from giant gorilla to spittin' image of the Hamm's Beer bear.

No proof was ever found of the existence of this creature, except for a few possibly faked footprints. Yet it was always fun to read about the latest alleged encounter.

I understand that, after the environmentalists put the loggers out of business and the pot growers took over the mountains around Redding, the reports became more imaginative. But those folks probably had more monster and alien sightings than Buffy the Vampire Slayer.

Anyway, if there really is a Bigfoot, why would the big hairy resident of the Pacific Northwest suddenly show up in Arizona's hottest destination? Is he nearing retirement age and finding wet winters of the Cascades a bit too much? Is he going to be a full-time resident or only a simian snowbird? What kind of RV does a Bigfoot drive?

Perhaps the creature is planning on spending his golden years here in Bullhead City compiling a Yetish-English dictionary. He could still make a few bucks doing local television and radio commercials as a spokescreature for Purina Pet Chow.

And, if he has established residency properly, he could join the race to become Bullhead City mayor. Wouldn't the debates be fun? I'd be interested in how the almost mythical, reclusive Bigfoot might react to allegations of government secrecy from the legendary Great White attorney candidate. That particular race is already interesting with the two presently involved having about the same relationship with each other that the mayor and the shark did in the movie "Jaws."

On the positive side, if Bigfoot's campaign started to fall a little behind, he could be his own Rally Monkey.

Then again, Bigfoot could be a little too sensitive for Bullhead politics. After all, Bullhead City politics was once considered for a spot in the Olympics as an audience participation blood sport. BF would have to make sure he was not too cozy with the good ol' boys and at the same time avoid being improperly thought of as a union organizer (hint: leave the club at home).

Would old BF support building a dog park in the city? If he did, he would have to assure residents that he would not use it as his own personal dessert buffet. He would also have to promise to serve a full term and not resign to accept a place on the ballot as a candidate for Vice President in Ross Perot's next campaign.

Another question would be: How could any big, hairy, foul-smelling creature who grunts and growls gather enough monetary support to run a campaign for office? Answer: The same way they did in the last election — Clean Elections.

To avoid the destruction of his political efforts, BF would have to be very careful in what he says during media interviews. He would have to be concise and avoid discussing certain topics. For instance, if he says he does not believe in unidentified flying objects, there are those who would probably blast him as an unenlightened, closed-minded, establishment Republican.

Now that I think about it, for his own safety and sanity, old Bigfoot probably should hightail it back to the redwoods as soon as possible.

Quite often a simple day of news coverage would lead to a flight of column fantasy. Linking Bigfoot sightings to local politics is quite silly but therapeutic to this editor who also dealt with wild and wooly campaigns and the daily business of elected officials.
It's best to laugh, because the alternative is not healthy.

9. Random Thoughts

From the last half of 2005 through 2012 I became a spokesman (public information director) for the unelected departments of Mohave County, Ariz. Being a government flack was unique for me, in that I was able to observe from the inside how the county operated. During that time, I wrote AP-style news releases concerning county department personnel, actions and services. However, sometimes when the county was publicly attacked by unethical political activists or officials, I was able to communicate a point of view a few times with proposed guest columns and cartoons, all approved by my boss, the county manager.

My belief is that government information should be released in journalistic style with full attribution so folks will understand who makes which statements. I also believe that opinion columns and editorial cartoons are governmental communication tools the same as standard press releases. It's just that most public information officers don't have those skills in their tool kits. I still do not understand why some congressmen or senators haven't thought of drawing their own editorial cartoons to respond to newspaper artists. Surely some elected officials must have that talent.

Luckily, I worked for a very experienced and ethical county manager who wouldn't buckle to threats from those who wanted to use county personnel, funds and properties for improper activities. That manager and all three supervisors were Republicans who didn't believe in wasting constituents' tax dollars. The law, being very specific about what county officials can and cannot do, was the guide we all followed in our actions.

Sometimes the county came under attack over issues and actions. When those attacks were found to contain legitimate viewpoints, the Board of Supervisors would work to solve the issues. But, often, attacks came from dark corners of society that may have been coordi-

nated by a cloaked power group with hidden political agendas. We usually held fire and didn't respond to wacky activist allegations except in extreme situations where we believed a tongue-in-cheek guest column would communicate logic to the residents so they would fully understand an issue or action.

Some of the following are examples from that time period.

The first is from 2006 and deals with a flamboyant state senator who, with the help of another senator and two pigs as props, held what I'm sure he considered an entertaining press conference regarding taxes. He didn't, however, consider any of the opposition responses, including this column, entertaining.

Local control under fire from pig-totin' senators

Arizona Republican State Sen. Ron Gould considers Mohave County services as a "trough" and those who value those same services as "piggies." This senator, known for flying his Confederate flag at his Lake Havasu City home, must see himself as the last of the mountain rebels who wants to make those who disagree with him squeal like a piggy. Ned Beatty, watch out!

Gould and his pig-totin' partner, Sen. Jack Harper, each recently rented a pig to squire to a press conference. As they both walked the red carpet with their hired escorts, they told the throng of reporters that they are strong tax-cutters. And, although their dates were probably embarrassed by the senators' behavior, Gould and Harper were able to pose for glamour shots while getting their chops in against county governments and anyone who opposed their dictates.

This is the same Sen. Harper who attempted to get one million tax dollars to build a culvert in an area of Hackberry, in Mohave County, where it wasn't needed. Mohave County Supervisor Pete Byers said, "I know that area and, for the life of me, I can't figure out why a million-dollar culvert needs to be built where it would benefit just a couple of residents who have another road to use if flooding occurs. This is not Harper's district. Why is this self-proclaimed 'tax cutter' looking to spend a million tax dollars in someone else's district where it isn't needed? That doesn't seem kosher to me."

I understand that, during the senators' press conference, one of the pigs actually delivered an opposing view on Sen. Harper's jacket.

It's amazing how our senator from Mohave County can go to Phoenix, team up with the Maricopa crowd and campaign against local control of his home district and in opposition to the 55 county supervisors from across the 15 Arizona counties. And that's just what Gould is doing. He is pandering to the Type 1 businesses – mining, gas, utilities and oil companies – by supporting the mislabeled "Truth in Taxation" proposal. This bill, championed by the Arizona Tax Research Association (ATRA) and other lobbyists for big corporations, is a huge gift of hundreds of thousands of dollars to those same companies, who are themselves responsible for much of the inflationary pressures on homeowners, while placating homeowners with approximately $10 a year each off of their property taxes.

If our legislators were really interested in fairness to homeowners and small businesses, they would target property tax relief to seniors and other Arizona citizens who really need it.

We understand why a legislative cabal from the Great State of Maricopa wants to dictate to the rural parts of the state – because they can. They have the numbers; they have the dollars; they have the huge growth in businesses, jobs, residents and homes. They also want that growth to continue, and to do that, they want to stop competing growth in rural areas and centralize all of the resources and political power under one roof at the Capitol.

Great balls o' fire, Sen. Gould! What part of your Articles of the Confederacy tells you to build a strong centralized government at the expense of rural areas?

We understand the conservative concepts of limited government and fiscal restraint. But Gould and company are sending a message that local government, and public schools, cannot be trusted while only his Politburo, I mean Legislature, can make decisions.

Mohave County government is looking at ways to hold down homeowners' property tax burden and has supported several proposals. But we want to target it to homeowners, not oil companies. One such proposal, which was ignored by Gould and the majority of the Legislature, was for the state to stop taking so many county tax dollars to support state-mandated, state-managed programs. This year alone, the state is taking more than $10 million county dollars for its Arizona Health Care Cost Containment System/Arizona Long Term Care System (AHCCCS/ALTCS) programs. They have increased that amount by an average of 16 percent per year. It seems the state Legislature leadership increases the size of state programs and pays for them by taking more and more county tax dollars. No wonder the state commissars want to dismantle what's left of local control.

God only knows why Gould has turned against his rural constituents in favor of the Maricopa County power structure. We know that most rural representatives end up being impotent against the big-city power mongers, but at least they could put up a little fight for their constituents. Perhaps promises of committee leadership positions have him bowing to the Maricopa Mecca. One wonders what has been slopped in *his* trough.

I believe if rural Arizona residents take a good close look at Gould and friends' TNT proposal of corporate welfare for mining and oil interests and their continued lack of support for homeowners, small businesses and public schools, they might just "ditto" the editorial statement that one of the pigs did on Harper's jacket.

The attached cartoon depicting Lake Havasu City resident State Senator Ron Gould along with state Sen. Jack Harper accompanied the proposed guest column to a variety of publications. Gould didn't care for it either. Oddly enough, Gould is currently a Mohave County Supervisor.

I was able to get my point across on other more-general issues through a bit of sarcasm once in a while. Such is the case with the following proposed guest columns. They landed in a limited number of publications.

Government issues change with the times

While attending Mohave County Board of Supervisors meetings, I find the many subjects the Board deals with quite interesting as well as the variety of public input offered by individuals.

For instance, any agenda item with the word "water," "development," "tax," "budget" or "polygamy" will bring out a variety of people who want to bring their views before the supervisors. Speakers range from developers seeking a change, to competing developers, nearby landowners, out-of-state investors, activists and concerned individuals.

Some public input is exceptionally helpful to the elected officials while some is lacking in expertise and may even be way off base or abusive. Interesting issues always seem to bring about unique discussions and sometimes surprising media attention.

Mohave County has been around since 1864 and, I would think, has had many newsworthy Board meetings during that time. I wonder how civil those early meetings were. Although there were no video cameras, internet streaming of meetings or use of Tupperware and toilet-paper rolls to help communicate points of view back then, I'm sure those meetings were just as interesting as today's – in some cases, probably more interesting.

Recently I took a cursory look at some of the Board actions from the middle 20th Century. Political correctness has certainly changed as well as what is socially acceptable.

One document is credited to have come from the County Board of Health in 1923. According to present-Clerk of the Board Barbara Bracken (she wasn't around in 1923), no signed document or recorded minutes exist to prove the proposed resolution made it to the Board of Supervisors or was ever put into effect.

The document states, "…it is made the duty of the County Board of Health to prosecute diligently any and all violations of the criminal statutes relating to offenses against public health and safety…. any person found spitting or expectorating on any sidewalk or stairway, or in and about any public building or public gathering place in the Town of Kingman, will be arrested and prosecuted to the full extent of the law."

This could have been the launch of an Old West version of MCTUPP (Mohave County Tobacco Use Prevention Program). Obviously, in those days, tobacco-chewin' cowpokes needed a little reining in.

Today's civilized society avoids smoking, drinking and cursing "on any sidewalk or stairway, or in and about any public building, or public gathering place" in Kingman and elsewhere. Behaving in such a manner today could bring a hefty fine. But in 1923, if McGruff the Crime Dog existed, I don't believe he would have needed to read anyone his or her rights before he took a bite out of tobacco-spittin' crime.

A sign-of-the-times resolution from 1946 recorded the Board of Supervisors acceptance of a generous donation from the Kingman Elks of a remodeling of the "West End of the Mohave County Hospital Veranda, making a room that is to be known as the 'Iron Lung Room.'" Although the Kingman Elks continue their generous community spirit, I hope the tragedies of Polio and donations of Iron Lung rooms stay in the ever-increasing distant past.

Resolution 137 and Ordinance 138 from December 4, 1950, recall another aspect of a simpler era. In 1950, American troops were fighting Communists in the Korean War. Mohave County Resolution 137 required every county employee to sign a pledge "that he is not now, nor has been within a period of three years preceding the signing of the affidavit, a member of the Communist Party or the Communist political association or any organization declared by the Attorney General of the United States to be subversive, nor is affiliated with, or supports any organization that believes in or teaches the overthrow of the Government of the United States, either by force or any illegal or unconstitutional means."

Ordinance 138 requires "every person over the age of 21 residing in Mohave County, Arizona, on January 1, 1951, either permanently or temporarily, who then is or within a period of three years preceding said date has been a member of the Communist Party," and/or all those other things stated above, "is hereby required within ten days from and after said date to register with the Sheriff of Mohave County…"

Those Commies were given three days to register or face $100 fines "or imprisonment in the County Jail for a period of not to exceed 30 days, or both…"

That's a pretty simple concept to keep an eye on people who support the enemy in time of war and also keep them out of government jobs. In those days, Communist Party members, like American Nazi Party members, would not be trusted very far by their government coworkers and by the people they were supposed to serve. Come to think of it, those kinds of subversives shouldn't be trusted today. Of course, I could be a little bitter, since Communists did their best to off me in Vietnam.

I wonder what the public had to say about the local roundup of Reds during that December 1950 Board meeting. Oddly enough, Clerk Bracken said there is no record of Resolution 137 or Ordinance 138 ever being revoked.

Recently, some verbally active current residents are on a quest to "take back the government." Is this where they want to take it back to? Do they want to take it away from the "subversive" elements in our community? Or are these folks the subversives who, like the proletariat in the 1917 Russian Revolution, want to storm the seat of government and develop a "People's Republic?" Some want to override offices elected by the majority. Many don't want to pay taxes and yet they are living on government checks and demanding free government services. In 1950, these folks would have been on a list.

The question then comes up as to whom these people might designate as subversives if they take power. Will they register the rest of us? Will they agree with Shakespeare on the worth of attorneys? Will they register members of the media, talk radio hosts and other conspiracy theorists? Worst of all, once they "take the government back," where will they put the tobacco-spittin' bloggers?

That one was just a fun look back at our history. Yet, if Commies were still (rightfully) considered anti-American and they had to be on a list, it would have certainly simplified U.S. Rep. Eric Swalwell's dating activities and saved him a lot of ridicule.

Mayor Hakim bites the only hand that feeds Bullhead City seniors

Bullhead City Mayor Jack Hakim engaged in more mincing, prancing and profiling during Tuesday's City Council meeting than Joel Grey's performance as the Master of Ceremonies in the musical "Cabaret."

Mohave County Supervisor Tom Sockwell and Department of Public Health Director Patty Mead attended the meeting to clarify some misinformation concerning the County Senior Program that Hakim and local attorney Steve Moss have been touting throughout the community. Unfortunately, it was obvious from the beginning of the meeting that the county representatives were there to be ambushed by Hakim, who never let a fact get in the way of an attack.

It was made clear early in the meeting by Hakim and Councilman Sam Medrano that it was going to be a bash Mohave County night when the Council approved the agreement with the Fort Mojave Indian Tribe to provide jail space at a lower cost than Mohave County. Medrano said the County wouldn't work with the City on lowering the fees for housing City criminals. In other words, they were upset because the County wasn't going to make property taxpayers pick up the City's costs.

Mohave County applauds the Tribe for the entrepreneurial spirit to come up with a lower-cost alternative for the City. The County will also save money by not housing the City's bad guys because the cost of housing each inmate in the County Jail is actually more than the charge amount the mayor and councilman were whining about.

Hakim then decided it was time to attack Mohave County Manager Ron Walker. Hakim seemed to think it was an outrage that someone who is unelected should criticize an elected official of his eminence. He also questioned whether Walker had written the guest column that questioned Hakim's attack on the County for not spending more property tax dollars on a program where Hakim funds nothing. Ron Walker has several college degrees including two master's degrees and many years of budgeting experience with even larger entities than Mohave County. Ron Walker is certainly intelligent enough to write his own material. I'm not sure Hakim can put facts in order, though, in that his recent hissy fits are rather disjointed and quite embarrassing.

I am writing this column because I was appalled while witnessing the mayor's personal meltdown Tuesday night. Assisted by Moss, the discussion of County Senior Programs was a setup reminiscent of a 1950 House Un-American Activities Committee tribunal. Of course, Hakim has had a lot of practice at the Tri-City Tribunal, which has about the legitimacy of a press club/picnic society. Rather than learning from each other on how city issues are handled in the other cities, that organization tries to call county officials and staff before them to be lectured on how the Tribunal wants them to manage. "Are you or have you ever been a member of Mohave County?" I guess you can call that act "Hakimism."

For a second Council Meeting, Moss, chairman of the non-government, non-profit Bullhead City Senior Nutrition Site Council, gave a confusing statistical analysis not based in the real world on program funding. I wonder why the man has such a problem with County fiscal decisions and had nothing to say about a bad check for $2005 cashed against his Meals on Wheels by a former Site Council member to make a mortgage payment.

According to the Bullhead City Police Report, "On 08/24/10 at unknown hours.... K. (Kathy) Bruck discovered a large amount of money was taken from the savings account..." The report stated that the former Site Council member had made the withdrawal from a Bullhead City bank. Yet when confronted by police, that suspect denied making a withdrawal "from any account" and had "done no banking on their behalf during her tenure on the board." A bank employee who had supplied the police with a video of the transaction contacted the former Site Council member who "suddenly remembered obtaining a cashier's check for $2000 to pay her mortgage."

The police report states the money was paid back. Charges were not filed, but the report was forwarded to the Mohave County Attorney for review.

Could Moss and the Site Council be embarrassed by the fact that this happened on their watch? If he can't keep Meals on Wheels money safe from possible misuse, how can he lecture the agency that funds Senior Programs with the $396,426 grant and $250,000 of General Fund money, which is six times the necessary matching fund to get the grant?

Hakim pranced over in front of a news reporter with a congregate meal on a tray for his outraged photo-op denouncing the meal as not worth the suggested donation of $3. (I wonder if a senior showed up to the Center and wasn't able to get a meal because the mayor took it.) Mead explained to him that senior-meal menus are designated by the Western Arizona Council of Government (WACOG) dieticians, not the county. Like the other facts Mead offered, his eminence ignored that.

Mohave County takes care of Mohave County seniors, not Bullhead City. When times got tough and revenues dwindled, the county continued to fully fund that program for three years while the size of government shrank by more than 15 percent. This year, the county had to tighten this non-mandated program, but the three supervisors ensured the Meals on Wheels program would not shrink. Meals on Wheels participants go through an eligibility process with WACOG. They are the most vulnerable of our citizens.

I get a little ticked when government types who believe they know better how to spend other people's money just don't know when to stop lecturing. Besides Walker and Sockwell, the mayor also criticized Board of Supervisors Chairman Buster Johnson for not kissing his ring. I just wonder if the last time Hakim went on a junket to Washington, D.C., to schmooze with high-priced lobbyists, if President Obama named him Whining Czar. He puffed up, wrapped himself in the flag and told Supervisor Sockwell the County needs to do more for seniors and veterans.

The County is the only agency that takes care of Bullhead City seniors. As for Hollywood Hakim's right to talk down to real veterans, where was he when Sockwell was serving in the U.S. Army in Alaska and then working a long career building weapons delivery systems and surveillance satellites at Hughes Aircraft to defend America? Where was he when Johnson was serving in the U.S. Army in Korea followed by a career in law enforcement? Where was he when Ron Walker was serving two tours on aircraft carriers off the coast of Vietnam; on the U.S.S. Saratoga, whose air wing captured the Achille Lauro hijackers, and when they bombed Libyan terrorist Kaddafi? Navy Capt. Walker served more than 26 years in peacetime and war. Where was Ho Chi Hakim when I was on patrols and search-and-destroy missions in the Highlands of South Vietnam?

Perhaps he was hanging out in Hollywood with the Ozzy Osbourne crowd.

Mohave County is continuing to find ways to fund services in this tight economy because of the long-term planning of Walker and the Board of Supervisors. Wages and hiring were frozen in 2007 and a reorganization occurred, that Comrade Hakim doesn't understand, which streamlined the chain of command, eliminated redundancies and saved more than $550,000 per year. That was the deputy county manager-approach, which eliminated several budgeted positions and created a one-stop shopping for county permits. Bullhead City, on the other hand, came up flatfooted throughout the economic downturn with staff layoffs, pay cuts and furlough days to try and balance out its overspending.

Hakim needs to lighten up and realize when he attacks this agency, dishing it out, he better be able to take it as well. He should also learn that one does not have to be an "elected" official to respond to his blather.

And, the next time he behaves like Joel Grey's Master of Ceremonies from "Cabaret," he needs to sing about his own agency's "Money, Money, Money," not Mohave County property taxpayers' money.

Long-time Bullhead City Councilman and the Mayor Jack Hakim was not a fan of my cartoons and columns when I was at the newspaper. Many times he went to the publisher seeking to control coverage and silence the editor on the opinion page. Eventually, his successes led to my leaving the paper to join the county. I remember the last November (Thanksgiving) I worked at the paper when I had a reporter put together an article by asking all of the elected officials in the area what they were thankful for. Hakim's response was that he was thankful that Purcell wasn't allowed to draw cartoons anymore. I was surprised; at last an honest answer. Hakim obviously had a talent of gathering political influencers to assist his efforts to build political power.

'Moderate voice' touts incorrect information

Thursday's (July 22) *Kingman Miner* newspaper featured the creation of an organization that claims to be a "moderate voice for gun owners." Unfortunately, the group's first shot out of the barrel is a misfire.

The former editor of the now defunct *River Cities Business Journal* and publisher of the no longer viable MohaveBusiness.com, whose name was misspelled in the *Miner* article, was quoted concerning the newly formed Citizens Rights League of Mohave County. The self-anointed gun expert writes an occasional column for the *Miner*.

When it comes to interpreting the law, I recommend people listen to attorneys, not advocates. As we have been told from childhood on, ignorance is no excuse for breaking the law. In other words, if you follow the advice of an advocate and break the law, you will be held responsible.

Mohave County government has many well-educated, experienced attorneys who spend a lot of time in court prosecuting lawbreakers, defending clients and interpreting the law. Our chief civil attorney states the *Miner*'s gun guru is dispensing inaccurate information that could lead to the arrest of anyone who attempts to break the law by trying to sneak weapons into a county building.

I'm gonna pause this one right here, as I am a pro-2nd Amendment guy. At that time, the Board of Supervisors meetings had become increasingly outrageous with some advocates spouting threatening remarks during meetings and on a few online blogs. (One blogger claimed I wasn't worth "the powder to blow" me "to Hell!" Later, two supervisors, the County Manager and I each received letters containing a powdery substance. But that's another story.) County Manager Walker followed state law on how weapons should be secured to avoid a mass shooting or assassination attempt. According to the law, the Board had to put in manned metal detectors and individual lock-boxes to keep the weapons safe for their owners while they attended the meetings. Unfortunately, there were activists who wanted to bring their pistols, semi-automatic rifles and one pitchfork into the Board Chamber.

My internal remarks on the subject were to let them be armed, but also allow county employees the right to carry weapons in the facility. That didn't go over well. And the situation became a big political kerfuffle. Anyway, back to the guest column.

———————————— 99 ————

The *Miner* (did I spell that right?) reporter paraphrased the gun guru's remarks with, "State law does not give the county permission to search or screen everyone that enters the building, he said. And what about gun owners with concealed weapons permits? The permits are supposed to allow a resident to carry a gun into any public building that isn't secured...."

The guru cites jails and courthouses as examples of secured buildings and states that the County Administration Building is not a secured facility. Click! Misfire.

Our attorney's legal opinion is that the activist is spouting claptrap. Entering a public establishment with a deadly weapon after being requested to remove it and offered storage of same is misconduct involving a weapon *(state law)*. Public establishment is defined by law as "a structure, vehicle or craft that is owned, leased or operated by this state or a political subdivision of this state." It is not limited to "secured facilities."

The *Miner*'s gun guru wrote his legal opinion in one of his published columns early in June. He claimed at that time as well that, "the law cited at the County Administration Building will not allow county officials to force concealed weapons permit holders to relinquish their weapons."

I don't know if he wants local law-abiding folks, who may follow up on his advice, to get arrested or that he just believes that the laws are for other people. I do know that, back in March, this activist brought a gun and a pocketknife to the Admin Building to test the county's security efforts. He questioned the actions and demanded information, which was supplied by the county risk manager. According to the risk manager, he described himself as "working for the *Kingman Miner*." That caused me to wonder if any newspaper publisher or editor ever asked a reporter or freelance representatives to test the security efforts of a governor's office, bank, school or jail concerning deadly weapons. That instance and the advocate's full-page column that followed were not high points in local journalism.

The key here is all laws are to be followed by everyone. Mohave County will continue to follow and enforce the laws. Our security measures will include everything legally possible to ensure the safety of our citizens and employees. To do anything less would be unethical, ignorant and tantamount to accepting liability for the possibly violent actions of others.

And, we will continue to get our legal opinions from law school graduates who have passed the State Bar and have engaged in years of legal practice – and not from the *Miner*'s "moderate" gun guru.

This column made many of the unique individuals in the Kingman, Golden Valley area unhappy with me to the point that they labeled me a "liberal," of all things. I'll bet even Attila the Hun giggled.

The process is working

How many of us are so sure we are right that we would accept the bending or breaking of the law to achieve our desires?

There are extreme philosophies which will accept an "end justifies the means" act. In justifying such activity, some people may win a battle but will, in the long term, lose all credibility for themselves and their cause.

For instance, most businesses follow all regulations and are concerned about their products' impact on society as much as their profit margin. America's free enterprise system is, after all, responsible for much of our continuing technological advancement – and the better the product, the better the profit. Of course, there are some unethical human beings, so every now and then a business owner, manager or employee will be arrested for illegal activities such as fraud, theft or illegally dumping dangerous materials.

In the same category, most people who consider themselves "environmentalists" are concerned individuals who want to protect wildlife and our natural resources. However, some "environmentalists" will also break the law through violent acts such as tree spiking, SUV burning or attacking someone for wearing fur, among others.

And, as we have all become so painfully aware in recent years, there is a small percentage of religious leaders who truly do not have a prayer.

The bottom line is the old cliché, "Your right to swing your fist ends at my nose." The law protects and serves all of us and no one is justified in breaking the law. Our democratic republic system has many avenues of changing laws some people may consider intrusive, individually punitive, ineffective or just wrong. One only needs a majority to agree with him or her to make changes. At the same time, our Constitution protects us all from having majorities take away our individual civil rights.

I assume readers by now understand I am a believer in the American system of rights, laws and justice. And, most importantly, I know the value of our right to free speech.... even very unpopular speech. Some people even use this right to, publicly, advocate criminal actions. I find such attempts to subvert our freedoms as distasteful, but an acceptable necessary evil of our system.

Before World War II, some Americans opposed going to war against Nazi Germany. In fact, the American Nazi Party was quite large prior to our entry into that conflict. And although most of those Americans crawled back into the woodwork during the war, that organization still openly spouts hate today, as do many other racist groups. Many Americans opposed the Korean and Vietnam wars for a variety of reasons. Some actually supported the Communist enemy during those years. Once again, these are illustrations of people using their First Amendment right to free speech to support those who would not only silence the rest of us, but would probably have exterminated the rest of us.

If we Americans choose to silence stupid or evil people just because of their words, where would we draw the line? Therefore, we must tolerate sometimes-hateful rhetoric.

The overwhelming examples of the benefits of freedom tremendously outweigh the irritation of those who misuse it. Because of our acceptance of diverse values and expressions, America is the birthplace of many great innovations. Our libraries contain the treasures of free thought. From unique and thoughtful political perspectives and historic references to creative fictional scenarios and some just downright wastes of ink, we have freedom of choice in our literature. America's theatrical and other artistic endeavors also have had no limits to creativity. Although some complain, Americans presently enjoys jazz, rock 'n' roll and a myriad of motion picture and live theater choices as well as the ability to applaud or curse editorial cartoons without setting anything on fire.

We have all read the ongoing reports of economic growth in Mohave County. Some developers are working very hard to build "master-planned" communities and some people are working very hard to stop them. In the middle is the lawful process that will not lean in either direction.

Mohave County and the State of Arizona have checkpoints all along the road to development: mandated public hearings, permits, inspections, and commission and board approval. Officials look at the viability of a development site; onsite infrastructure needs and all access needs to the site; environmental necessities; water allocation; code compliance and the developers' insurance liability, personal background and possible motives.

Public hearings are held all along that road to allow developers to present their projects to the public, the public to offer suggestions and value judgments and the press to have access to every possible document and statement involved. Permits and inspections are continuing. Water allocations are being sought. County and state requirements must be met.

In an effort to further their dictates, some "activists" are making hateful allegations, some quite slanderous, against those officials involved in the process. Although, officials are "public" and therefore open to harsh criticism, so are activists who continually attack all those except their own sycophants. Many of these people have Internet blogs with a history of that kind of hateful rhetoric. I was very surprised by one local activist's blogs that included attacks against Christians, the President, and the war and had harsh words for just about everyone except Saddam Hussein.

And I applaud her use of her First Amendment rights. She certainly offers her opinions and I found them to be very enlightening on her possible motivation for attacking lawful processes.

The bottom line is, people are offering their views on all sides and officials and, hopefully, those same people are listening. The law is being followed; the process is working; and, in the end, most participants will still have their integrity.

This is the last of my governmental flack attempts to explain processes and services to the public.
I'm glad I don't have to do that anymore.

The 2012 election brought change to Mohave County, Ariz. With that change, I retired before the new order took office. That governing agency took on a new focus with unique "ideals." Leaving my position did not, however, end my desire to make my, now extremely, politically incorrect positions clear. The first private-citizen guest column appeared in a couple of local weeklies.

A New Order takes charge at Mohave County
January 2013

Former Prime Minister Winston Churchill once said, "Never in the field of human conflict was so much owed by so many to so few." In reference to the recent Mohave County General elections, Never in the field of local politics were so few, with so little credibility, responsible for doing so much TO so many.

To be specific, I have to compliment a small gaggle of wactivists who, through a variety of measures, were extremely successful in their political endeavors during that recent election. These folks (let's just call them the Golden Valley Mensa Society) were not encumbered with college degrees or career experience. Yet they were able to frame the political discussion with what they called "horse sense" (I called horse manure).

They created issues that didn't exist and successfully campaigned on them. 1. Guns weren't an issue until nut jobs held an armed protest on county grounds. That confrontation led to the reaction they wanted for their campaign. 2. Senior nutrition services were not a problem until a mayor and his protégé spouted bogus statistics and outrage, thus fabricating another issue. 3. They repeated the false claim that four years of county property tax decreases were actually increases. 4. The wactivists alleged conflicts of interest regarding county employees, yet their own human failings went unquestioned.

This Mensa group is not new to political activism in that anyone who gets within a few feet of these folks knows they are committed to water conservation.

I don't have to go on as you have all read the wactivists' side of things in certain local publications. And although I find their behavior ludicrous, I do have to give credit where it is deserved. Their slapstick activities, which, if filmed, would have made the Ritz Brothers walk out of a theater in disgust over the lowbrow conduct, were successful in getting their slate of new supervisors (a new majority) elected to the Mohave County Board.

Now, 2013 is well underway and the new Board members have already started paying the activists back for their efforts.

The first order of business was to bestow the county Board's first "Call to the Public," in which anyone can step up before the elected body (on video) and make the supervisors aware of important issues such as a federal government conspiracy to poison Golden Valley residents through the use of commercial jumbo jets; the use of Unidentified Flying Objects (UFOs) to spy on certain wactivists' homes; the 75 cents per year one mother pays for the county Television District tax that is forcing her out of her home; visitors must have the right to carry pitchforks, machetes, bayonets and other tools they deem necessary into the county facilities at any time; and a prize should be awarded to the visitor wearing the funniest hat at each Board meeting.

Bullhead City Mayor Jack Hakim is garnering a lot of the political payback for his support. Bullhead elected two supervisors, although one claims to represent unincorporated areas south of that burg. These two self-proclaimed "fiscal conservatives" have already given that city the senior nutrition building, thus saving Bullhead the dollar-a-year lease. The mayor is delighted to save the dollar at a large cost to county taxpayers. He is also pleased that he is being promised a bigger amount of Flood District dollars to be taken from areas such as Fort Mohave, Mohave Valley and, believe it or not, Golden Valley.

Hakim is appropriately being rewarded for his coalition with the Mensa team. As a former recording industry promoter, he took then-candidates Steve Moss and Hildy Angius under his wing and mentored them like he did in the old days with upcoming musical talent. Hakim was as successful in controlling the media to his and the candidates' benefit as he was as a young man building careers for such luminaries as Ruth Etting, Russ Columbo and Joe Penner. It's said that Hakim was first noticed by the Victor Talking Machine Company when he allegedly uttered the now-legendary statement, "Lose the megaphone, Rudy."

The two "conservative" Bullhead supervisors seem to be joined at the hip with Hakim (who not that many years ago endorsed Janet Napolitano for governor) and don't seem to have any problem with his attempt to increase city taxes by 50 percent.

Having already mentioned Winston Churchill, I now predict that, very much like another former British prime minister, Moss will, following a short period of payback, be pictured in the local newspapers waving a piece of paper and announcing that he has achieved "peace in our time" with Mayor Hakim.

"Broomhildy" Angius spent a good part of her campaign on a witch-hunt for "corruption." Her vitriolic allegations were only surpassed by her outrage when the facts illustrated she was full of beans. She may have made more traction with her allegations of conflicts of interest had she practiced by looking into the recent leadership of the Republican Central Committee. Had she given a hard look at the internal behavior of some officials and members of that outfit prior to the Primary Election, she may have met the enemy and had a Pogo-epiphany.

But she has branded herself as a MUAC (Mohave Unangius Activities Committee) corruption fighter and I'm sure she will continue her witch-hunts.

Now, all potential conflicts of interest for county personnel are to be placed in individual folders, which is probably a good thing. That can help keep the public perception of conflict out of all issues. For instance, I'll bet all those civil cases (found on the court website) involving attorney Moss will be placed in his conflict folder, as he certainly shouldn't be voting on issues involving developers and businesses he has represented or opposed in court. And although his own words concerning conflict perceptions are coming back to haunt him already on his office building lease from campaign donors, I'm sure it was just an unnoticed error on his part. Of course, in voting on court issues as a whole, the fact that two of his former law-firm partners are now Superior Court judges certainly leaves the impression of conflict.

With all of the Planning and Zoning and court issues that come before the Board of Supervisors, Moss may have to abstain from a lot of votes. I'm sure, though, that he could keep busy during meetings by handing out his business cards to chemtrail advocates who slip and fall in the Board Auditorium.

The wactivists and their candidates parlayed very little except noise into real success. So congratulations to the victors and their entourage. I will continue to watch as they redefine county government. And I can't wait to see what the New Order will bring.

The following cartoon depicting all of the supervisors, the above-mentioned mayor and a gaggle of local activists was sent to the media along with this column. It is noted that they were published in two weeklies. But not one of the dailies, including my former publication, wanted to rock that boat. And, noted, after a few years former attorney Moss resigned his supervisor position to be named a judge of the Mohave County Superior Court.

Son of a gun if that didn't feel good. Anyway, here are a few more somewhat cynical, critical views concerning news events and issues from recent years that I found needed a touch of pot stirring.

No more assassins!
June 2017

It's been a week since Socialist-Democrat James Hodgkinson shot Republican U.S. House Majority Whip Steve Scalise, among others, on a baseball practice field not far from the U.S. Capitol. And we've had the usual demands from the left that guns were responsible and more anti-gun legislation is needed – in spite of the fact that none of the targeted Republican officials were armed.

Others have decried the current climate of "hate" coming from whatever side they aren't on politically. The Left believes that any traditional-value statements conservatives make are actually genocidal, homophobic, racist, etc. The Right sees the violent protests in Berkeley and other places as a Communist, Fascist, anti-democratic rebellion. Add in the death threats that many elected officials have been receiving, and it becomes quite difficult to see any softening of the rhetoric and attempts to find middle ground.

Many of these folks are the people who have yet to accept they lost the 2016 presidential election. Even though they celebrated the prior President's statement that, "Elections have consequences," they deny the legitimacy of the current White House occupant. Therefore, they support a comedienne who posed with a fake bloody head that looked like their elected enemy, applaud an updated production of Julius Caesar where their hated President is slaughtered, and blame the 2nd Amendment for the attempted assassination of Republicans.

Even though nutcase Hodgkinson broke a hell of a lot of laws in his attempt at mass murder, the Leftists want more laws that restrict all of us from our rights of self-protection. That kind of thinking would pretty much ensures that future mass murderers will have sitting ducks for targets. It certainly wouldn't stop any killers from getting weapons. They don't obey laws.

Those on the Right think we have enough laws and that maybe we should be enforcing the current ones a little better. Illegal immigration comes to mind. But the Leftists say those laws don't matter. They want laws enacted that crack down on honest people, not illegal aliens and gang members. They blame guns and not shooters, especially if the shooters are proponents of their beliefs. I'm surprised they haven't demanded banning cars and trucks since fanatical Muslims are now using them to murder pedestrians.

This political schizophrenia needs to be cured. Are we or are we not a culture that believes in the Rule of Law? Shouldn't all laws be enforced equally? Whether guns, trucks, machetes or poisoned banana cream pies are used in an attempted assassination, shouldn't the killer or killers be personally blamed – and punished?

Which gets me to my point. Mass murder and assassination attempts are seriously insane, disgusting and illegal. I believe there should be a mandatory death sentence for such crimes. Capital punishment IS a deterrent, and certainly a one-hundred-percent cure for recidivism.

Normal people see these wacko perpetrators as nuts, but that doesn't mean they should be able to escape justice, like John Hinckley Jr. He shot President Reagan, yet he was found "not guilty by reason of insanity." He is now a free man. Arthur Bremer shot presidential candidate George Wallace, yet he also is now a free man. Manson-family weirdo Lynette "Squeaky" Fromme and garden-variety nut Sara Jane Moore tried to kill President Ford and, you guessed it, they're walking the streets today as well.

Skinhead mass murderer Jared Laughner, who shot U.S. Rep. Gabrielle Giffords and killed six other innocent people including a nine-year-old girl, is serving a life sentence in a prison medical center. Jew-hating Palestinian Sirhan Sirhan, who killed presidential candidate U.S. Sen. Robert Kennedy in 1968, is still in prison, but comes up for parole again in 2021. James Earl Ray, the man who murdered Martin Luther King, continued to breathe for 30 years after King was shot, until he died in prison.

Luckily, law enforcement terminated Hodgkinson. Otherwise, he would probably have slaughtered several of his Republican targets and then been sentenced to live out his life in prison, or worse, be eventually released to join Hinckley and others.

Now, I'm going to agree with the Left on a few things. In spite of the disgusting messages of the updated version of *Julius Caesar* as well as other anti-administration "works of art" and stupid protest-march slogans, our First Amendment protects even evil free speech. The "feel-the-Bern" Socialists and election-denier Hillaryists have every right to espouse their hate. Even that unfunny orange-haired woman has the right to pose with any fake body part she wants. Of course, consumers also have the right to stop purchasing items from her sponsors.

And our Second Amendment protects the rights of the rest of us to defend ourselves against crazy murderers who, for whatever reason, want to kill us.

As for the law, I believe it is time to say enough is enough to those who want to slaughter us. Attempted mass murder and attempted assassination should be restrictively labeled capital crimes with a mandated death sentence. There is no justification for such traitorous acts of terrorism. Perps should not be able to excuse their behavior because of their childhood, alleged social injustices, or voices from inside their heads.

Both the Left and the Right need to unite on this and say, no matter which side their targets stand, "No more Hinckleys, no more Sirhans, no more Laughners and no more Hodgkinsons!"

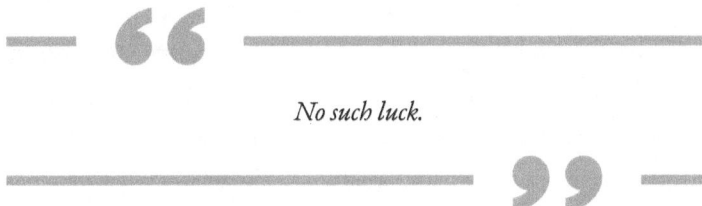

No such luck.

Is anybody else sick to death of terrorists?

June 2017

I find it amazing that western civilization now takes terrorist attacks in stride. In fact, those wacky Muslim extremists have pretty much been given the benefit of the doubt both before and during their deadly acts, thanks to politically correct news reporters and celebrities.

For instance, London has received its share of the Islamic extremist foreign policy over the last month. And even with our current instantaneous television coverage of such events, it takes hours before officials will label deadly assaults as terrorist acts. Wow! We see bridges being blocked off, police officers running toward a situation while civilians run in the opposite direction – some stopping to tell reporters of the death they witnessed. And the news crawl will explain that officials have yet to use the word "terrorism."

In such situations, it doesn't matter if it's Muslims with guns and knives celebrating Rama Lama Ding Dong, college millennials with Bill-Ayers-style nail bombs protesting a trimmed free-lunch menu or Canine Lives Matter activists sending cats with explosive vests into Korean lunch counters. Any deadly assaults against peaceful citizens going about their lives at ice cream parlors, rock concerts and tourist attractions are acts of terrorism. And those involved deserve the ultimate penalty, as do all who assist in their acts of war.

Now, I'm sure some of the folks at CNN would disagree with my take on the subject. But then again, if today were 1940, Joseph Goebbels would probably have his own show on that channel. They do try to keep their "independence" while behaving in an "unbiased" manner. Of course, unbiased can come off as unbalanced when a news pontificator attacks a democratically elected American President for saying nasty things about a form of government that won't allow women free speech, the ability to drive or speak their minds but does allow men to rape women (whether said victims are one or two of their wives or not), stone them to death for showing their faces and throw gay people off of buildings.

You'll notice I didn't add the part about Islamists videotaping the beheading of people for being American, Jewish, Christian or just not Muslim enough. That's because beheading is a sore subject these days. One over-the-hill "comedienne" with bottle-orange hair (and I'm not talking about Carrot Top) seems to think beheading is hilarious. And, of course, she believes it's a right-wing conspiracy that most people don't agree with her (other than a few leftist celebs and anchors who don't remember Daniel Pearl).

The Ayatollah Cockamamie-crowd hates everyone who doesn't kiss the rings on their unclean hands. Just like the Nazi SS concentration camp guards, their beliefs have no wiggle room. They want all of us dead. They consider us weak and laugh at our continued attempts to negotiate peaceful resolutions. But, during our invasions of Iraq and Afghanistan, they learned America does, or did, have a backbone. Around 2009, the backbone went somewhat soft. But now, America is stiffening back up, and several civilized Muslim countries are with us in our attempts to bring down ISIS and that gang's wackadoodle supporters.

And just like Hitler's followers, our Islamic enemy will wake up one day to find out they are no longer the meanest dogs in the junkyard. Surviving sheikhs will see the remains of their palaces, a bit like certain bunker dwellers once did in Berlin, and decide that peace does have its benefits. Until then, besides the bomb-wearing murderers, we will still have America's Fifth Columnists preaching from late-night television and the California governor's office. But if we do what's right and stand up to the enemy, we can send today's terror acts into history like the union and Bolshevik bombings of the very early 20th Century.

And when that happens, CNN and leftist celebrities can join together in creating and supporting Hanoi Jane's Fund Raising for Homeless Ex-Terrorists.

And speaking of terrorists, here is a final cartoon from 2017 concerning three murderous dictators, Iran's Ali Khamenei, Syria's Bashar al-Assad and their benefactor Russia's Vladimir Putin.

10. B-Western Therapy

The simple world of B-western good guys vs. bad guys, clear definitions for right and wrong, classical American morals and justice-prevails endings is therapy for anyone who finds current events to be frustrating and stressful. The following columns, which appeared a few years ago in a couple of weekly publications, are a calm way to relax, take a breath and step away from the news channels and incessant political blather to think about the things that make life so darn good – family, friends and doing the right thing.

Calming Our Minds With the Code of the West

To quote a great American thespian, historian and philosopher, "Dadgummit! Life ain't what it used to be, you young whippersnapper!"

It's hard to picture the late George "Gabby" Hayes wearing a smoking jacket and ascot while seated in a winged-back chair in a library, let alone resting one hand on a stack of leather-bound classic literature as he holds a Meerschaum pipe in the other. And yet the often-cantankerous characters he portrayed in a multitude of low-budget western films professed more than a bushel and a peck of common-sense messages to mankind which were far superior to just about any modern-day talking-head news commentator, Ivy league professor or radio shock-jock.

Hayes worked in vaudeville and had been successful enough to retire at the age of 43. After the stock-market crash of 1929 wiped him out, he tried his hand in Hollywood. The rest is history, as he became a popular western-movie sidekick to Hopalong Cassidy, Roy Rogers, Gene Autry, Wild Bill Elliott, Randolph Scott and John Wayne. His characters not only supplied a sagebrush-Dr. Watson to the lead cowboy's Sherlock as a storytelling device, but his dialogue offered laughs to the children in the audience and sage advice to everyone. That's because the storylines all echoed the lessons of the Code of the West: Crime doesn't pay. Good guys are kind to women, children and animals. Heroes never fight dirty. Good guys never lie, cheat or steal. And, most importantly, good always triumphs over evil.

And Gabby never failed to punctuate the films' lessons on morality, justice and American patriotism with a firm, "Yer durn tootin'!"

If you're like me, trying to make sense of the current political, cultural, economic news of this country and the world the last couple of years is a bit like trying to swallow a whole porcupine, tail first. I would think the news channels would take a hard look at their content, then cancel all those Medicare-supplement, car-insurance and special-pillow commercials to make room for Tums, Rolaids, Maalox, Alka-Seltzer and (depending on what state you're in) legal recreational drugs commercials. They might make more money and they'd be doing a public service for their victims, I mean viewers.

For those of us who have industrial-strength headaches from trying to understand arson, looting and rioting in the name of social justice, burning the American Flag and killing law enforcement officers of a variety of races as a protest for racial diversity, and assaulting the nation's Capitol while carrying the stars and stripes and yelling about supporting law and order, you know what I mean. My mind spins when my thoughts turn to multi-billion-dollar, high-tech companies banning members of the pro-capitalist political party from social media, as well as main-stream media; members of the political party that created the Confederacy and went to war to keep their slaves, then developed the Ku Klux Klan as their party's enforcement vigilantes, tearing down statues of Abraham Lincoln because he didn't do enough for people of color; local governments ordering their police departments to stand down while crazy people burn and loot small businesses; city officials demanding which sexual images a Christian bakery can design for wedding cakes; and seeing a rag-tag group of misfits, who really looked like they should be float-wavers on a Frisco pride parade, break into the Capitol building in Washington while calling themselves conservative patriots. Gabby would call them "consarn sidewinders!"

Enough! Turn off the news and find a good streaming service that offers classic B-westerns. If you have young children, get them to put down their electronic devices for an hour and join you for an exciting, adventure-filled, escape into a long-ago, black and white world of good guys, bad guys and wonder horses. Expose your kids to hard-working ranchers and farmers who had to fight to survive against the criminal element of those days. Enjoy heroes like Rocky Lane, the Three Mesquiteers and the Rough Riders, and heroines like Gail Davis as Annie Oakley and Barbara Stanwyck in the Big Valley, taking on the black-hatted varlets of the Old West.

Got a family member who objects to all the guns in your average western? In those films guns aren't the problem. They're the answer. Just like today, villains carried guns. But in the westerns, good guys also carried guns. Without them, a bad guy could simply shoot all the unarmed innocent people, like in a lot of contemporary situations. But the films teach that an individual who has the right moral code can stand up to bullies and win.

Actually, you can just forget all the morality and justice themes and basically enjoy a clean action adventure – with no swearing (other than a dadgummit or two), extreme violence or sex acts – that is designed for both kids and adults. There aren't any CGI effects, as most of the old western stars were also rodeo champions who started their film careers as stuntmen. You won't walk away wondering why Liam Neeson tortured all those people or why he shot so many of them when, in real life, he pontificates about gun control. And when the old-time western stars extolled patriotic viewpoints, you knew they meant them, as most of them had served in either The Great War or World War II. Some volunteered for both. There's no hypocrisy there.

Basically, step away from the all-news-all-the-time insanity and into a B-western, where good, justice and peace of mind still live. The films may not be historically accurate but, at this time in history, the messages are super therapeutic.

> This column and the following ramblings deal with my fascination with B-western movies and serials from the 1930s, '40s and '50s. You just read why I enjoy them so much. In fact, I also write and illustrate a series of neo-pulp novels and short stories that are set in the early days of talking pictures. I concentrate the action to fit alongside what took place in the old Saturday matinee serial chapters while I illustrate them in the style of pulp publications of the same era.
>
> My writing process includes researching a time period where certain actions could have taken place, finding which movies were being filmed during that specific time and bringing actual characters and events together to mix with my fictional characters and scenario – if that makes sense. My western novels are the Hollywood Cowboy Detectives (HCD) series, which can be found in paperback and Kindle format on Amazon. (I also write the Man of the Mist and Vermin books, among others.)
>
> My first HCD novel, "Mystery at Movie Ranch," was published in 2014. Although I was retired at that time, I continued to submit news and feature columns to a couple of weekly publications, mostly to plug my books. This first column's headline is a paraphrase of a line we used toward each other in Vietnam, quite a lot.

Don't sweat the small stuff

Anyone who has read a few of my columns probably understands by now that I like to take issues and have a little fun with them. After all, anything I might say isn't going to change the world.

When I was young, I took things far more seriously than I do today. Many of my editorial cartoons of that era went directly for the jugular and were harsh and unfunny. Now I try to find the silliness in life to play with on the drawing board. Of course, there are those folks who have said the cartoons I've drawn over the last 20 years weren't funny either – usually politicos who didn't like to be caricatured (I could still name a few).

The same can be said for my writing. These days, however, if an elected official, celebrity or television talking head does or says something that raises my blood pressure, I don't run to the computer or the drawing table to immediately react. I give the situation a day or two to digest while I decide whether I want to have a little fun with them or just yawn and move on.

For instance, last week we were all inundated with pictures and videos of frowning, over-paid football players on their knees while the National Anthem was being played. They said they had a point to make and, I'm sure, American patriots, military members, veterans and police officers certainly understood what that message was. But rather than join the throng of writers that expressed their displeasure with those shoulder-pad-wearing nuts and the idiot Steelers coach who was outraged because one team member, a military veteran, stood to honor our Flag, I wrote about Halloween shopping. It was more fun and it didn't cause me to want to throw a beer at the television.

I guess it has a lot to do with being retired. I'm no longer on a daily deadline to crank out any "hard-hitting" opinions. And, when I do things, I try to do fun things that I enjoy. That's not to say that I don't enjoy making fun of Hillary and Obama. But it's a lot more pleasurable to just poke a pencil at some of the more benign topics in our world, like Halloween shopping, PETA proposals and old B-westerns.

And to those who have read all the way through one of these columns and continued to read the italic blurb at the bottom concerning my book series, thank you. Just like what I was getting at a couple of paragraphs ago, when I retired I decided I needed to write something that would bring ME pleasure.

After all, there really isn't a great need for B-western adventure books in the 21st Century. And any folks (other than me) who know who Hoot Gibson, Ken Maynard and

Tim McCoy were are probably more interested in the early bird special at their favorite casino than they are in reading modern pulps.

But, I do it for me. It may just be a sign of impending dementia, but I really enjoy writing a bunch of wacky characters into a serial-style cliffhanger predicament, only to find a way out for them in the next episode, I mean chapter. I get to create evil villains like the Viper, the Arizona Dragon, the Alien Banshee, the Horned Monster and others, as well as aliens, demons and enemies from beyond the grave. And, in contrast to real life, the good guys always win.

What I'm saying is, in this time of radical insanity don't let the crazies get you down. Find something you enjoy doing and do it for your own happiness. Take a class at the community college just for the fun of it. Go dancing, or in my case, hobbling. Get a book on woodworking or some other craft you've always wanted to try and give it a shot. And, even though western movies are about as rare as saber-toothed ferrets, try writing and illustrating 1930s western pulps.

Values of the Code of the West

"Who's your favorite cowboy?"

I remember debating that question with other children on the playgrounds, backyards and pastures during my youth in the 1950s. Depending on the year, the answers were Hoot Gibson, Ken Maynard, Lash LaRue, Tim McCoy, Tom Tyler, Rex Allen, Tex Ritter, Hoppy and other great B-western heroes whose movies of the 1930s and '40s were saturating early television. We often watched the films with our parents who had enjoyed them during their first runs in theaters. In the late '50s and early '60s, television series stars such as Steve McQueen, James Garner, Richard Boone, Will Hutchins and James Drury were added to the discussion.

It was a great time to be a kid. And it wasn't just us guys who got a kick out of these shows. I remember watching Annie Oakley save her little brother Tagg and Deputy Lofty Craig from some villainous situation or another every week for a few years. They were truly fun adventure programs. Gail Davis' Annie Oakley character lived by the same standard as the male cowboy heroes. In later years, major motion picture star Barbara Stanwyck rode herd on television's "The Big Valley."

These wonderful action stories contained very important morality lessons for the children of the 20th century. Thinking back, I believe the Saturday matinee westerns were probably the only sermons on good versus evil that some of the children of the Great Depression, and later, came in contact with. And, likewise, those of us from the late 1940s into the early '60s all wanted to grow up and be strong, good and heroic. And although that didn't work out for all of us, it was a good start on life. As we became adults and reality started to smack us around, most of us did our best to hold on to those western values.

These movies and early television characters all shared their visions of the Code of the West. They taught the beliefs of self-reliance, honesty and fair play. Every leading B-western star was a straight shooter who always told the truth, paid his debts, was kind to animals and courteous to the ladies. Only bad guys lied, stole, cursed, back-shot, and mistreated horses, women and children.

Good guys always fought fair, no matter what sleazy tricks the bad guys used. In the long run, bad guys were always brought to justice. Honesty, fair play and self-responsibility were tenets of life.

That's why today I still love the old B-westerns. When I've read or heard too much bad news about war, crime and politics, I simply pop in a DVD and watch Ken Maynard round up the rustlers, Hoot Gibson take down the crooked banker or John Wayne and the Three Mesquiteers save the settlers from the clutches of an attorney's evil land scheme. You can call it therapy; I think of it as pleasure.

I've always followed local politics closely. The things I read about that just scream political cronyism or payoffs to members of small-town political machines could very well be re-imagined into a B-western script. Of course, in that situation Randolph Scott would ride into town and clean things up within 90 minutes.

Although great western films can still be seen on some cable stations as well as at Internet sites, today's children quite often debate their favorite video games or "reality" shows. I would love to see youths rediscover B-westerns like so many have with the classic films of Bogart and Chaplin. I think they would be amazed at the trick riding found in the 1930s Gibson and Maynard films, which contain no Computer Generated Imagery (CGI) special effects.

When we watch these films today, the stars of that bygone era live again, as does the Code of the West message that justice always wins. I believe those classic characters will continue to share their world of always doing the right thing for many years to come. If asked, "Who's your favorite cowboy?" today I have to answer, "All of them."

Adventure serials offered weekly thrills

The great B-westerns serials of the 1930s are still the best when it comes to action.

Many top western film stars also worked in multi-chapter serials. Matinee heroes like Buck Jones, Johnny Mack Brown, Dick Foran, Gene Autry, Ray "Crash" Corrigan and Hoot Gibson stepped out of B-western features and into serials to cheat death during 12 to 15 cliffhanger chapters. The low-budget episodes featured amazing action scenes that most assuredly bruised up many stars and stuntmen.

Designed to bring kids back into theaters every weekend, each episode ended with a death-defying situation where the hero or heroine is stabbed, shot, thrown off a cliff, blown up in a building, crushed in a cave or eaten by some terrifying creature. When one returned to the theater the next week, the new chapter would show how that star escaped death only to run into another cliff-hanger ending where there was no way he or she would survive.

Often, the week between seeing each episode allowed for some unique fudging on film editing. But with today's DVDs, one can watch the ending where Tom Mix is on a cliff in a cave shootout; he is hit in the chest; and falls forward off the ledge. With the next chapter beginning immediately, one sees Mix in the shootout; he rolls off the ledge; steps down to the next level and escapes. Aw, c'mon!

But even with the ability to catch film-edit fudging, these serials are great entertainment.

My two favorites are Ken Maynard in "Mystery Mountain" and Tom Mix in "The Miracle Rider." Both are produced by lowest-of-the-budgets Mascot Pictures.

"Mystery Mountain" (1934) has Maynard (as Ken Williams) battling an unknown villain who calls himself The Rattler. It takes 12 chapters to unmask The Rattler, as he is a master of disguising himself as other characters in the film. The plot is a re-imagining of the John Wayne railroad serial, "The Hurricane Express" (1932), where the Duke seeks to expose The Wrecker.

"Mystery Mountain" was Maynard's only serial. And, in spite of an Ed Wood-level budget, it is exciting and a lot of fun. Every time someone learns the Rattler's identity, we find out the perpetrator was in a disguise. Maynard is assisted by Syd Saylor's character, Breezy Baker, who is a not-too-bright but enthusiastic reporter. (Nobody's perfect.)

My other favorite serial, "The Miracle Rider" (1935) was the last film of Tom Mix. To protect Indian lands, his character, Tom Morgan, battles veteran villain actor Charles

Middleton (Flash Gordon's Ming the Merciless) as Zaroff. There are a lot of great action scenes that show Mix, at 55 years old, was still an athletic western hero.

I always loved "contemporary" westerns such as this where cowboys meet up with (1935) technology and science fiction elements such as the "Firebird" rocket plane and a mysterious explosive found only on the tribe's reservation.

One of the uniquely jarring parts of the film was after Mix has dispatched the villains. The young Indian girl who has obviously been in love with Tom throughout the picture is sad that her hero is leaving to go back east for a better job. Instead of Mix taking off his hat and holding it up to cover a kiss to show they will be together, he shakes her hand and offers her a job as his secretary.

I guess we can all thank 1935 political correctness for that.

Black Hats Matter

One key element that all western films have in common is the battle between good guys and bad guys. And, in the classic B-westerns of the 1920s into the '50s, the good guys wore white hats (except for Lash LaRue and Hoppy) and the bad guys wore black hats.

Film villains in those days were usually saloon owners, bankers and attorneys with pencil-thin mustaches and smarmy smiles. It didn't take an A-student to identify a B-western bad guy within the first five minutes of a Saturday matinee presentation. (I only wish it were that easy in real life prior to an election.)

The great character actors who wore black hats and perpetrated dastardly deeds in many western films were usually the best actors. People like Charlie King, Myron Healey, I. Stanford Jolley and Barton MacLane appeared in countless films as delightfully wicked scoundrels. Where the white-hatted heroes were strong, handsome and, usually, quite stoic, the villains were able to mug for the camera and chew scenery while carrying out their evil attempts to steal the ranch, rustle the cattle, rob the bank or force the schoolmarm into an unwanted marriage.

The King of the Black Hats was Charlie King. His bushy black mustache and deep Texas accent made him a popular rascal in close to 400 motion pictures during his career. Although he appeared primarily as a villain, King also played a variety of parts in oaters, including comedic roles. Virtually every B-western hero (Ken Maynard, Hoot Gibson, Tex Ritter, Bob Steele, Lash LaRue, Buster Crabbe, etc.) engaged in memorable on-film fistfights with King.

Myron Healey's bad-guy characters were usually clean-shaven. But young audiences began to recognize his villainous smile as a sure sign he was up to no good.

Healey landed his first scoundrel roles post-war at Monogram Pictures where he faced off with Johnny Mack Brown, Whip Wilson and Jimmy Wakely, and also wrote some of the film screenplays. That led to a long career in film and television westerns.

Barton MacLane was another great character actor who became known for his cowboy villains. During his career, which lasted from the '30s into the '60s, MacLane also successfully portrayed gangsters, cops, military officers, newspaper editors and protective fathers. His recognizable face can be found in B- and A-feature films as well as television. He worked with Humphrey Bogart, Randolph Scott, the Marx Brothers, Glenda Farrell and other greats in films with singing and non-singing cowboys, pirates, Dr. Jekyll, the Mummy and Jeanie from the *I Dream of...* series.

Although his name isn't often recalled, I. Stanford Jolley, whose acting career lasted from the '20s into the '70s, is instantly recognizable as a western villain. He portrayed all kinds of characters in motion pictures and television, yet his look personified the mustached black-hatted blackguard who would shoot a preacher in the back for the coins on his plate. Young matinee audiences would begin hissing the minute he appeared onscreen and then break into a cheer at the end when the white-hatted hero would dispatch him to his un-heavenly reward.

Mr. Jolley's family and friends have remembered him as one of the kindest men in the business. Now that's a real actor.

The classic cowboy stars of the past could not have existed, let alone been so heroic, if it were not for the wonderfully evil black hats who were out to get them.

Classic cowboys team up to battle evil

My recent column, titled Black Hats Matter, reminded me that so many of the old western movies dealt with individuals battling against cultures of power – villains united to further their own evil goals.

On the silver screen, the rugged individual stood by the Code of the West philosophy (do the right thing) while fighting against a black-hatted, set system that didn't allow for opposing thought (silence all opposition). In today's world, such evil can be found in the growth of political correctness (PC). When one group of citizens (or non-citizens) can get away with stopping traffic, breaking windows and shouting down opposing speakers just to stifle any viewpoint other than their own, PC evil triumphs over freedom and democracy.

On film, the good guy always defeated evil while teaching everyone else to stand up for their neighbors' rights. Today, individuals are silenced quickly by the PC culture. We see patriotic gatherings being attacked by large squads of shouting, black-masked thugs who see nothing wrong with using signs as clubs, burning American Flags and torching police cars. These modern outlaws, brown shirts, whatever you want to call them, get away with their tactics because today's average American will step back thinking that this activity is only temporary.

It isn't!

Thanks to our capitalist system, producers of B-westerns during the 1930s and '40s decided that, if one cowboy hero could bring in a profit, three heroes would be a jackpot. That was the beginning of the western team-up films. Those films taught pre-war and wartime audiences that, sometimes, rugged individuals needed to team up with other like-minded allies to be able to defeat powerful villains.

Probably the most popular of the teams was Republic's Three Mesquiteers (based on characters created by William Colt MacDonald), which at one time or another consisted of John Wayne, Ray "Crash" Corrigan, Max Terhune and/or Bob Livingston, Tom Tyler, Bob Steele, Duncan Renaldo, Guinn "Big Boy" Williams, Rufe Davis, Jimmie Dodd, Raymond Hatton, Kirby Grant and Ralph Byrd, among others.

I enjoyed all of the different team-ups of the Mesquiteers, as well as the follow-up Range Busters series. Monogram's Trail Blazers with Hoot Gibson, Ken Maynard and/or Bob Steele and Chief Thunder Cloud were also fun.

But my favorite B-western, team-up series is The Rough Riders from Monogram. They were a bit on the cheesy side, but starred two of the greatest real-cowboy stars ever, Buck Jones and Tim McCoy. Raymond Hatton rounded out the team as a worthwhile sidekick who wasn't just around for laughs.

Each movie begins with the three leads, at their homes in different states, receiving notice they are needed somewhere. They would then unite at the scene of the action with undercover identities to assist their investigations. At the end of each film, the trio waves to the audience and says, "So long, Rough Riders," and they ride off in three separate directions.

For a low-budget series, the dialogue is excellent (or maybe it's just the ability of the three veteran actors to bounce their characters off of each other). Jones played Marshal Buck Roberts, McCoy was Marshal Tim McCall and Hatton portrayed Marshal Sandy Hopkins.

The three appeared together in eight Rough Riders features. A ninth picture, "Dawn of the Great Divide," was made after World War I veteran McCoy had gone back into the military for service in World War II. Rex Bell replaced him. And, sadly, the film was released right after Jones' death due to the Cocoanut Grove nightclub fire.

Hatton continued to portray Marshal Sandy Hopkins in a series with western star Johnny Mack Brown.

One of the strangest, and most enjoyable, team-up B-westerns was a 1938 oater with Smith Ballew and Lou Gehrig. In "Rawhide," the singing cowboy, Ballew, and baseball-great Lou Gehrig battle a corrupt "protective association" and a crooked sheriff. Small-town politics gone over to the dark side had to be whipped back in shape by the unique heroes. Plenty of action and some surprisingly good acting in Rawhide led me to give this B an A.

"Rawhide" was released right about the time Gehrig started having physical problems. He looks good in the film and, if he had remained healthy, would have probably been able to do well in the movie industry.

Western books and films have always celebrated rugged individualists who fight for justice. The B-western team-ups show that friends can unite and, by following the Code of the West, overcome evil. Even in 2017, that's one lesson worth remembering.

Sharing the West

Those of you who have read any of my books or occasional columns realize by now that I am a big fan of western films. And I don't consider myself alone in my enjoyment.

There are a lot of us who still thrill to the sound of "the thundering hoofbeats of the great horse Silver," and other classic lines that bring Pavlovian smiles to our faces. Whether it is the beginning of a 1930s matinee serial, the yodeling of a 1940s singing cowboy, the "William Tell Overture" from radio and early television, the theme to "The Good, The Bad and The Ugly," or even Frankie Laine singing "Blazing Saddles," our attention is captured.

But, it is a common situation that spouses don't always share the same interests. My wife, for instance, has not been a big fan of westerns. She doesn't know Ken Maynard from Congressman Ken Buck and, when I mentioned the Three Mesquiteers recently, she asked if Annette Funicello had been a member. It's a sad situation. However, being a modern, enlightened sort of guy, I figure that I can find a way to bring her around. Cowboy films are something that couples should share.

There is a slight difference in our film tastes. For instance, when we were first married, the wife asked me to go see a British comedy with her. I thought she said "Benny Hill." I was delighted. When the lights came on in the theater, I had been stuck watching "Notting Hill." The memory of that terrible night still haunts me with HCFDSS (Husbands' Chick Flick Delayed Stress Syndrome). I probably should have reported her to the Geneva Convention.

Anyway, I'm over it. And I have a plan to improve her film interests. Christmas is coming up and, instead of getting her a new iron or set of dishtowels, this year I plan to shower her with DVDs that will certainly put a smile on her face.

Knowing that I have been thinking about holiday gifts, the little woman has been tossing out hints on things she would enjoy receiving. Just last week she was watching the Travel Channel and remarked how she would like to see more of the country. So, for her geographic knowledge, I ordered Buck Jones and Tim McCoy in "Down Texas Way," Dick Foran and Leo Carrillo in "Riders of Death Valley," and Randolph Scott in "Abilene Town."

And while watching the Hallmark Channel, she mentioned how much she enjoyed romance films. You guessed it. I bought "Romance on the Range" with Roy Rogers and Gabby Hayes.

One of the things the two of us agree upon is our support for law enforcement. Therefore, I think she will really appreciate the DVDs of "Law of the Lash" with Lash LaRue, and "Guns of the Law" with Dave O'Brien.

Now, obviously you have picked up that I've subtly taken her suggestions slightly to the west. And, by doing so, I have chosen the perfect Christmas entertainment that will inspire her to become a western-film aficionado. To cap everything off, I've included a 2017 calendar so she can keep track of family events. I can't wait to see her eyes light up when she opens it to see the large, beautiful, color photos from the last 20 minutes of Sam Peckinpah's masterpiece, "The Wild Bunch."

Who said romance is dead?

Okay. It had been a while since I had offered my Valentine's Day expertise. In reality, my wife doesn't watch B-westerns with me. And I don't have to watch Hallmark romance films with her. We do, however, both enjoy British and American detective films.

Good westerns have heart

I believe most current theatrical western films lack the heart needed to rebuild the genre's popularity.

In explaining my views, I'll throw in a little history while champing at a bit of opinion that could cause one to see me as a man of my age cursing at children to get off my lawn. And perhaps I have listened to The Statler Brothers' brilliant "Whatever Happened to Randolph Scott" far too many times.

Under the studio system of the first half of the 20th Century, B-westerns were cranked out to fill theater seats at Saturday matinees. Adults supported their children's interest in the films because of the Code of the West all-American values they embraced. Even at 10-cents per ticket, low-budget westerns were profitable.

The great talking A-westerns, beginning with starring roles for Gary Cooper, Richard Dix, Preston Foster and Warner Baxter, kept the white-hatted value system espoused in the Bs while expanding storytelling and humanizing subjects for an adult audience. John Ford and John Wayne, among others, polished the genre to an art form that, with "The Searchers," focused a Rembrandt-level spotlight on what a western could be.

Suddenly television took over the role of the Saturday matinee and B-westerns filled the small screen. Cooper, Wayne and Scott, who were joined by veterans (in more ways than one) James Stewart and Audie Murphy, kept western fans coming to the movie palaces.

Then the 1960s happened. Cooper died. Scott retired. Producers found it was less expensive to film a car chase on Los Angeles streets than to truck horses and actors farther and farther out of town. Many of us were sent to Vietnam with our hands tied, to fight Communists – eventually leading to gutless politicians negotiating a loss for America. Cynicism began to replace the Code of the West.

As the American film industry struggled, the B-western immigrated back from Spain and Italy. The producers and directors of those low-budget films put a European slant on the genre. There were no good guys, only bad guys with supernaturally fast draws killing even worse guys. The so-called Spaghetti westerns were caricatures of America's films. Yet, they were profitable, for a while.

Then former TV cowboy Clint Eastwood returned to the states and began to recreate the American western, using the quick action and ultimate revenge of the European films while bringing back a bad-assed version of the good guy taking out the bad guys for the right reasons.

By 1980, very few cowboys rode the silver screen west – until recently. "Bone Tomahawk," "The Revenant" and "The Hateful Eight" were touted as the long-awaited revival of western films.

I don't believe strangely non-empathetic characters spouting 21st Century views while engaging in scenes of agonizing torture and murder are going to inspire western fans to return to the theaters. Quentin Tarantino (The Hateful Eight) ignored the art that John Ford honed while embracing the worst of the European caricatures, making his film a bad imitation of not very good films.

But, like the message in many classic movies, there is always hope. And I hope the remake of "The Magnificent Seven," which seems to have been a success, has enough heart to prompt other filmmakers to attempt the genre. It ain't Randolph Scott, but it's a start.

Okay. So recently produced western films are lacking in therapeutic value. All the more reason for all of us to look within ourselves and find our own simple B-western Code of the West. When activists, candidates and elected officials stir the pot with lies, threats and clueless behavior, Hoppy would tell us that they have the First Amendment right to spout their claptrap. But he would also say that we have the same right to share our opinions and/or ignore theirs. And if we keep smiling, and use our words or cartoons to laugh at stupidity, we can say a lot while discounting others' angry rhetoric. And Gabby would probably add, "Yer durn tootin'!"

I hope you enjoyed my slightly sarcastic, sometimes over-the-top, look back on local, state, national and international issues. I also hope you appreciate that I placed my B-Western chapter at the end, as a sort of cleansing of the palate to help remove the taste of some of my political rants. Mayors, county supervisors, governors and presidents have come and gone. But, as I look back on them, today's issues seem to be pretty similar. Federal administrations are still debating how to defeat an enemy. City and county governments continue to fight with the states against centralized control. And some of the surviving newspapers are doing their best to hold on to ethical coverage of the political arena.

Basically, things haven't changed that much in local issues and actions during the last almost 30 years. State and federal political scenarios are just as wild and crazy, as well. But right here in the Southwest, specifically Arizona, free speech still trumps political correctness. And although, like in California, sometimes the PC crowd was able to impact my work, they were never able to completely silence me. I think that's the theme of what I have been saying by some of my over-the-top rants. Never give up. Speak your mind. Don't let the woke alligators get you down. That's what we do in the Southwest.

Obviously, my viewpoints have evolved over the years (really!). Although I'm sure many people probably would still see me as being on all fours in the evolution chart. We need to continue to discuss the issues openly. Colleges need to reject "safe spaces" where opposing views are forbidden. Whiners should learn to debate rather than use the excuse of hurt feelings to silence or cancel their political opposition. And violence toward a governing body, innocent people or businesses is not the answer.

There is a reason our nation's founders placed Freedom of Speech as the number one priority in our Constitution. When we can no longer speak, write or draw our viewpoints, democracy will have become an illusion.

End

The Author

Darryle Purcell has had a variety of jobs during his lifetime – including soldier, illustrator, editorial cartoonist, newspaper managing editor and government flack.

He served in the Army as an infantry paratrooper in the First Cavalry Division in Vietnam and then stateside as a medic, first in the 101st Airborne Division, then in the 82nd Airborne Division. Following the military, he worked his way through college, graduating with an art degree from Cal State University Long Beach, which led to a career as a cartoonist in magazines, newspapers, educational comic books and Saturday morning animated television shows.

Purcell's political cartoons garnered quite a few awards in California during the 1980s and early '90s, while his work as a newspaper managing editor in the later '90s and first few years of the new century led to many statewide awards in Arizona for news columns and editorials. From 2005 through 2012, he was a public information director for a county in Arizona.

Purcell currently writes and illustrates the *Hollywood Cowboy Detectives*, *Man of the Mist* and *Vermin* pulp adventures from his home in rural Arizona, where he lives with his wife Patricia.